Race and ethnicity in
a welfare society

Race and ethnicity in a welfare society

Charlotte Williams and
Mark R. D. Johnson

Open University Press

Open University Press
McGraw-Hill Education
McGraw-Hill House
Shoppenhangers Road
Maidenhead
Berkshire
England
SL6 2QL

email: enquiries@openup.co.uk
world wide web: www.openup.co.uk

and Two Penn Plaza, New York, NY 10121-2289, USA

First published 2010

A catalogue record of this book is available from the British Library

ISBN-13: 978-0-33-522531-6 (pb) 978-0-33-522530-9 (hb)
ISBN-10: 0335225314 (pb) 0335225306 (hb)

Library of Congress Cataloging-in- Publication Data
CIP data applied for

Typeset by RefineCatch Limited, Bungay, Suffolk
Printed in the UK by CPI Antony Rowe, Chippenham and Eastbourne

The **McGraw·Hill** Companies

Contents

Praise for this book

Introduction
'Race' and ethnicity in a welfare society

In recent years the term 'race' has gradually been erased from government discourse and documentation. Politicians prefer to speak about communities, diversity, or cohesion and employ all sorts of alternative language to acknowledge forms of social division in contemporary society, rather than deploy the term 'race'. As UK equality law is undergoing change, with the single equality act poised to replace the Race Relations Amendment Act, so the signifier 'race' will become muted within the body of anti-discrimination legislation, bringing Britain into line with other parts of Europe where there has been a general reluctance to deploy such explicit terminology. There are good reasons for suggesting that 'race' is a redundant and outmoded concept. The connotation with biological and scientific classifications alone makes it somewhat of an irrelevance today. It has also proved to be an awkward concept in its application to what is now acknowledged to be a highly differentiated set of social relations between minority and majority groups in contemporary society (Rex 2001). Among ethnic minority groups themselves the term has an ambivalent status, as there is concern not to differentiate oneself from others, and to stress a common humanity. In addition many individuals feel the term does not accurately describe their status. Nevertheless, and more than 40 years after the UN scientists' Paris conference in 1967 (UNESCO 1968) declared that the term 'race' had no scientific validity, it remains a potent term, capable of generating angry denial or heated argument, and a word that can set headlines alight. In other words, the term 'race' is known and imbued with meaning, if not welcomed, as a shorthand for describing a particular social positioning.

We have deliberately adopted the term 'race' in the title of this text to speak to a set of historical relations as they are manifest in welfare arrangements and welfare relations today. More accurately, we seek to acknowledge the way in which some groups are *racialized* within society with a negative and enduring impact on their well-being and to demonstrate how racisms that arise from some or other conceptualization of 'race' are embedded in welfare practices. This works both ways: 'racialization' makes explicit or codifies assumptions about people based on a phenotypical (visual) description and classification of them, and it also creates assumptions or 'necessary' expectations by essentializing these differences, and using them as an explanation for relative inferiority (or, less often, superiority). Our central task, however, is to demonstrate how difference and diversity, in this case as marked out by membership of one of the minority ethnicities, including minorities described as 'exotic' or non-autochthonous by reference to their religion, language, or descent group (for example 'asylum seekers'), is (or is not) accommodated in welfare delivery. Our aspiration is towards the creation of a *welfare society* – one in which the well-being of all is central and in which welfare arrangements are owned, shaped and co-produced with the active engagement of all citizens.

History tells us that social policies and welfare practices have been consistently imbued with fundamental racisms that have undermined the potential for well-being among Britain's ethnic minorities. The structure and implementation of immigration law has provided the overarching context in which welfare entitlement has been differentiated and inclusions and exclusions marked out. Against a range of measures the traditional Beveridgean welfare state failed significantly to enhance the well-being of ethnic minorities. Its architecture and its bedrock philosophical approach would ultimately render it ineffective in meeting the needs of an increasingly diverse society. But this is almost too simplistic a picture to carry through into the twenty-first century. The picture of a lumbering dinosaur resistant to change or of an archaic computer jinxed to deliver a corrupted program will not suffice by way of explanation of the relationship between Britain's ethnic minorities and contemporary welfarism. Ethnic minority groups and individuals have always been engaged in the production of welfare for their co-ethnic compatriots and for others and in lobbying for more appropriate service delivery. Their full potential is yet to be tapped, but they are active agents in the process of change that is underway in the contemporary scene.

Since the 1980s welfare delivery has been radically restructured and reformulated from its socialist collectivist origins to what some have called a post-welfare market state. The neo-liberal New Labour project of modernization has produced a very different set of welfare arrangements, in which many of the old assumptions of post-war welfarism have been undermined or rejected. Society has also significantly changed – economically, socially and demographically, and a number of processes have served to unsettle the old welfare certainties. It is no longer possible to conceive of the welfare state in isolation from the global context. International migrations and transnational welfare provisioning are fundamental to the sustainability of all Western welfare states. Processes of exchange, mutuality and movement defy national borders and there cannot easily be any simple equivalence between national borders, citizenship and the state. The welfare apparatus as it was originally conceived has been further challenged by the introduction of reciprocal rights and expectations across a 'common market' of goods, services and labour in a new and expanded European citizenship, where our continental neighbours have seen dramatic improvements in their own welfare services and social provisions. At the same time both multiculturalist policy making and the dynamics of multicultural society have undergone transformation. More latterly, wider issues of risk and security have come to the fore in the post-9/11 world and been linked in political discourse to issues of collective welfare. Gradually the politics of multiculturalism itself has been contested, undermined and rejected by both the right, and, increasingly the liberal left. Thus, many of the assumptions that underpinned the post-war welfare contract have been unsettled.

The sad fact is, however, that deep and entrenched inequalities for racialized minorities persist along every axis of need – in health, in education, in housing, social care services and in terms of basic income and social security. Despite state attention to combating a basket of inequalities, related to disability, gender, age, sexuality, religion and race/ethnicity, the last category has the greatest potential to endure and to form the basis of political division, while the others are more frequently sites of united struggle. The 'ethnic penalty' is still a regrettably clear marker of disadvantage (Heath and Cheung 2006), as are the processes of exclusion based on ethnicity. Policy actions and the administrative infrastructure have compounded this situation with a gaping hole between policy intentions and implementation. Welfare professionals and other stakeholders have been obliged to reconsider their ethical codes of practice, their skills and competencies in responding to ever increasing diversity of need, and been found wanting. It is now a decade ago that the Parekh Commission on the *Future of Multi-Ethnic Britain* set out a number of proposals on ways of countering racial discrimination and disadvantage and making Britain 'a more confident and vibrant multicultural society at ease with its rich diversity' (2000: viii). Many of its recommendations were directed at governments but they added: 'we do not believe that all social change comes prepackaged in legislative paper, and we also address business, local government, health bodies, police authorities and community organisations. Not least we address the general reader and the individual citizen' (p.11), indicating a wider responsibility for concerted effort.

In this book we explore issues of ethnic minority need and well-being in the context of the changing framework of delivering services within a mixed economy of welfare. Our approach represents a shift in analysis away from the impacts of specific policies or within specific policy fields such as health, housing and so on, to consider the organization of welfare in specific sectors of the mixed economy, the repositioning of welfare subjects and their relationships with welfare organizations and service providers. Attention is here focused on the processes involved in the production of welfare, what is produced and offered, how it is experienced and used and the role of professionals in the interface with ethnic minority service users.

In this text we adopt the term 'welfare society' to signal not simply the neo-liberal conceptualization of the changing nature of relationships and responsibilities between the state, the individual and communities in welfare delivery but to argue for a holistic perspective to a consideration of ethnic minority welfare. We posit *welfare society* as a way of thinking about interconnections between welfare arenas in the mixed economy of welfare and welfare contexts where struggles and contestation over welfare outcomes are played out. We also suggest welfare society as a way of thinking about social relationships, human action and agency in interplay with structures and systems. We suggest the term somewhat normatively to signal ownership of the new politics of welfare by a wider set of actors involved in the design and delivery of welfare arrangements as communities themselves are becoming governmental. Our argument is that cultural diversity has for too long been seen as problem for welfare delivery rather than as a resource to it: a resource for building a flexible welfare framework and a resource in terms of solving the issues presented by increased diversity. This avoidance of the positive potential of diversity has given rise to negative, reactive and contradictory policy making which has historically characterized the response to migrant settlement. There have been many high-profile examples of this reactive response to new encounters with diversity in all policy fields – the Climbié case in social work, the Honeyford case in education, the Macpherson report in policing, Scarman on housing and Cantle on community cohesion among others; all in turn reveal a negative politics of welfare in which the people become the problem and/or marginal adjustments are made to the institutional workings.

It is a sad fact that social welfare practice has consistently failed to consider minority communities as a resource in building the welfare framework of the nation(s), and a resource to solve the problems and issues posed by increased diversity. The issue therefore becomes how to harness this resource effectively within the mixed economy of welfare to mutual benefit. It is our contention that the social relations of welfare remain largely monocultural and that the model of welfare assimilationism which prevails means that welfare delivery will continue to fail to meet the needs of diverse groups. The current focus on consultation and co-ordination in the new governance, while leaving the mainstream structures untouched, will not resolve this ineffectiveness. What is needed is a thoroughgoing deconstruction of the predominant models in use to accommodate more significantly the principles and approaches of social development, founded on negotiation and contestation over welfare outcomes.

A welfare society is one in which the actions of governments alone will not secure well-being. It is based on the forging of new sets of obligations across civil society, new relationships between the state and the individual, fostering sustainable social development and social cohesion. An exploration of the notion of 'welfare society' raises a number of **key policy questions** fundamental to a refreshed discourse on 'race' and welfare with which we hope to engage in the ensuing pages of this text and in our conclusions:

- Can we afford a multicultural welfare state?
- Who is entitled to welfare goods and services? Why?
- What are the appropriate structures to deliver welfare in a multi-cultural society?
- How to protect the rights of minority groups?
- How to combat persistent inequality among minority groups?
- How to fix the solidarities and reciprocities vital to sustaining welfare?
- How to respond effectively to diversity of need?

We do not propose definitive answers to these questions, but seek to illuminate the debates and discourses that surround them inasmuch as they reveal values and assumptions about entitlement, ideas about integration and cohesion and about the responsiveness of service delivery. This book is above all about the transformations that are occurring across all the sectors in terms of organization and delivery of welfare and in terms of transformations to welfare practices and how these are being negotiated. Such an analysis demands attention to **structure** – those enabling or inhibiting features of societal arrangements that are institutionalized and that provide the context to understanding of change, and at the same time it requires attention to the role of individual or group **agency**, those actions of individuals or collectives that have transformative potential. Each chapter seeks to explore the interplay between these considerations. In between these two resources or constraints, lies **process**, which we hope will be illustrated by the examples we use, and demonstrated to be universal and not particular or deterministic – in other words, people, and institutions, can change and can be changed by individuals and actions.

Chapter map

The text is organized in three sections. The first considers the state(s') response to multicultural welfare delivery, from the perspective of the central state and the devolved administrations. In Chapter 1 we consider in more detail the issues and debates surrounding the response of the central state to multi-cultural welfare delivery. We provide an overview of changing policy agendas and consider the discourse on 'race' and welfare as it has been formulated in different political eras. We review the response of New Labour to the issue of racial diversity and consider how the neo-liberal approach produces an ambivalent policy stance towards Britain's ethnic minorities. This chapter concludes by considering some of the key questions that shape the debate on 'race' and welfare. Chapter 2 addresses legal and regulatory measures as a means of bringing about change. It considers the push towards institutional reform and the bureaucratic regulation of race equality, concluding that legal measures alone cannot produce change to widespread inequality without wider preconditions in civil and political life. Chapter 3 concludes the section by offering an analysis of the impact on devolution as part of the new welfare relationships. It considers whether devolution has changed the picture of contemporary multiculturalism or the patterning of racial inequality and reviews how this rescaled citizenship has impacted on ethnic minorities' welfare, participation and well-being.

In the second section of the book we turn our attention to the wider framework of welfare delivery within the sectors of the mixed economy. Here we explore the changing nature of the interrelationships between these sectors and state policy and practices. We look at the available evidence of change within these sectors and consider the implications of the changing nature of the relationships for Black and minority ethnic groups. Chapter 4 opens the section by looking at the historic and contemporary organization of ethnic minorities at the level of civil society. What has been their role in the development of welfare and how do they sit in the new governance arrangements? In Chapter 5 we consider the dimensions of care giving and care reciprocities in the informal sphere, primarily within the family and community networks of social life, where it is likely that the majority of care giving actually takes place. Policy makers and many practitioners have consistently misunderstood the nature and functioning of minority ethnic communities and families, and avoided responsibility with the famous (and inaccurate) phrase 'they prefer to look after their own'. We highlight the responses of the communities to this challenge. In Chapter 6 we consider a fast growing but little discussed arena of welfare delivery, the private sector, and consider how the massive expansion of private welfare services helps or hinders well-being among minority groups. Contemporary transformations to the notion of multiculturalism include a more rounded consideration of those not living within urban conurbations. Chapter 7 explores the way in which the territorial distribution of ethnic minorities shapes their relationship to welfare policy and practice. This raises a much broader question than the simple geography of the matter, alluding to the more structural consideration of territorial inequality and its implications for citizenship rights. Does the social contract extend universally across the land or is it confined to areas where minorities have garnered political strength through population concentration?

In the final section we look towards changes and developments in welfare delivery for ethnic minority individuals within the workplace (Chapter 8) and in terms of the professional response to diversity. Implementation relies on good practices – responsive and reflective practice. Can the professions deliver on this? In Chapter 9 attention is drawn to the issue of self-regulation and the professions, the role that professionals can take in reformulating public service values and the crafting of a welfare society. Finally in Chapter 10 we return to our theme of welfare society and consider what constitutes a multicultural welfare, what needs to change, what we can draw from this sector by sector exploration, and ask what the new framework means for ethnic minorities and where the most fruitful seeds of hope lie.

There are some important opening considerations relating to the ways in which we categorize and enumerate ethnic minority groups, to which we now turn by way of preamble to the text.

Describing and enumerating people and groups

Throughout this text, we shall be using a variety of terms to describe ethnic or 'racial', cultural and migrant groups. There is at present no national (let alone international) consensus on the use of these words. It is important to recognize that language, like culture, is a living and constantly changing thing. Debates between practitioners, campaigners and politically active people over the proper use of words have occupied many hours, and there have been many papers on the definitions of group membership and the meaning of 'race', 'ethnicity' and 'culture'. We do not believe that we have the final answer, but present below some of the issues and our preferred solutions. Where we quote from, or rely on, other people's research and policy papers, we shall use the terms they have used, and elsewhere we have attempted to follow our own strategy, as described here. In reference to official statistics and for general use, we shall normally, however, rely on the terms adopted for the national (UK) Census of Population by the Office for National Statistics, recognizing that these have changed over time as well (see below).

First, we need to recognize that 'race' is not a scientific concept, although nineteenth-century and early twentieth-century scientists used this term freely. Indeed, much of the social or medical scientific efforts of Hitler's Germany during the Third Reich (i.e. during and just before the Second World War, 1939–45) was dedicated to proving that there was a 'German', or, at least, Aryan 'race' that was in some way superior (Bhopal 2005). It is now recognized that these old notions were based on a fallacy, and that there is greater genetic variation within population groups, however defined, than between them. The United Nations convened a UNESCO Experts Committee on Race and Race Prejudice in 1967 at which a consensus of world scientists agreed that there was no scientific justification for the use of the term, although it was recognized that there was an issue of racism, based on the popular use of the concept to justify or explain discrimination and conflict (Rex 1969).

Those who use the term tend to assume that there is a genetic basis for behaviour and ability, and that this is inherent in distinguishing between the position and experiences of (among others) Black and white people – perhaps most recently expressed in publications such as *The Bell Curve Wars*, which argues differences in innate intelligence between these categories of human being (Fraser 1995).

On the other hand, 'culture' is seen as an option, or at least infinitely variable and capable of being adopted by choice, and hence of less importance. Culture has many aspects – popularly, it includes things sometimes labelled 'high culture' such as art, music and literature, but it also refers to morals, ideals, diet and family traditions. Fundamentally, it is a sort of shorthand for ideals, values and expected patterns of behaviour or ways of life. Anthropologists and ethnologists suggest that it was well described by a British anthropologist, Edward Burnett Taylor in 1871 as 'the complex whole which includes knowledge, belief, art, morals, law, custom and any other capabilities and habits acquired by man as a member of society' – that is, a shared system of meanings. As Hofstede (2001) shows, these affect the ways in which groups and societies respond, their organizations and behaviour. However, one can be a member of multiple cultures – defined by age, gender, religion or sexual orientation, as well as some of those attributes being associated with, or affected by one or more particular national or ethnic cultures. A voluntary association with a particular behaviour or cultural value may not mean that it is lightly abandoned or negotiable.

Increasingly, there has been a tendency, at least in social sciences and demographic statistics in the English-speaking world, to use the term 'ethnicity' and 'ethnic group' labels (Afshari and Bhopal 2010). This refers more directly to identity, although again not denying that people can have multiple identities, including those based on their impairment or disability, as shown by the 'D/deaf' movement (http://www.aslinfo.com/deafculture.cfm). By adopting a specific label or ethnic identity, people may be making a political statement, or campaigning for its recognition in official statistics. All of this, clearly, will affect how people react to, and identify with, specialist welfare, health and care services, and how health and care workers relate to and approach them.

The implication of all this is that there is no simple, single and enduring way of advising on the use of language to describe groups. What is more, we use words differently in different contexts. Especially, there are often differences between the use made in legal, administrative and official language of terms – which may have technical or legal implications that would be ignored in ordinary conversation among the general public. That form of discourse reflects, and is reflected by (and often accentuated in) the media, particularly when a campaign is running, or to make 'snappy' headlines. We should also be aware of the words that disabled people or people and communities from minority ethnic, religious and cultural backgrounds use and understand about

Table I.1   The roots of terminology in race and ethnicity

	Primary characteristics	*Origin*	*Associated perceptions*
Race	Inherent, physical, nature/ natural	Genetic – descent	Permanent, with sequelae (i.e. causative)
Culture	Behavioural expression of preferred lifestyle	Upbringing – learned	Capable of being changed, optional
Ethnicity/ Ethnic group	Identity, multi-faceted, 'political'	Socially constructed – internal or external – or legal	Situational, negotiated

themselves, including 'nicknames' that are not intended or expected to be used by 'outsiders'; and finally, there is academic language.

The majority of publications and government policy documents at present use the term Black and minority ethnic or BME, rather than ethnic minority. The sequence here suggests that it is the minority status, rather than the ethnicity itself, which is the focus of attention. In most of mainland Europe, however, terms relating to ethnicity are rarely used, since the focus, even when referring to people who were themselves born locally to parents who have come from abroad, is on the 'migrant' status (or origin), whether as economic migrants or refugees and asylum seekers. In such discourse, a more appropriate or acceptable term might be 'migrants and (ethnic) minorities'. Other authors and agencies use BAME, where the A is taken to refer variously to Asylum seekers (and sometimes, Refugees), Asian (since there is a resistance among many south Asian and Chinese people to being described as 'Black'), or possibly capitalized And, to demonstrate that not all 'minority ethnic' groups are 'Black' either in appearance or in the historic use of the term, but that many people of white European origins are now organizing and presenting their needs in minority ethnic terms. Refugees and asylum seekers, whose legal position is distinct, as well as 'undocumented' migrants, have their own ethnic and national identities on top of their citizenship-related status.

These issues will continue to exercise academics, practitioners and policy makers for the foreseeable future. The following section and examples come from a discussion by members of the electronic discussion group 'Minority-ethnic-health' (www.jiscmail.ac.uk/minority-ethnic-health):

> The question was raised as to whether it was appropriate or desirable to use the capitalised letter B in writing 'Black'. The majority of contributors accepted that the use of the capital letter was analogous to its use by members of the D/deaf community, to indicate that the word is being used as a political or social marker of group identity, rather than

as a purely descriptive adjective. One member of the group recalled early implementation of this usage:

> 'In this context *b/Black* is not a colour, it reflects the relation of a group or individual to power', I remember being told in 1980s London at GLC Equality meetings. This was under Ken Livingstone's direction, the 1st time around and an approach which provoked some odd distinctions. These did vary, over time and setting. At one point mainland Greeks were called 'white' for the purposes of discussion groups at Equality meetings, while those from Cyprus and their fellow islanders of Turkish heritage were *'b/Black'*. This term was also applied to those whose links were with the Turkish mainland/Kurdistan. Later Cypriots were *'w/White'*. I also recall that there was some heated debate among women attending from communities with a heritage in the subcontinent of India (*Asian*). This focused on feelings around rejecting or accepting the externally ascribed definition of *'b/Black'*, with those from Southall Black Sisters & similar activist groups keen to actively embrace the term while other Asian women; perhaps older ones or those from faith/ neighbourhood /specific sections (e.g. some 'Kenyan Asians') seemed less happy about this ascription.
>
> (Lindsey Ahmet, Middlesex University, on the jiscmail electronic discussion group, October 2009)

Other contributors noted that their local authorities and health trusts were adopting slightly different approaches, one rejecting the notion of 'ethnic' in favour of 'Black and other racial minorities' (BRM). Another was driven by more mundane but equally significant pressures:

> Last time I had to decide, I chose to capitalise – partly because of this statement I came across from the University of Sussex style book (1997):
>
> Formerly, the words *black* and *white*, when applied to human beings, were never capitalized. Nowadays, however, many people prefer to capitalize them because they regard these words as ethnic labels comparable to *Chinese* or *Indian*: e.g. 'The Rodney King case infuriated many Black Americans'.
>
> (Prof. David Ingleby, in electronic discussion, October 2009)

As he commented, 'Chinese' and 'Indian', however, are capitalised because they are derived from the names of countries – so that argument is not really watertight. Nevertheless, one needs a way to distinguish between the social categories 'Black' and 'White' and the adjectives 'black' and 'white'. The former refers to ethnic identity, the latter to skin colour. However, in his view, using lower case to refer to the ethnic groups encourages the view that these are natural categories rather than social constructions while using capitals emphasises that they are a matter of convention or choice.

The numbers issue

For many years after the beginning of the twentieth-century welfare state, it was possible for policy makers and practitioners in Britain to argue that the numbers of people from minority ethnic backgrounds were so low that it was not practicable or cost-effective for them to make 'special provision' for the 'special' (or as we would prefer, specific) needs of the groups. Even today in the twenty-first century, this argument sometimes is raised and particularly in relation to rural areas. However, populations do change, and with this, the politics of decision making can be seen to have developed. In particular, the national statistics of the United Kingdom have begun to reflect the need to record, and allow people to register, their ethnic identity (Johnson 2008). For much of the twentieth century, the only evidence about origins that could be drawn on was the place of birth of individuals enumerated in the decennial Census, or recorded on their birth and death certificates and compiled into reports by the office of the Registrar General.

As the politics of immigration developed in the post-war years, increasingly restrictive legislation was passed to reduce the ability of migrants from the so-called 'New Commonwealth' (i.e. those of African and south Asian 'racial' origins) to enter Britain. In 1968, the Commonwealth Immigrants Act withdrew the automatic right of settlement hitherto held by 'subjects' of the Queen, unless they could demonstrate a 'close connection' with Britain. In practice, this was interpreted to mean descent from a British-born parent or grandparent. The 1971 Immigration Act made this explicit, with the so-called 'patriality' clause. The decennial Census of that year was marked by the addition of a question about the birthplace of parents. This was opposed as a racist and discriminatory act (and a filter for immigration controls) and debate began to consider the inclusion of a less pejorative question, asking about 'ethnic group', although not without controversy (JRSS 1983). However, reportedly on the initiative of the then Prime Minister, Margaret Thatcher, the first attempt to include an 'ethnic' question was abandoned at the last minute just before the forms for the 1981 Census were printed. Debate on the subject continued, and the first question on ethnic identity was included in the 1991 Census, providing a baseline for future equality and diversity statistics. This was revised and refined, reflecting both the response of users (such as the desire of Irish people to self-identify) and the needs of services and government departments to reflect changing realities of demography, such as the growth in people of 'mixed' or dual heritages (Sims 2007). The question asked in 2001 has, where possible, been used as the basis for statistics in this volume (see also Johnson 2001), while we are conscious that the 2011 Census will include new categories and show significant changes from its predecessors, both in quantity and 'quality' (or, at least, label) of the groups identified.

In 1951 the Census showed that of the total population of Britain, then 48.8 million people, 1.6 million were 'non-UK born' (3.3 per cent), of whom only 200,000 had birthplaces in the 'New Commonwealth' (NCWP: Asia, the Caribbean and Africa other than South Africa, also excluding the Commonwealth territories of Canada, Australia and New Zealand). While there may have been a few people of Black and minority ethnic origin born in the UK at that time, they would have been heavily outnumbered by the children of expatriate British staff and civil servants working in the colonies and associated states of the Commonwealth, most of whom would have been white British, in modern terms. Most of the other non-UK-born population would probably have been of European origin, but many were refugees or 'European Voluntary Workers' (displaced people) from central and eastern Europe, following the events of the Second World War. A proportion of between 0.4 per cent and 0.5 per cent would, however, be a fair estimate of the Black and minority ethnic population of Britain at the time. Even in 1961, the non-UK-born population had only grown to 2.2 million out of 51.2 million (4.3 per cent), and those of NCWP background were still a small fraction of this (Runnymede Trust 1980). By 1971, however, the total non-UK-born population had grown to 3 million out of a total of 53.9 million (5.6 per cent), of whom 1.2 million (2.2 per cent) were of New Commonwealth birth. However, the 1966 Census (the last time that a 'sample' census was conducted in between the decennial counts) had demonstrated that one in three of the 'Indian-born' were in fact white people of 'colonial' families. In 1971 it was still estimated that 300,000 of the Indian-born population were white, against a possible 500,000 British-born Black, Asian and 'mixed' population. Consequently, it was estimated that the population of 'New Commonwealth and Pakistan' origin was about 2.4 per cent of the national total (Owen 1993). (Pakistan rejoined the Commonwealth in 1989.) The loss of the 'ethnic question' in 1981 meant that the Census had to analyse data using the proxy variable of 'head of household born in the New Commonwealth or Pakistan' in order to get some estimates of housing conditions and needs. On that basis, it was estimated that the Black and ethnic minority population was about 4.2 per cent of the national total in 1981. The introduction of the 'ethnic' question in 1991 produced the first reliable estimate of ethnic diversity for England and Wales (questions in Scotland and Northern Ireland were less detailed), showing that 5.5 per cent of the GB population (three million out of a total of nearly 55 million) were of minority ethnic origin. This was, however, heavily concentrated: nearly half (44.5 per cent) of the Black and minority ethnic population lived in the Greater London area, compared to only 10.3 per cent of the white population, and a further 14 per cent of the Black and minority ethnic population lived in the West Midlands. By 2001, the proportion of Black and minority ethnic people for England and Wales had risen to 7.9 per cent, or 12.9 per cent including 'other' minority ethnic origins, and there were some signs of a spread beyond the most heavily urbanized areas.

For practitioners, it is important to recognize that the UK 2011 census will provide more accurate and detailed statistics than ever before. The additional information included will enable better understanding of the key dimensions of discrimination and exclusion, and enable further refining of the provision of services to ensure that they are culturally and linguistically appropriate. New questions to be asked include English language proficiency, national identity, and citizenship (in the form of a question asking if the person holds a British, Irish or 'other' passport). This latter question may be less helpful, but in the 2007 'Census Test', nearly two thirds (69 per cent) of those giving their ethnic origin as Bangladeshi stated that their nationality was British. There will again be a question of faith or religion, and the 'ethnic group' question has been developed especially in respect of 'mixed or multiple' origins, and to include an Arab ethnic category as well as one for Gypsy or Irish traveller.

The 2011 Census is expected to indicate a rise in the Black and ethnic minority population on the 2001 figures to approximately 12 per cent (CRE estimates). This is a relatively small increase. What may be more significant is the increasingly diverse nature of this population, shifts in its internal demography and new and emerging identity formations (Fanshawe and Sriskandarajah 2010). Factors such as increased numbers of mixed heritage children, new associational and identity affiliations, the increased numbers of older people from minority backgrounds and concentrations in particular cities such as Birmingham that will produce a White minority (Finney and Simpson 2009) will be of much more significance in terms of the delivery of welfare to which we now turn.

PART 1
The State

1 Delivering welfare in a multicultural society

Themes, issues and debates

Introduction

Contemporary multiculturalism poses a number of challenges for the design and delivery of welfare services. Indeed, multiculturalism has come to represent one of the most profoundly unsettling processes in the renegotiation and reconfiguring of welfare services across Europe and beyond. As public sector services are being modernized and restructured into a new welfare framework, considerations of difference and diversity are being inserted into the heart of service delivery and will provide a litmus test of the efficacy of any system in years to come. Yet at the same time the fact of multiculturalism, while widely acknowledged, is not necessarily accepted. Too often, contemporary governments appear reluctant to recognize the basic rights that mobility throws up and too often they compromise potentially progressive policy strategies in order to retain widespread popular appeal. In an era of deep insecurities about the impacts of such change, questions of entitlement – who should have rights of citizenship, and questions of integration, cohesion and solidarity are hotly debated. Within this complex political dynamic, welfare arrangements are being renegotiated with the overarching aim of being sufficiently flexible and responsive to diversity while at the same time remaining equitable and cost-effective.

Service delivery in the UK in respect of Black and ethnic minorities has historically been poor. In the post-war era, addressing the welfare needs of groups considered racially, ethnically and culturally different from the majority ethnic group has been variously characterized by reluctance, neglect, incompetence and at times outright resistance on the part of governments. It is a shocking reality that some sixty years on from the establishment of a comprehensive framework for addressing the British population's welfare needs, poor service delivery and unmet need is more typical than not for minority ethnic groups and that unequal welfare outcomes remain the norm. The legacy of this state of affairs is ever apparent. In 2007, to mark its closure, the Commission for Racial Equality (CRE) published a summary report on its 30 years of existence entitled *A Lot Done, A Lot To Do.* This report noted the sad fact that an ethnic minority British baby born on an NHS ward today is still more likely to go on 'to receive poor quality education, be paid less, live in sub-standard housing, be in poor health and be discriminated against in other ways than his or her white contemporaries' (CRE 2007:1). A complex combination of factors contributes to this state of affairs, not least the dynamic and differentiated nature of minority communities themselves but it is also beyond dispute that the political and professional practices of defining and determining need and shaping delivery systems impact on the welfare experiences and outcomes for all ethnic minority groups. It is these policy decisions and practices that are held up for inspection in the contemporary welfare arena. Challenges are increasingly made to the universalist assumptions of public service delivery, to public service values, to notions of professionalism and to the discriminatory practices that serve to replicate the relations of privilege and power between different categories of citizen. Ethnic diversity is still far from being an embedded feature of public service delivery. We are still far from realizing a welfare framework that can appropriately address ethnic minority needs and indeed still far from agreement that this is necessary and desirable.

In the context of a 'modernized' welfare arena and the emergence of the new multi-sectorial, multi-layered, multi-funded framework of delivery, new perspectives and lines of enquiry exist for exploring the responsiveness of welfare provisioning for ethnic minority groups and individuals and their engagement with systems of welfare delivery. These widespread transformations in the public sphere are coupled with ongoing challenges to the universalist assumptions of the public service ethos and the liberal values that underpin them. No longer is the 'one size fits all' approach to delivery an accepted norm, nor the expectation that the individual will 'fit' into predetermined categories of need. Multiculturalism has produced transformations at the heart of contemporary welfare delivery and continues to do so. The idea of a welfare system geared to some homogenized understanding of the national collective has been undermined, as the contemporary reality of heterogeneity, fluidity and change unsettles the notion of a common national identity. At the same time traditional multicultural models of welfare provisioning are being disrupted by change within minority communities themselves. Complex, multiple and newly emerging identity patterns defy the easy categorization of minority groups for the purposes of policy intervention (Fanshawe and Sriskandarajah 2010). All of these factors contribute to the need for a refreshed consideration of how best to meet ethnic minority need(s).

This chapter opens up the central concerns of this text, the pursuit of appropriate, flexible and equitable forms of welfare delivery in a multi-faith, multi-ethnic society, by considering the issues and key debates that underpin

this endeavour. It considers the legacy of the past, contemporary transformations in the welfare arena and transformations to the idea of multiculturalism
itself that impact on welfare delivery. It asks how racial and ethnic 'difference'
can be accommodated in social welfare policy and practice and engages theor-
etically with key questions that are implied by the notion of multicultural
welfare.

The legacy of the traditional welfare state

Any review of where we are now or where we are headed inevitably opens
in dialogue with the traditional welfare state. The now established story of
'race' and welfare summons the unwieldy apparatus that was the Beveridgean
welfare state to demonstrate that policy making, governance and the performance of public bodies has been consistently found wanting in addressing
minority needs across all policy fields and across some considerable period of
time (Jacobs 1985; Williams 1989; Parekh Commission 2000; CRE 2007; Craig
2007b). The welfare state was not built to respond to diversity and very quickly
proved largely unable to adapt to the emerging reality of a multicultural society. The consequence of this is evidenced by a plethora of data that demonstrates widespread inequalities for ethnic minority groups across a range of
indicators (Walby *et al.* 2008) but is also evident in the experiential narratives
of minority individuals themselves (see for example Bryan *et al.* 1985 or
Phillips and Phillips 1998).

The original architecture of the welfare state, its assumptions and values
should concern us here only in as much as it continues to determine sets of
relationships, discourses and ideas and indeed practices that have proved
resilient to change. So, for example, even in the light of changes brought about
by a globalized economy, trans-national relationships and the loss of Empire,
particular notions of national citizenship and the national collective continue
to shape the boundaries of the welfare state (Clark 2004).

The traditional welfare state had fundamentally nationalistic and imperi-
alist foundations which gave rise to a very restricted view of citizenship.
Perhaps the most classic statement in the academic literature demonstrating
the interconnection between racist ideology, policy making and practice comes
from Fiona Williams (1989). Williams's analysis takes us through three historical eras, each inter-related but each reflecting a dominant narrative of the
'othering' of Black and minority ethnic peoples. From the 1905 Aliens Act,
through the influence of Eugenicist ideas in the inter-war period to the
exclusionary nation building project of the post-war period, Williams illustrates the ways in which racist assumptions have determined policies of exclusion for Black and ethnic minorities. From this perspective, the failures of the
welfare state in relation to ethnic minorities are attributable to a very exclusive

notion of citizenship rights based on an essentially racialized imagining of national identity. In this imaginary, the nation as the boundary of eligibility for access to services is essentially white and fundamentally homogeneous in terms of its values. Britain and Britishness are largely equated with whiteness and thus by definition Black people (and ethnic minority people of colour) cannot be British. Interestingly, what Williams alerts us to is the relevance of the pre-war attitudes to minorities in the crystallization of political views and debate that followed the large migrations in the post-war era. In doing so she and others identify a distinctly racialized orientation, directed to people of colour, rather than to difference *per se*; a factor noted by Kathleen Paul who contrasts the treatment of Commonwealth and European immigration pre- and post-war (Paul 1998).

Although post-war policies implied an equitable, fair and universal system of delivery for all British citizens, the notion of Britishness itself that was conveyed in policy papers and in welfare practices was clearly differentiated in a colour coded hierarchy. This hierarchy placed white Britons on the top of the list of those deserving, and Britons of colour at the bottom, reflecting tier after tier of gradations of eligibility (Paul 1998).

The perennial concerns that have underpinned post-war approaches as the core aims of public policy in the area of ethnic diversity and the liberal paradigm that shapes them have been:

- to encourage the adjustment and assimilation of existing ethnic minorities within the context of liberal universalist welfare provision (while restricting further immigration);
- to use regulatory agencies and measures to promote greater equality of opportunity and remove discriminations;
- to ensure better community/ethnic relations and thereby societal stability.

This approach has as its overarching aim the levelling out of diversity in order to sustain the homogeneity of the British nation. Restrictive and oppressive immigration legislation has continued to narrowly define and redefine British nationality with the aim of restricting eligibility to welfare resources and curtailing the flow of principally 'non-white' migrants into the country. These policies and enactments have produced what McLaughlin and Baker (2007) note as negatively differentiated citizenship whereby different tiers of citizenship status operate to confer particular sets of rights, with (by and large) the rights of a variety of old and newly racialized groups being restricted relative to those who are defined as part of the 'majority' society.

The enduring impact of this coupling of immigration legislation and welfare policy plays out on the contemporary scene in a number of ways: producing and reproducing inequalities along racialized lines, fuelling anxieties about immigrants as welfare scroungers and significantly deploying the welfare apparatus as a crucial mechanism in the surveillance and control of the lifestyles of Black and minority ethnic individuals and communities (Hayes 2000). In this way 'race' has been an orchestrating construct in government welfare policy and will continue to be while immigration policy and welfare policy remain so critically aligned. It has been a particular political ploy of governments of every hue to signal the institutions of the welfare state, and in particular the National Health Service, as representative of the very essence of Britishness and British values, symbolically coupling the welfare system with a very particular conception of the national collective. Inevitably, therefore, any perceived threat to the institutions of welfare and its bedrock values becomes a threat to Britishness itself.

This strategy, bolstered by media reporting, has effectively ensured the rise of 'popular' fears of immigration and cemented a discursive chain positing immigrants as a drain on limited welfare that remains central to welfare debates to this day (Goodhart 2004). Those early migrants of the 1940s and 1950s, like their contemporary counterparts, were vital to service delivery and yet deeply resented as consumers themselves of scarce welfare services. Migrants are generative of wealth and well-being in society and at the same time seen as presenting a demand on those very resources. A notable legacy of post-war welfarism is the reluctance to make any political capital of the contribution (quantitative or qualitative) made by migrant labour (see Chapter 6). There has been an abject failure on the part of policy makers and politicians, and indeed in the social policy research and literature, to capture and quantify this effort, to characterize the fundamental importance of cross-national and global interconnections to the survival of welfare institutions and welfarism in Britain. Thus the master narrative of the drain on welfare services has prevailed over the contributions narrative.

As a consequence the common myth that migrants and minority ethnic groups 'place a strain on public services' too often lies unchallenged (see, for example, the site of MigrationWatchUK – www.migrationwatchuk.org). Well-argued rebuttals of the notion of the welfare-dependent minority can be found elsewhere (see, for example, Finney and Simpson 2009, and the websites of ICAR – the Information Centre on Asylum and Refugees – www.icar.org.uk, or the Institute for Public Policy Research – www.ippr.org.uk, or what was possibly the earliest example of a careful examination of this question: Jones and Smith 1970). It is worth, however, revisiting the conclusions of all such studies:

1   Immigration overall has been, and continues to be, economically beneficial for states.
2   As a rule, migrants are most likely to be young, healthy and economically active, and well qualified or willing to take jobs that are 'hard to fill'.

3   Migrants are net contributors to national revenues through taxation.
4   Minority ethnic groups and migrants counterbalance the demo-
     graphic tendency for national populations to age and increase their
     dependency ratios.
5   Minority ethnic group members underclaim on the benefits to which
     they would be entitled.
6   There is no evidence that points to clear 'additional costs' in deliver-
     ing services to diverse minority ethnic populations (Szczepura *et al.*
     1998; Clark *et al.* 1998).

It may well be that migration of dependent relatives and older people has
continued to add small numbers of people who will need special attention
in terms of language needs and advice, given unfamiliarity with British
institutions (Green *et al.* 2009). On balance, however, there is little evidence to
support the 'drain on public services' arguments but considerable evidence of
how these arguments have been deployed in the debates on race/ethnicity and
welfare provisioning. Thus our argument in this text is that 'race' has mattered
in discourses of welfare and in policy making and continues to matter. It is not
simply a question of 'difference' that we are grappling with, or how to manage
service responsiveness in the light of increasing diversity, but that welfare
policies and practices have been intimately aligned to racialized divisions that
endure.

At an operational level the traditional welfare state as a system proved to
be riven with racisms and discriminations, sometimes intended, sometimes
benign, that contaminated service delivery, ensured low take-up and resulted
in inequitable outcomes. The bedrock of universalism on which the system
rested would always ensure that it fell short for Britain's growing ethnic minority population. Service users and service user organizations have long expressed
their frustration at the ineffectualness of welfare professionals that patholo-
gized their lifestyles and extended little more than the punitive arm of the
state towards them, and at the colour blindness of service delivery that
served to neglect or marginalize their needs (Bryan *et al.* 1985; Webster 1998).
Dissatisfactions and discontent would manifest themselves in open conflicts
on the streets, in both localized and national struggles over welfare outcomes
such as campaigns against the use of Depo Provera, campaigns for the recognition of sickle cell anaemia, or the uprisings in direct protest about poverty,
housing, education and policing as in Toxteth and Brixton. Such frustrations
resulted in the withdrawal into segregated and alternative provisioning. But
the incursions of such social movements were easily sidelined by the hier-
archical and bureaucratic structure of the welfare state which proved resilient
to ethnic minority welfare mobilization. As Miller (2004) has pointed out, the
edifice that was the welfare state, with its combination of the focus on expert
power, top-down central planning and collective security, left little room for

the active citizen or for wholesome community engagement. Ethnic minority-led welfare services would largely remain marginal to its operation, under-funded, lacking in capacity, compartmentalized and outside the policy wheel of evaluation and learning (see Chapter 4).

A legacy of mistrust ensues from these experiences at the front line of welfare services: a *Windrush scepticism*, as we might call it, that is proving hard to shake off. This loss of trust emanates from the day-to-day discrepancy apparent between formal and substantive rights of citizenship. Even those with access to the formal rights of citizenship as a legal status are excluded from exercising those rights in a myriad of ways, overt and banal, as 'un-belonging' from the national collective is communicated to them. Two problematics emanate from this particular history. The first is the 'Black disadvantage model' which has defined ethnic minorities in post-war multiculturalist policies as homogeneous collectives geographically contained in largely segregated areas of disadvantage. The policy vision of minority need has been set in this particular cast irrespective of other factors such as class, gender, locality, the differentiation of ethnic identities and social and spatial mobilities. Secondly, and significantly, a discourse on racial disadvantage based on the Windrush politics of the post-war period has been internalized by minority activists without too much reworking in the light of contemporary change. Old wounds take a long time to heal and an ongoing scepticism embedded in these politics is difficult to shift. This inevitably has led to the crisis of multiculturalism evident at the turn of the twenty-first century. The forging of a refreshed discussion on 'race' and race equality beyond the highly politicized strictures of originating debate was opened up by the Parekh report (Parekh Commission 2000), which we turn to below. Suffice to note here that the race relations discourse of the post-war period has furnished the language, concepts and analytical trajectories that have increasingly come under scrutiny.

The post-war consensus on multiculturalism and welfare has focused on the problematic nature of diversity, with only a cursory acceptance of its positive effects. It has lacked strategy and intent beyond the commitment to containment and control of 'the race relations problem' evident in defensive, reactive and negative policy making. Governments have been slow to accommodate the reality of settled minorities and the social implications of an increasingly globalized economy. Successive restructuring of the welfare state over decades produced no real shifts in terms of the well-being of ethnic minorities. In the late 1970s organizational reform of the welfare state under Margaret Thatcher did nothing to improve the situation for Britain's minorities. The radical restructure of welfare was driven not by a concern to produce a more responsive welfare framework but by a desire to create a more economically efficient system and one that would break the monopoly of the state and the dominance of public sector professionals. Indeed, policies on 'race' under Thatcher ensured the further marginalization and sidelining of minority concerns into a range of specific short-term initiatives, alongside an inflammatory discourse of immigrant scroungers (Lewis 2000b). Public service organizations were subject to marketization and service users became consumers of services obliged to mobilize choices across a spectrum of providers in the mixed economy of welfare. Under Thatcherite policies the vulnerable were to become more impoverished and inequalities more entrenched.

A number of very tangible impacts arise from this troubled history. The well-being of ethnic minorities remains an enduring concern. The Labour government's equalities roundup (HM Government 2007), noted a patterning of entrenched and persistent inequalities over decades with no small amount attributed to deep-seated discriminations. The evidence is indisputable. A vast literature on ethnic minority disadvantage provides a consistent message that minority populations living in the UK struggle to realize their citizenship rights within the context of inappropriate and unresponsive systems of welfare delivery and against the backdrop of widespread socio-economic disadvantage and social exclusions. The so-called 'ethnic penalty' retains a perennial hold, distorting opportunities, denying access and compromising substantive citizenship rights. A number of well-rounded accounts adopt the Beveridgean 'five giants' approach indicating across all the major policy fields: health, housing, poverty, education and caring, exclusions, discriminations and concomitant inequalities for racial and ethnic groups (*inter alia* Ratcliffe 2004 on major sites of exclusion; Ratcliffe 2004 on housing; Tomlinson 2008 on education; Law 2009 on social security and Nazroo 2010 on health inequalities; see also Parekh Commission 2000; Walby *et al.* 2008).

A review of discrimination in service provision undertaken by Chahal (2004) for the Joseph Rowntree Foundation looked at key messages arising from a body of research evidence. Chahal identified as problematic the ways in which mainstream services were often inappropriate to the needs of ethnic minorities with service responses based on assumptions and stereotypes about what these needs may be; and that while religious, cultural and multiple identity is very important to many people, this was rarely responded to by mainstream providers. The experience of racial discrimination and prejudice led to ethnic minority users seeking alternative specialist culturally competent services and yet, as Chahal identified from the studies considered, a number of barriers face voluntary and community sector organizations in responding to this need and the limitations of informal family support in many minority communities lead to high levels of unmet need (Chahal 2004).

Piecemeal advances in the field of welfare have been realized largely in response to crises and scandals – for example the Honeyford case (1985) and the issue of multicultural education and the Scarman Report (1981) on poverty and disadvantage in the 1980s; the death of Stephen Lawrence (1994), prompting the Macpherson Report (1999) and police reform in the 1990s. More latterly, examples are the Victoria Climbié case (2003) and child care reform and the Cantle report (2005), which influenced ideas on community cohesion in the 2000s. This populist-fuelled reactionary policy making has been riven with contradictions and poor implementation, characterized by lack of leadership and inept professional practice alongside an ongoing anti-immigration rhetoric. Some go as far as to argue that the state has been 'constantly hostile to the presence of Black, Asian and now other minorities' (Craig 2007b: 605).

The New Labour era – modernization and 'race'

The 1997 election of the Labour government came after eighteen years of neo-liberal politics and provided an opportunity to reconsider the organization of the welfare system and its responsiveness in meeting social needs. New Labour's social reform programme provided an alternative set of policies aiming to reclaim the sense of solidarity, collectivism and social citizenship lost during the Thatcher years, but at the same time signalled a distinctive shift away from the post-war Fabian model of welfare that had been so roundly undermined. It was dubbed the 'Third Way'. It was clear that post-war structures were not going to meet the realities of a complex, diverse society and shifting social attitudes. Old centrist and universalist tendencies of government were to be replaced by a distinctive shift towards the individual, communities and regions in determining their own needs and priorities. This would provide the key to a more responsive welfare framework. New Labour also sought to retain the redistributionist tradition of the party but with a break from the 'something for nothing' approach of the past. There were clear concerns to acknowledge and celebrate the spectre of a changing and vibrant multicultural society and communicate a vision of a modern and inclusive society. The *modernization* project therefore re-emphasized the role public services could play in promoting such solidarity and social cohesiveness.

Modernization has remained the dominant theme of successive Labour administrations and has been gradually extended across a range of service sectors. The core ingredients of this agenda are partnership working and joined-up policy thinking between a plurality of service providers both inter-agency and inter-professional. There is a clear restatement of the public service ethos and a greater reliance on evidence to guide practice. In addition the role of the citizen has been transformed from passive recipient to active agent, crucially involved in the planning, delivery and evaluation of services. Greater participation at all levels of government has been facilitated by the creation of new structures of engagement. Greater forms of devolution have been encouraged, allowing for differentiation in public service delivery and the extension of choice between service providers. The state's role accordingly has shifted towards regulation and building service quality, ensuring a national framework of minimum standards and building the capacity of citizens to engage within new structures of governance. Alongside this the state's direct provider roles have diminished. Several writers have critically commented on the various elements of the New Labour reforms (for example Levitas 2005; Vidler and Clark 2005). This general critique cannot engage us here. The themes of public engagement, new and evolving forms of social citizenship, capacity building and transforming the performance of public sector institutions and professionals *vis-à-vis* issues of race and ethnicity are issues for critical discussion in the forthcoming chapters of this text. It is worth pausing here, however, to extrapolate some key observations on New Labour's public services agenda on 'race'.

Perhaps the most significant characteristic of the New Labour project is its contradictory positioning in relation to 'race' issues. It has arguably been both progressive and regressive in its policy stances. In the aftermath of the 1997 election several significant developments indicated a government willing to embrace multiculturalism. It dropped the primary purpose clause in immigration law which prevented people bringing their spouse to settle in the UK. It signalled its vision of a cohesive and inclusive society which would underpin its modernization of services through a series of political speeches and high-profile events hosted by the then prime minister, Tony Blair. The government quickly committed itself to combating social exclusion, framed in terms of extending equality of opportunity rather than a focus on equality of outcome. In the first term of office it established the Social Exclusion Unit and a number of social development initiatives such as the Sure Start programme and the New Deal for Communities and a number of redistributionist programmes such as its promise to eradicate child poverty. By the second term it was notably beckoning in a groundbreaking new era of equalities policy. As a direct response to the Macpherson Report on the Stephen Lawrence Inquiry (1999) it placed institutional racism firmly on the political agenda, instituting far-reaching duties on all public authorities under the terms of the Race Relations (Amendment) Act 2000 (see Chapter 2). Despite clear caveats about its implementation in practice, this piece of legislation has been seen as potentially transformative and representative of a major benchmark in British race relations. In addition this was a government that clearly embraced European expansion, and the open borders policy for new economic migrants which saw the influx of some 750,000 migrants from Eastern Europe between 2004 and 2008 (ICC and LGA 2007).

However, a deep ambivalence quickly became apparent in its approach to racial and ethnic diversity. Against these progressive steps in the sphere of domestic politics stood a strident anti-immigration rhetoric which gained momentum in response to populist fears following the terrorist attacks of September 2001 and July 2007 and the riots in northern towns in 2001. No fewer than four pieces of immigration legislation have been passed in the 2000s by a government keen not to be seen to be out of step with widespread anti-immigration sentiments. The anti-immigration rhetoric was twinned with a powerful discourse of assimilationism. Early sporadic controversies under Jack Straw in the Home Office relating to issues such as the wearing of religious insignia and the wearing of the veil, and the David Blunkett English test for immigrants as a mark of citizenship, formed part of a refreshed and concerted discourse of assimilationism. In 1998 a high-profile Commission was convened by the Runnymede Trust, an independent think tank, to consider 'The future of multi-ethnic Britain'. From their deliberations what became known as the Parekh Report (Parekh Commission 2000) was published and it provided an impressive array of policy recommendations which could have been an important turning point in the politics of 'race' and welfare had it not been interpreted as an attack on the idea of Britishness (McGlaughlin and Neal 2004). The report examined the range of social policy fields in relation to progress on race equality and set out a far-reaching agenda for change. It offered a more nuanced and complex concept of multiculturalism beyond the rather fixed and essentialist groupings that characterized the post-war under-standing, which included considerations of new migrations, hybridity and mixedness and the position of national minorities such as the Welsh and the Irish. The report called for an integrated strategy of *reimagining* the national story and identity, for a balancing of equality and difference, liberty and cohesion and for confronting and eliminating racisms (2000:105). Its affront to the idea of Britishness, however, was too out of step with the New Labour project, effectively ensuring that no government agenda would arise from it.

From the second electoral victory in 2001 New Labour discourse began a more targeted restatement of the notion of Britishness and the search for common values. Gordon Brown, as Chancellor, led this prominent political agenda, giving several speeches aimed at establishing the key ingredients of these shared values. A plethora of managed integration strategies such as citizenship ceremonies, community cohesion policies and directives on limiting the use of interpreting services flowed. These policies effectively switched the focus away from institutions as the focus of the problem towards blaming the communities and people themselves for their disadvantage as a result of their failure to integrate. The self-segregation thesis of the Cantle Report (2005) into the uprisings in the northern cities crystallized this thinking and the death knell of multiculturalist policies had been rung.

In the third term, amidst widespread disaffection with multiculturalist policies on all sides of the political spectrum, within the academy and in populist thinking, New Labour effected its distancing from what it saw as an outdated model of multiculturalism. The dominant discourse on multiculturalism, it was argued, was based on a seventies model of discrete and essentialized groupings (Alibhai Brown 2000; T. Phillips 2005) that led to divisiveness and conflict and worked against the ambitions of a cohesive society. This new direction was marked by clear shifts in the policy language (Worley 2005) and the gradual move away from single-strand equality policies towards generic approaches to equalities. By 2006 the government had signalled its intention to disband the 'silos' approach to addressing discrimination by replacing the specialized equality commissions with a single equality commission, the Commission for Equality and Human Rights (now EHRC) in 2007 and moving towards a Single Equality Act. Its 2007 *Equalities Review* (HM Government 2007) signalled a new methodology for quantifying inequality which effectively disaggregated 'race'/ethnicity as a composite political constituency and focused on the evidence of particular vulnerabilities within and between ethnic groups (see Chapter 2). The gradual shifting away from race-specific policies has continued. In February 2009 the government undertook a consultation on 'Tackling racial inequalities' and produced a discussion document (DCLG 2009) from which its vision document *Tackling Race Inequality: A Statement on Race* (2010) was produced. This sets out the government's vision for embedding race equality within its broader equalities vision and commitment. The document discusses five key public service areas: education, employment, housing/regeneration, health and social services and criminal justice in terms of impacting on racial inequality and sets out 21 strategic questions for consideration. The statement is underpinned by a Tackling Race Inequality Fund of some £6 million for supporting projects aligned to identified priorities. The launch of this statement was met with some cynicism in the press, primarily because the thrust of its argument that poverty and class largely outweigh race as the key variables in disadvantage once again displayed a government reluctant to confront head-on the issues of widespread racism, discrimination and prejudice. It is not difficult to see the issuing of this *Statement on Race* as a transitional and placatory strategy within a broader shift away from the single-strand politics of race.

> There is also an important point about ensuring that our efforts to promote equality, to achieve fair outcomes for everyone, are in themselves fair and seen to be fair. We have to avoid the perception that some groups are singled out for special treatment. When we target help at one group, we cannot allow others to be left behind or to feel disconnected, otherwise there is a risk that our efforts will be exploited by those who would distort them to drive people apart. The over-riding message must be that regardless of class, race, beliefs or anything else: in every community, in every corner of the country – we are on people's side. No favours. No privileges. No special interest groups. Just fairness.
>
> (DCLG 2010: 12, para 1.22)

What is evident from an overall review of New Labour's policy stances is that Labour policies are essentially both apparently progressive and at the same time deeply repressive, reflecting the dilemma at the heart of the New Labour project. Back *et al.* (2002) explore the tensions underpinning New Labour policy and conclude that it is riven with 'incommensurable commitments and aspirations' (2002: 5.7). New Labour policy, they argue, has attempted to both respond to the demands for economic growth and the need to be responsive to the impacts of global economic forces and at the same time retain popular appeal by protecting the integrity of nation and nationhood. Thus New Labour needs to both placate its voters if it is to retain power and provide the circumstances conducive to the growth of capital. Stuck between two very contradictory demands, New Labour is, as Back *et al.* argue, prone to a very particular 'stress' (Back *et al.* 2002).

This dilemma has become more acute in successive Labour administrations and been given more fuel within domestic politics by discourses that suggest increased migrations weaken the very fabric of welfare systems. David Goodhart, editor of *Prospect* magazine, dubbed this contradictory positioning 'the progressive dilemma' (2004). For Goodhart this is a dilemma facing all left-wing governments wishing to appear favourable to the realities of multiculturalism yet at the same time not wishing to be out of step with the populist anxieties about immigration, asylum and undocumented migrants. Goodhart controversially suggested that 'too much diversity' undermines a common sense of citizenship, trust and reciprocities so fundamental to a risk-sharing welfare system (Goodhart 2004). His argument is that people are generally motivated towards give and take relationships along discrete co-ethnic lines and that ethnic segregationalism serves to erode the potential for societal redistribution and for the building of solidarities that are the essential glue of any welfare system. What Goodhart-type arguments fail to capture is the contribution migrant labour has made and is making to the resource base and development of welfare systems. This type of argument also implies that welfare reciprocities work along co-ethnic lines with ethnic minorities preferring to gift to their compatriots rather than to fellow citizens. There can be no real justification for this implication other than the fact that wider structural inequalities have spatially segregated large numbers of ethnic minorities who then necessarily become self-supporting. In this respect this is a circular argument that blames minority communities for their community spiritedness and begs the question: where is the evidence that they are self-serving and self-segregating?

Integration has accordingly become a key strand of New Labour policy targeted through a range of cohesion policies. This civic assimilationism and the inclusion agenda of New Labour tussles uneasily with the paradoxical injunction of contemporary multiculturalism as it looks towards the fostering of community but also away from it, seeking to break the bonds of the ethnically tied community. On the one hand ethnic minority groups are regarded as communities for the purposes of institutional state-orchestrated multiculturalist policies; at the same time policy is reluctant to acknowledge them as discrete groups as this is a potentially divisive force to wider integration. Public policy is now being steered away from recognition of such place-based territorially or ethnically segregated entities. The paradox is, however, that New Labour's rhetoric of locality, individual responsibility, community and regions is pitched exactly towards such smaller units of self-government. Herein lies an inherent tension, for it is apparent that for New Labour *some* types of community are favoured while others are not. The community of ethnically homogeneous groupings is clearly viewed sceptically. The mosque, the synagogue, the faith school or the ethnic 'overseas' students' association are no longer the haven of solidarity, welfare support and evidence of a vibrant civil society but are suspect, as the potential seat of conflict and dissent or even of terrorism (see Chapter 4).

In many ways, therefore, New Labour has sought to walk the fine line of encouraging community association and disputing its relevance. Nowhere has this been more publicly contested of late than in relation to the issue of faith schools and faith organizations. Greater and greater degrees of surveillance have emerged to monitor the activities of such communities. In the contemporary climate of fears and uncertainty, public service professionals are increasingly deployed in such vigilance across a range of welfare domains – teachers in schools and colleges must look for 'suspect' activities and forms of association and intervene to stop pupils from turning to terrorism by promoting common values; university lecturers are required to monitor closely the attendance of students who are on immigration visas for fear that this is a gateway to illegal immigration, and health visitors must subject asylum children to health tests to verify their age status. The apparatus of welfare has been mobilized toward higher levels of surveillance as suspicion of certain communities mounts in the public imagining.

While the New Labour era boded well for a number of significant redistributive reforms it has proved to be an era of missed opportunities. Its preoccupation with culture and faith has served to divert attention away from the issues of class-based disadvantage and inequality such that the promised tangible redistributive impacts on issues such as poverty, child welfare, poor health, educational outcomes and safety increasingly reveal a record of broken promises. It has pursued a largely liberal agenda of seeking to open up equality of opportunity and the removal of the most conspicuous barriers of discrimination for those Black and ethnic minorities 'at home' while pursuing ever more restrictive immigration policies towards migrants and asylum seekers. It is not difficult to argue, therefore, that the post-war assimilationist strategy retains its ascendancy in public policy and the modernization project is but another phase in a story of tinkering and incremental piecemeal responses to 'managing' the race issue rather than being driven by a concerted effort to establish race equality.

Conclusion: what does a multicultural welfare framework demand?

It will be clear from the aforegoing discussion that the pursuit of a multi-cultural welfare is not without contention and dispute. The search for a welfare framework that respects, accommodates and is responsive to diversity has far from popular support. Ethnic and racial heterogeneity is nevertheless a fact of modern British society. It exists, and efforts to publicly acknowledge and insti-tutionalize this heterogeneity have resulted in a variety of policy responses we can broadly call multiculturalist policies. The familiarity of this argument belies some of the deep complexities and pragmatic challenges posed for wel-fare provisioning in a multi-ethnic, multi-faith society – complexities that throw up for review not only infrastructural arrangements to meet need but ideologies, values and philosophies that underpin policy making and service delivery. These puzzles and policy dilemmas carry immense import beyond the search for pragmatic and workable solutions to meeting need. The con-cerns are not simply about how to tackle the challenges posed for delivering welfare in a diverse society but strike to the heart of assumptions of the liberal state and raise normative questions fundamental to contemporary society about how we live together, about the web of social relationships, reciprocities, solidarities and the everyday interactions that constitute individual and soci-etal well-being. All are highly contested.

There are evidently new opportunities posed by welfare reform in the last decade. Greater levels of self-governance, involvement in the shaping of wel-fare delivery and more democratic processes in public services open up the potential for more responsive services which could benefit Black and minority ethnic groups. Newman (2007), in her analysis of the process of moderniza-tion of welfare states, notes three major discursive shifts that are serving to unsettle public sector service delivery and that point towards a new politics of welfare. The first relates to the transformations in the public sphere itself, away from the centralized state monopoly of the delivery of services towards the market and towards the more personal domains of the voluntary and informal sector. This decentring of the state and dismantling of the public sector breaks what she calls the links in the discursive chain that assumes an equivalence between public sector institutions and public service values. As governance has become more open, so the values that inform welfare design, priorities and delivery have become more plural. Thus the notion that the state reflects a common public service ethos is undermined by this dynamic of the mixed economy. Secondly, she notes challenges to a discursive chain that suggests the public sphere as neutral, rational, open and tolerant in its dealings. She suggests this discourse has offered a relatively narrow politics of the public sphere – limiting counter claims for voice and justice and operating 'unjust' colour blind policies (2007: 59). Finally, she notes how the discourse that links the nation state to core ideas of shared national citizenship, universalism and commonality has been steadily and consistently weakened by the emergence of claims from a multicultural, multi-ethnic, multi-faith society.

The issue of competing values and aspirations is one that has come to confront significantly the assumptive world of public service delivery. The fact of multiculturalism has challenged the liberal values of Western bureaucratic forms of organization as being open, tolerant, meritocratic, impartial, rational and fostering equality of opportunity. These values have been criticized on a number of levels by Black and minority ethnic user groups, by professionals and academic theorists who have demonstrated them to be ill-equipped to mediate questions of social diversity. They argue that administrative actions are rooted in and reflective of wider social relations and that the social relations embedded in institutions are clearly mono-cultural. Modern-day dilemmas such as competing ideas about parental discipline, 'forced' marriages, the role of faith schools and the role of segregated welfare provisioning are given the apparel of deliberation but ultimately subsumed within the over-arching framework of liberalism. Yet the state is far from neutral. In social welfare, writers have argued against the cultural universalism of services organized around 'white norms' (Atkin and Chattoo 2007). Atkin and Chattoo, for example, argue that the recognition of difference and diversity has acted to illustrate that the 'white norm' of public institutions is no longer securely invisible and its exposure challenges the professional self and the professional ethos.

The issue of competing values in a plural society is a debate the Parekh Report (Parekh Commission 2000) sought to address. The report called for transformations to the public realm, to its conceptual languages, forms of speech, patterns of thinking and standardized responses (2000: 223). In a similar vein, Newman (2007) calls for a *rethinking* of the liberal public sphere. She argues that the state is far from the transparent, neutral arbiter of competing claims but has proved itself to be out of step and unable to respond to competing claims for recognition and justice. These writers offer a critique of the idea of common values; shared values, they suggest, are essentially liberal values and non-negotiable. Accordingly, reworking the structures of the welfare state but leaving untouched its assumptive world (its values) can only produce a never-ending cycle of ineffectiveness in response to multiculturalism.

The emerging welfare framework is in development. There is now more than ever before greater potential for involvement, responses and resistances in the process of *remaking* welfare. A new localism, greater forms of devolution, flexibility and responsiveness in service delivery, new forms of alliance, increased public participation and capacity building to promote wholesome deliberations over service outcomes are all part of the new arrangements. The concept of a welfare society engages with these new forms of public participation, with potential new and novel alliances between providers, users of services, policy actors and academics and citizens in general. It is not based on a structure or set of structures but an emergent property of these new processes of engagement. The search for an overarching structure, as in the creation of the welfare state, is to overlook the impact of serendipity and to deny the significance of struggles, actions of radical professionals and others over welfare outcomes and to misread the available framework for securing change. In such a framework issues of power, enfranchisement and equality will be critical to the success or otherwise of a multicultural welfare system.

Typically, cultural diversity has been seen as problematic rather than as a resource to the development of welfare. The conundrum is how to effectively harness this resource to produce more responsive service delivery in the context of *a welfare society*. Strategies for change include actions on a range of levels, to reduce racisms and discrimination, to tackle inequalities and to promote increased participation and interactions between the range of people of all ages and backgrounds in society. The remainder of this text explores in more depth the various aspects of contemporary welfare practices via this multi-tiered, multi-funded, multi-sectorial welfare delivery, highlighting issues that need to be addressed to ensure progress towards the challenge of multicultural welfare.

2 Equality and social welfare
Legal duties and regulation

Introduction

The protection of rights and the securing of equity and equality were established as fundamental principles of the post-war welfare system and remain core ambitions in public service delivery. It has long been recognized that legislation alone cannot secure these ends but legislative instruments remain critical levers to change. The valedictory report of the Commission for Racial Equality (CRE 2007) noted that many changes had taken place in the climate and practice of 'race relations' during the previous thirty years. This is attributed in part to the development of legislation, and in part to changing mindsets and policy frameworks. In this, the report appears to echo the recommendations of the Parekh Report (Parekh Commission 2000) that pointed to the positive effects of the 1976 Race Relations Act. Its chapter on health and welfare suggested a series of coordinated actions, policies and regulatory changes, including requirements for data collection and monitoring, to underpin legislative developments. There have been a large number of such proposals, initiatives and regulatory innovations: not all have had an immediate impact or can be shown to have been successful, but the totality of their existence has undoubtedly had an effect on corporate cultures and on practice. However, some, most notably the multiple requirements for monitoring, appear still to be more marked 'in the breach rather than the observance' (as Shakespeare once remarked in a different context: *Hamlet*, Act 1, Sc 4, 1603). At the end of the first decade of the twenty-first century, equalities legislation has undergone significant transformation. A new legislative approach has been introduced that represents a rebalancing of effort from an emphasis on enforcement and sanctions to an emphasis on self-regulation. Within the new welfare arrangements the protection of rights and the promotion of equality involves a significantly extended remit for public bodies and public service professionals, and a strong legal framework and effective enforcement are recognized as critical levers to ensuring better outcomes for ethnic minority groups (DCLG 2010). This chapter considers the history and development of legislation for race equality in the context of wider changes that have taken place at the level of the European Union. It comments on the strengths and limitations of statutory drivers in taking forward the equality mandate and concludes by considering some of the issues raised for equalities practice within the contemporary welfare economy.

The history and development of legislation for equality

There has been in Britain, since the start of the twentieth century, a tension between the principle of protecting the persons and rights of migrants, refugees and minorities and the political imperative to satisfy 'democratic' demands from the general population who have, for much of that time, seemed opposed to any incursion on their own rights and privileges. This has been to the point of resisting the access of any migrants and the rights of anyone who might be described as belonging to a minority other than their own. Thus, in 1905, the Aliens Act was introduced to restrict the flow of Jewish 'aliens' (i.e. non-citizens) to Britain, and to insist that any migrants granted entry should not become a 'burden' on the state, or, more specifically, have recourse to welfare provided by the then apparatus of the 'welfare state' (the parish system). Indeed, at that time, Jewish refugees were accused of both taking British workers' jobs *and* of living on welfare at the same time (Brown 1995), in the same racist and self-contradictory mythology which opponents of migration continue to employ in the twenty-first century. During the period of maximum immigration to Britain, immigration law and anti-discrimination legislation marched more or less in step on the premise that 'Without integration, limitation is inexcusable. Without limitation, integration is impossible' (a catchphrase attributed to the Labour politician Roy Hattersley in 1965). It is worthy of remark that this came not long after the then leader of the Labour Party, Hugh Gaitskell, stated in 1961: 'The Labour Party is opposed to the restriction of immigration as every Commonwealth citizen has the right as a British subject to enter the country at will.' This right of citizens was 'unconditional', and it was made clear that there should be no restrictions on grounds of health or criminal record (Jenkins 1999). However, this was the run-up to a period of serious debate and anti-minority politics, which included the famous 'Rivers of Blood' speech by Enoch Powell, the Minister of Health who perhaps more than any other politician did so much directly to recruit internationally to staff the NHS.

During the 1960s race was to become a major public issue in British politics. It was, however, immigration which became the focus of attention and not the question of racial equality. In the eighteen months before the passage of the Commonwealth Immigrants Act (1962), over 200,000 Black migrants had arrived in Britain. This period was marked by a sharp and negative shift in public opinion (Layton Henry 1992). In 1962, a few months before the passage of the Act, 62 per cent of the public favoured controls and 23 per cent favoured free entry but by April 1968 the corresponding figures were 95 per cent and 1 per cent respectively. Party leaders and prominent spokesmen (there were few high-profile female politicians at the time) did little to counter this shift, but rather sought to jump on the bandwagon and harness the energy for their own party. Thus, it was clear that both major parties subscribed to the view that immigration should be controlled, on the grounds that immigrants placed great strain on employment and housing. The rhetoric, further, continued to elide the distinction between migrant and minority ethnic, so that by the time Britain's first civil rights law, the Race Relations Act 1965, had been passed, for many, 'Blacks' had become synonymous with 'immigrants'.

Moreover, prior to the Local Government Act of 1966 (with its groundbreaking provisions in Section 11), the general laissez-faire attitude of central and local government meant that virtually nothing had been done to cater for the problems that many immigrants experienced in housing, education and social welfare (Johnson *et al.* 1988). It is also worth noting that the only reason that this particular piece of legislation was so liberal is that it contained a plethora of incentives to urban local authorities to support its reforms, by promising Home Office monies for those which could demonstrate that they suffered from a diversity of handicaps such as the presence of a major port or airport of national significance – and therefore 'carrying a burden' on behalf of the nation which could and should not be funded out of local taxation. Section 11 included among these burdens the presence of 'significant numbers' (2 per cent) of the population being of 'non-English cultural background'. A modern parallel could be drawn with the funds offered to areas with large airports or waste disposal sites.

While it seems agreed that the first 'equality and diversity' legislation to have real impact was the Sex Discrimination Act (1975), the model for nearly all such activity was the 1965 Act, and the approach was first tried in relation to racism. This drew heavily on the example of the United States of America following the riots or urban uprisings and civil rights campaigning that reached a peak in and around 1967 and, especially, the Report of the National Advisory Commission on Civil Disorders or Kerner Report, published in 1968. One significant difference, however, was the avoidance of any attempt in Britain to emulate the Affirmative Action policy proposals which had been initiated by President Kennedy in 1961 (Executive Order 10925 mandated 'affirmative action' to ensure that applicants are employed, and that employees are treated during employment without regard to their race, creed, colour, or national origin). That approach was reinforced by the Johnson administration and subsequent US governments.

In Europe, and especially perhaps in Britain, there has been considerable suspicion and opposition to what has been termed more commonly 'positive discrimination', and indeed, UK and EU legislation explicitly forbids this in relation to race. There is, however, some difference between equality strands in this respect. For example, there was a long-standing expectation (often ignored) that employers should recruit a minimum quota or target of people with disabilities – not only in the UK but also in other Member States of the European Union. In countries such as France and Germany quotas are regarded as an intrinsic element of disability employment policy. Moreover, Article 7(2) of the EU Employment Equality Directive provides additional protection for positive action in respect of people with disabilities. It states that:

> with regard to disabled persons, the principle of equal treatment is without prejudice to the right of Member States to maintain or adopt provisions on the protection of health and safety at work or to measures aimed at creating or maintaining provisions or facilities for safeguarding or promoting their integration into the working environment.

Similar attitudes have been expressed in relation to gender discrimination, especially since the 1999 Treaty of Amsterdam (Article 141(4)), which states that:

> with a view to ensuring full equality in practice between men and women in working life, the principle of equal treatment shall not prevent any Member State from maintaining or adopting measures providing for specific advantages in order to make it easier for the under-represented sex to pursue a vocational activity or to prevent or compensate for disadvantages in professional careers.

Such an approach has never been attempted in relation to minority ethnic groups or to counter discrimination based on race. Certain provisions of the UK Race Relations Act (1976) could be interpreted as permitting positive actions in relation to employment, noting that there may be 'Genuine Occupational Qualifications' inherent in the ability to speak a language, be of a specified gender, or belong to a culture or faith – in very limited circumstances. The 1976 legislation also allowed additional training to be provided to groups who were 'under-represented' – but there is little evidence that this had a significant impact on the situation of under-represented minorities.

The Labour Party manifesto for the 1964 General Election did contain a commitment to legislate against racial discrimination and incitement in public places. The working group, however, confined the scope of legislation against racial discrimination to public places, and to employment, rather than services. They further felt that racial discrimination should be a criminal offence, requiring official support for prosecution and a higher standard of proof than in a civil case. In the end, the case for a civil right was made, and a group of supporters, including Anthony Lester, impressed by the American experience that anti-discrimination laws were more effectively enforced by administrative machinery than by proceedings in the courts, presented proposals which in the end led to the creation of a Race Relations Board – the forerunner of the present Equality and Human Rights Commission. Their original proposal was in fact for a citizens' council with powers to investigate discrimination on the grounds of race, colour, religion, sex and national origin in the fields of education, employment, housing, insurance, credit facilities and the administration. At no point was health or welfare ever considered, which might well reflect a nervousness about reawakening the spectre of the 'welfare migrant'.

In passing, we might briefly reflect on the role of individuals and champions: Anthony Lester also helped Jenkins to write a memorable speech on racial equality in Britain, which he gave in May 1966, in which he defined integration 'not as a flattening process of assimilation but as equal opportunity, accompanied by cultural diversity, in an atmosphere of mutual tolerance' (1966 address to Voluntary Liaison Committees: National Committee for Commonwealth Immigrants). He subsequently was elevated to the House of Lords, and as Lord (Anthony) Lester of Herne Hill QC was an architect of the Race Relations Act (1976) and the Single Equality Bill (2009), which has been proposed as a model for lawmakers in creating workable legislation that is effectively enforced. Equally, it is true that he did not act alone, but was assisted in the early days by Lord Pitt, one of the first Black peers and, indeed, a GP of Caribbean origin who made a significant contribution to both the development of the NHS and UK race relations (http://www. 100greatblackbritons. com/bios/lord_david_pitt.html).

The changes introduced by the Race Relations Act (1976) marked a significant move forward from the 'enforcement' activity of the 1965 Act (albeit in a small area of social life) and the 'encouragement' activity of the Community Relations Commission set up by the 1968 Act which had few teeth and little concern for health and welfare. The 1976 legislation extended the meaning and scope of discrimination and replaced the Race Relations Board and Community Relations Commission by one body, the Commission for Racial Equality. It widened the ability of individuals to seek redress by allowing individual access to courts and tribunals and altered the criminal offence of incitement to racial hatred. Most significantly, for our concerns, in regard to the meaning and scope of discrimination, the definition now included indirect discrimination (Section 1(1) (b)) as well as discrimination by victimization (Section 2). The grounds on which discrimination were made unlawful were extended to cover discrimination on the grounds of nationality (Section 3). Contract workers (Section 7), partnerships (Section 10) and various professional and training bodies (Sections 12 to 15) as well as clubs with a membership of 25 or more (Section 25) were all brought within the scope of the Act (MacEwen 1991). In this way the ground was laid for the present legislation and the findings of the Scarman (1981) and Macpherson inquiries (1999), which led to the legislative recognition of 'institutional discrimination'. This took the responsibility out of the need to prove a single individual was culpable, and the sting out of accusations of 'being' or 'acting' in a racially discriminatory or 'racist' manner – which had been hard to prove and enforce and which had in fact been a barrier to changing practices. The Macpherson Inquiry into the murder of Stephen Lawrence defined institutional racism thus:

> The collective failure of an organization to provide an appropriate and professional service to people because of their colour, culture or ethnic origin. It can be seen or detected in processes, attitudes and behaviour which amount to discrimination through unwitting prejudice, ignorance, thoughtlessness and racist stereotyping which disadvantages ethnic minority people.
>
> [Racism] persists because of the failure of the organization openly and adequately to recognize and address its existence and cause by policy, example and leadership. Without recognition and action to eliminate, such racism can prevail as part of the ethos or culture of the organization. It is a corrosive disease.
>
> (Macpherson 1999: 28, para. 6.34)

The report also emphasized that this concept was one relevant to all bodies (e.g. the NHS):

> Racism, institutional or otherwise, is not the prerogative of the Police Service. It is clear that other agencies including for example those dealing with housing and education also suffer from the disease. If racism is to be eradicated there must be specific and co-ordinated action both within the agencies themselves and by society at large, particularly through the educational system, from pre-primary school upwards and onwards.
>
> (Macpherson 1999: 33, para. 6.54)

When in 2000, in response to the pressures arising from the findings of the Macpherson tribunal and the concerted actions of minority ethnic communities and groups (including the dignified and powerful representations made by the family of Stephen Lawrence), parliament passed the Race Relations Amendment Act (RRAA), significant and irreversible gains were made in combating discrimination and inequality, patching the gaps left in the original legislation. The establishment under this piece of legislation of the notion of a 'general duty' to combat inequality provides a powerful instrument for change, and has meant that no public (and few private) bodies can now deny that they have to take account of diversity, and none can take refuge in pointing to a 'primary' objective that overrides it. Indeed, every public body has to establish a published Race Code of Practice and undertake regular audits of policy against identified targets, including Equality Impact assessments (O'Cinneide 2001).

Contemporary developments at European level

There is now in operation a large raft of legislation affecting equality and diversity duties. Anyone who tenders for government contracts has to sign framework contracts that require bidders to assent to compliance with a range of these, from the Prevention of Corruption Acts 1889 to 1916, to the Employment Equality (Sexual Orientation) Regulations 2003 and 2007. Most far-reaching are the requirements to comply with regulations made under such legislation, which are continually updated. Some of these have great potential to improve the situation of Britain's Black and minority ethnic communities – if they were enforced. In particular, the drive to adopt European standards as expressed in the expanded community's Amsterdam and Lisbon treaties has widened significantly the potential for minority ethnic groups to benefit. This was itself something of a breakthrough, since the original Treaty and founding documents of the European Community paid little or no attention to racialized or ethnic discrimination, and it was for a long time held that the EU had no competence in these areas. All that changed with the introduction of the Amsterdam Treaty and the new approach of supporting 'human rights', which in turn developed out of incremental legislation and regulation.

The founding Treaties of the European Community, and its predecessors, the European Coal and Steel Community, and European Economic Community (EEC), contained no specific provisions on fundamental rights. Guarantees for fundamental rights slowly emerged from rulings of the European Court of Justice. In 1986 the preamble to the Single European Act included a reference to the promotion of democracy on the basis of fundamental rights. This stated that 'the Union shall respect fundamental rights, as guaranteed by the European Convention for the Protection of Human Rights and Fundamental Freedoms signed in Rome on 4 November 1950 and as they result from the constitutional traditions common to the Member States, as general principles of Community law' (Article 6(2), ex Article F.2). As European integration has progressed, the European Union has gradually widened its field of action and advanced these rights on behalf of residents, migrant workers and all who hold any form of European citizenship or legal residence. This does not, of course, necessarily include all migrants or minorities, especially those who are seeking asylum or have moved to seek work without formal documentation.

British legislation has had to take account of these changes, and, while initially more concerned with 'race' and ethnicity issues and welfare of migrant-descended minorities, it is perhaps now no more liberal than (and in certain respects may lag behind) the directives and treaties that form the corpus of pan-European rights. These include a number of main European Directives, initially primarily focusing on employment but increasingly concerning wider forms of domestic discrimination. Only one directly addresses the specific concerns of migrant/minority groups: Council Directive 2000/43/EC implementing the principle of equal treatment between persons irrespective of racial or ethnic origin.

The most significant change at a European level, however, was the incorporation of the new 'Article 13' into the Amsterdam Treaty, which enabled the Council to take appropriate action to combat discrimination based on sex, racial or ethnic origin, religion or belief, disability, age or sexual orientation, after consulting the European Parliament. This has led, in all the states of the Union, to moves towards new legislation and a wider human rights equalities agenda – on a supra national level. Clearly, the background to this was the context of wider European migration, and a wish to preserve the rights of migrant workers from one European country to another, but its provisions are equally applicable to those moving within a nation state, or into the Union – and those who are demarcated not by national citizenship but some other form of identity, such as ethnicity or 'race'. Yet, while these issues are debated at European level, and rights have been extended across Europe, there are some signs of withdrawal or restriction on entitlement within Britain.

In particular, it may be suggested that the move to compliance with the Single Equality Act has led to fears of the development of hierarchies of oppression, the loss of attention to the effects and realities of discrimination based on the 'race' word, and even competition between the equalities strands. The extension of equalities must, in the long run, be seen as a good thing, especially insofar as there is sharing of models and approaches, and a greater pressure to comply, especially if a wider constituency of disadvantaged people (a 'Rainbow coalition') places greater political or commercial pressure to change. There is some evidence that there are signs of this: the recent 'Pacesetters' initiative within the NHS (Pacesetters 2008) was focused on six 'strands', including not only 'race' but also faith, gender, sexual orientation, disability and age, and certain approaches such as the gathering of equality monitoring data were expected to progress across all of these. That said, the National Equalities Panel found little evidence for convergence across strands in relation to economic well-being and educational attainment (Hills *et al.* 2010).

In addition, in July 2008 the Commission of the European Communities published a new draft Directive which would prohibit discrimination on grounds of disability, religion or belief, sexual orientation and age, in access to goods and services, housing, education, social protection, social security and social advantage. This Directive was considered in a wide-ranging process of consultation and then the EU Parliament voted to extend EU anti-discrimination legislation on 2 April 2009 (http://europa.eu/legislation_ summaries/institutional_affairs/treaties/amsterdam_treaty/a10000_en.htm). The 2009 directive (if ratified) will apply to social protection and health care, social benefits, education and access to goods and services, including housing. However, transactions between private individuals outside professional and commercial activities will continue to be excluded: it is not totally clear how this will apply to certain 'care-related' transactions such as payments made out of Individualized Budgets and carer allowances.

New era equalities legislation in the UK

Based on the findings of the Discrimination Law review between 2005 and 2007, the Department for Communities and Local Government published a consultation paper, *A Framework for Fairness: Proposals for a Single Equality Bill for Great Britain* in 2007. This was followed in June and July 2008 by two Command Papers published by the Government Equalities Office: *Framework for a Fairer Future – the Equality Bill* (Cm 7431); and *The Equality Bill – Government Response to the Consultation* (Cm 7454). In January 2009, the government published the New Opportunities White Paper (Cm 7533) which, among other things, committed the government to considering legislation to address disadvantage associated with socio-economic inequality. The Equalities Bill, which became law in April 2010 as the Equality Act, brings together and restates all the enactments listed above and a number of other related provisions. It harmonizes existing provisions where appropriate to give a single equality approach.

In establishing a single equalities legislation, UK law now shifts from a specific to a 'generic' approach to equalities, encompassing all the equality strands and significantly moving from a reliance on negative duties toward greater use of positive duties (McLaughlin 2007:115). In contrast to the reactive approach of negative duties which provide for protection against infringements of rights, positive duties seek to pre-empt and prevent discrimination and inequalities by encouraging certain kinds of behaviours and practices. This represents a fundamental and important step forward, for the legislation now relies much more heavily on incentives to change practices rather than punitive measures after breaches of the law have been established. McLaughlin suggests these duties have three core characteristics. They include an organization adopting the ethos and approach of *mainstreaming* equality across all its functions (see Rees and Parken 2003), engaging in consultative policy-making processes, and undertaking anticipatory impact assessments on the likely effects of its policy decisions (McLaughlin 2007: 115). In this sense the new equalities apparatus includes extensive levers promoting change.

While most of the existing legislation will be repealed, the Equality Act 2006 will remain in force (as amended by the Bill) so far as it relates to the constitution and operation of the Equality and Human Rights Commission; and the Disability Discrimination Act 1995, and so far as it relates to Northern Ireland, thus preserving some aspects of the devolutionary settlements referred to in Chapter 3.

The new Act will strengthen the existing anti-discrimination law in a number of areas. It will:

- place a new duty on certain public authorities to consider socio-economic disadvantage when taking strategic decisions about how to exercise their functions;
- extend the circumstances in which a person is protected against discrimination, harassment or victimization because of a protected characteristic;
- create a duty on listed public authorities when carrying out their functions and on other persons when carrying out public functions to have due regard to: the need to eliminate conduct which the Act prohibits; the need to advance equality of opportunity between persons who share a relevant protected characteristic and those who do not; and the need to foster good relations between people who share a relevant protected characteristic and people who do not. The practical effect is that listed public authorities will have to consider how their policies, programmes and service delivery will affect people with the protected characteristics;
- allow an employer or service provider or other organization to take positive action so as to enable existing or potential employees or customers to overcome or minimize a disadvantage arising from a protected characteristic;
- extend the permission for political parties to use women-only short-lists for election candidates to 2030.

It will also make it unlawful to discriminate against, harass or victimize a person when providing a service (which includes the provision of goods or facilities) or when exercising a public function in respect of the extended list of characteristics – while retaining the original powers relating to 'race' but adding the concept of 'caste' discrimination to that. This protection is also reflected in the provisions that establish a general duty on public authorities to have due regard, when carrying out their functions, to the need to eliminate unlawful discrimination, harassment or victimization; to advance equality of opportunity; and to foster good relations (the 'general duty' of the 2000 RRAA), and the provisions which enable an employer or service provider or other organization to take positive action to overcome or minimize a disadvantage arising from people possessing particular protected characteristics. This exemption is similar to the 'genuine occupational qualification' which was retained as a concession in the 1976 Act, to permit female workers or people with specific language or cultural knowledge to be employed in welfare-related roles as well as in certain other settings such as entertainment.

A new equalities measurement tool

Alongside these developments the EHRC has been working with the Government Equalities Office, the Office for National Statistics and the devolved administrations to develop an equality measurement framework that can be used to assess equality and human rights across a range of domains relevant to twenty-first century life. This framework is based largely on the work of Amartya Sen's (1997, 2005) work on capabilities which focuses on those things in life that people say are important for them to actually *do* and *be*. Sen's 'capabilities approach' (2005) has emerged as the leading approach to thinking about issues of inequality and human development and underpins the previous Labour government's approach to equalities. For Sen a capability reflects a person's *ability* to achieve a certain level of well-being or functioning which reflect their choice or agency in doing so (or not) as well as structural determinants that compound group inequality. His analysis goes beyond consideration of economic inequalities to include evaluations of well-being more generally in terms of issues such as participation, freedom to lead a valuable life and enjoyment of positive states of being and doing. Examples of capabilities are being well fed, engaging in the labour market, caring for others, being healthy, many of which reflect the community-focused and functional definitions of health preferred by minority ethnic communities (Johnson and Verma 1998). The use of resource-based analyses (who has got what) does not permit us to consider how people differ in their abilities to convert resources into capabilities, due to limits placed upon them by social, economic and environmental factors such as a society's public infrastructure. Sen's approach, however, has been praised for its ability to accommodate heterogeneity and diversity through recognizing differences in people's ability to convert opportunities into outcomes, for its ability to accommodate human agency as well as drawing out group disparities based on factors such as age, race or gender and for emphasizing the fact that different people, cultures and societies may have different values and aspirations.

The Equality Measurement Framework (EMF), built on Sen's approach, will monitor the things in life that people actually value and achieve, such as enjoying an adequate standard of living, being healthy, opportunities for education and learning, legal security, and being free from crime and the fear of crime, as these relate to characteristics such as age, disability, ethnicity, gender, religion or belief, sexual orientation, transgender and social class. The EMF will not actually measure performance but provides a baseline of evidence against which progress can be evaluated and priorities decided by a range of public bodies in their responses to inequalities, and by the ECHR to discharge its legal duties to monitor social outcomes under the Equality Act 2006 (see www.theequalitiesreview.org.uk).

The limits of the law

Writing prior to the introduction of the Race Relations Amendment Act, the Commission on the Future of Multi-Ethnic Britain (Parekh Commission 2000) suggested that the founding race relations legislation had helped to 'curb the worst kinds of discrimination in employment and the provision of services' and 'had an invaluable impact on the general climate of opinion' (2000: 264), but conceded that considerable change would be needed if legislation was to be an effective tool for change. They looked forward to the broadening of the remit of the law to include 'institutional discrimination' and to the imposition of positive duties, and heralded a Single Equality Act and a single Equality Commission – all of which are now virtually in place. Despite this there remain concerns that the Single Equality Act will provide an effective response to the problems of structural discrimination and social exclusion (Dickens 2007; Malik 2007).

Regulatory drivers are important to prompting change but their limitations have long been recognized (Lustgarten and Edwards 1992). The considerable problems of seeking remedy and redress coupled with the vulnerabilities of disadvantaged groups have effectively operated to compromise rights established under the law (Genn 1999; Williams 2004). Individuals have traditionally been weak partners when seeking legal remedy against organizations, often lacking access to information, advice, representation and support in taking forward their cases (Malik 2007). Lustgarten and Edwards's summation of the potential impact of legal measures on inequality as being 'like trying to etch figures in glass with a pickaxe' (1992: 277) has been the enduring story of discrimination law (Dickens 2007; Malik 2007).

There is little doubt that equalities consciousness and action is now a mandatory dimension of organizational practice. The Parekh Report argued for just such organizational self-review as the most effective way forward and identified ten sets of questions to guide organizational change, covering a range of issues from monitoring, good leadership, consultation and partnership to training and staff development (Parekh Commission 2000: 282–3). In a similar vein, a plethora of guidance and 'standards' documents and 'light touch' equality toolkits have been available from the Audit Commission, Care Quality Commission, CRE and similar bodies (for example the Equality Standard for Local Government) to drive forward organizational competence. Evidence of change at an operational level is still sadly lacking, however. Bhavnani *et al.* (2005: 75), drawing on the Audit Commission Report (2002), suggest there is 'little empirical evidence that "race" equality policies have changed the social and discursive practices of racism . . .' The CRE in its final assessment of public sector bodies noted that, even within Whitehall departments, a large number had not complied with the existing race equality duty (*Guardian*, 18 September 2007) and its report (CRE 2007: 53) noted that in a recent monitoring round of 47 local authorities sampled, 30 were not compliant with the duty to promote race equality and all of the district councils targeted in the project were non-compliant. In a review of evidence from Wales spanning the ten years from the introduction of the 1995 CRE Standard on Race Equality, Hold and Williams similarly observed:

> lack of leadership and commitment to integrating equality and diversity work at the highest levels, authorities struggling with finding solutions to effective consultation with ethnic minority individuals and groups, that collaborative/partnership arrangements for taking forward work on equalities are weak and that monitoring performance data remained problematic. Despite significant drivers within the period since the 1995 CRE Standard, most notably the Race Relations (Amendment) Act requirements, authorities failed to make real their stated aspirations for change with much of the activity in the ten year period focussed on developing processes and preparing policies rather than on measurable outcomes that impact on the quality of life of ethnic minority individuals.
>
> (Hold and Williams 2007: 27)

The evidence available from Scotland and Northern Ireland paints no better a picture. The limitation of the positive duties in producing substantive shifts in equality practices and improvements in widespread inequalities has been the concern of a number of commentators writing in the context of Northern Ireland where positive duties have been in place for some time (Osborne 2003; McLaughlin 2007; O'Cinneide 2007). McLaughlin (2007), for example, argues that the emphasis of these duties on equality proofing the *processes* of decision making rather than on the *content* of the decisions themselves is necessarily problematic. Consultation processes may produce involvement but involvement itself does not automatically influence outcomes. There is a tendency for organizations to lean towards minimal compliance, adhering to the letter and not the spirit of the law. The tick box culture of modernized service delivery fosters a focus on procedural compliance and minimal statutory obligations rather than providing any substantive challenge to prevailing norms and cultural practices within organizations as required by the mainstreaming approach. The assumption underpinning the new legislation is of willingness on the part of public authorities to engage with and implement the duties. This clearly requires conditions in civil society that cannot be created through legislation alone, such as capacity building for wholesome engagement and higher levels of public participation. Widespread changes to the welfare framework from top-down, command and control cultures to more decentralized network-based frameworks imply an engagement with equality practices that extends far beyond the internal machinery and cultures of state organizations. New forms of engagement will require more flexible, creative and responsive approaches to prevent discrimination and exclusions taking place in these new arenas of association. This will inevitably rely on greater forms of self-regulation, based on self-generated policies and action plans and on a strong commitment to public service values. Nevertheless, changes of this kind can be encouraged by clear and transparent legal structures that facilitate good participation and strong accountability (Malik 2007). In its most recent *Statement on Race* (DCLG 2010: 13), the government commits the EHRC to:

- work with the government to help us to ensure that the Equality Bill is effective and fit for purpose;
- produce statutory Codes of Practice and guidance for public bodies, not-for-profit organizations and employers so that they know how to meet their obligations and responsibilities;
- undertake at least 100 legal actions within their remit and intervene in at least 70 cases annually to strengthen the protection available for individuals;
- improve the data which is publicly available so that organizations can see how their performance compares with others;
- ensure public bodies have access to the guidance they need to fulfil their duties and create networks to promote good practice;
- work with CLG and the Government Equalities Office to make sure that public sector bodies are not just meeting their legal obligations but also adopting best practice in areas such as positive action and procurement, which can support greater equality.

It should also be noted that the new equality duties focus on public sector bodies, and the private sector, which is responsible for 80 per cent of the workforce, remains largely beyond their remit. Here the reliance is on voluntary participation in equality standards and the levers of pay audits, procurement and contract compliance which have to date proved largely ineffective (see Chapter 6). An important function of the new Equality Commission should be to consider how it can influence and impact on the private sector, otherwise large-scale inequalities will inevitably persist.

The reaction of many grassroots activist groups in the minority ethnic communities to the proposal of a single Equality Commission and a single Equality Act was largely hostile and probably best summed up by Karen Chouhan's phrase 'one big equality mush' (*Guardian*, 30 November 2004). For all the CRE's failings it had served as a focus for Black and minority ethnic concerns: a single commission would inevitably fail to maintain a sufficient momentum for the debate on combating racism. Fears have been raised about loss of symbolic salience of the 'race' marker in the revised legislative and policy terminology (Worley 2005) and a loss of the energy and passion associated with specific-strand equality activism. The generic approach to equalities may exacerbate a loss of focus in practice on the particular dimensions of racial discrimination and an attrition of the more affective and moral elements that have been critical to driving forward change, by detaching the various stakeholder communities from the change effort and putting it in the hands of a professional elite of equality practitioners. Concerns that the new single commission would offer little more than a watered down 'one size fits all' approach have yet to be fully tested. In his review of the new Commission, O'Cinneide (2007) draws on lessons and concerns from the past and concludes that 'it is not inevitable that the CEHR will turn into a bureaucratic and complacent monolith'; pointing to the greater enforcement powers available to the commission and the ongoing expansion of anti-discrimination law. However, he cautions that the new body remains moulded in the image of its predecessors and subject to the inheritance of their inherent defects. Regrettably, his preliminary concerns have some apparent validity, as much of the media attention surrounding the Commission in its first two years focused on internal disagreements and infighting between the appointed Commissioners.

The impact of these proposed laws and assessment and evaluation frameworks will be seen in due course. The educational role of the debates around them, together with the impact of campaigns and a growing awareness of employers and employees, service users and those responsible for commissioning, planning and delivering services, should, hopefully, lead in the end to the changed mindset that both the CRE and the Parekh Inquiry saw as essential preconditions for change.

3 Devolution and multiculturalism

Introduction

In the opening chapter we considered the role of the central state in responding to an increasingly diverse and multicultural society. We demonstrated the ways in which the post-war nation building project operated to define a very particular notion of British national identity, to the exclusion of other identities, and how this in turn delineated access to welfare entitlements. But in many respects this type of analysis omits a consideration of the UK as a four-*nation* state, a confederation of four territories that are in some ways ethnically, linguistically and culturally distinct. The political reconfiguration of the UK under devolution was undoubtedly to have far-reaching implications for the reframing of the relationship between the state, welfare and ethnic minorities but it would also serve to bring into question the broader issues of national identity. With no small amount of foresight the Parekh Report (Parekh Commission 2000) quickly identified devolution as one of several potentially unsettling processes in transforming British multiculturalism and called on the devolved administrations to take responsibility for progressing race equality.

Now, some ten years into devolution, the impacts of the new welfare arrangements are beginning to be felt. At the most conspicuous level devolution has produced tangible differences in policies between the four countries of the UK – for example, free prescriptions in Wales, free university tuition fees and free personal care in Scotland. More substantively, however, decentralization and devolution have effectively rescaled citizenship to the sub-state level of regions or nations. Citizens now exercise a range of welfare rights through sub-national governments. In this respect devolution represents a departure from the post-war welfare settlement, based as it was on the affiliation of citizens to a *British* nation state and to the solidarity of a single 'national community'. As McCrone succinctly states:

> Back then Britain still thought of itself as mono-cultural, even a
> mono-national society, constructed on the twin anvils of warfare and
> welfare: especially with the experience of total war a mere generation
> previously and the homogenizing function of the Welfare State.
> Back, then, the British thought of themselves as a single, largely white
> society born and brought up in these islands.
>
> (McCrone 2006: 63)

Britain was, however, never as mono-cultural as assumed but neither was it
mono-national. The 'old minorities' of a four-nation UK, the Irish, the Welsh
and the Scottish, always posed a challenge to the assumed homogeneity of
Britain, as would the *new* minorities who arrived from the Commonwealth
countries in the post-war period.

The Welsh Assembly Government, the Scottish Parliament and the Northern Ireland Assembly were constituted in 1999. The then Labour government
envisaged devolution as a mechanism for enhancing social and political
engagement and for producing a more cohesive society by bringing decision
making closer to people. The claims for devolution cited the need for the
particular countries of the UK to develop specific solutions to their specific
social problems. This meant that devolution would produce discernible differences in policy in the four territories although it was never intended to produce differentiated sets of citizenship rights. The central state at Westminster
would be responsible for holding the ring in terms of equity across the territories. The radical potential, if not the realities of the implementation of devolution suggested, therefore, a reworking of the nation-state visioning of social
citizenship, a reworking of particular models of public service delivery based
on new levels of civic participation and engagement and a reworking of the
received tenets of multiculturalism.

For those from minority ethnic backgrounds, devolution was always
going to be a risky business. The possibility of a further tier of government in
the grip of a potentially narrowly framed nationalist sentiment, coupled with
a politically endorsed and long-standing neglect of issues of race equality
hardly made it an attractive proposition. Nationalism in Europe has rarely
been allied with a liberal attitude to strangers, and the British National Party is
not a name associated with multicultural enthusiasm. Fears that the exclusionary claims of nationalist party politics would impact detrimentally on
Black and other ethnic minorities meant that enthusiasm for devolution was
severely constrained, at least initially. Perhaps some of this angst was summed
up by the prominent political commentator Yasmin Alibhai-Brown when
she stated:

> It is astonishing to hear pundits and politicians speaking of the
> 'four nations' of Britain. Windrush and its aftermath is not even an

afterthought in this discourse. So when Scotland has got kilted up and the English have established their homelands far from the Welsh and the Irish, where do we, the black Britons go?.... When ethnicities are created on the back of bold decentralization, and identity is tied to history and territory, the results are not always what you want.

(Alibhai-Brown 2000: 271)

Yet devolution must be seen as an ongoing process. It is not an end in itself but developmental and one in which ethnic minorities would be empowered to engage and shape events. This chapter considers the influence of particular political and cultural contexts on shaping both patterns of discrimination and the policy process. It seeks to outline some of the key changes and transform-ations to approaches to race equality under devolution. It assesses whether devolution has produced more conducive welfare relations for ethnic minor-ities, or led to greater engagement of minorities in the design and delivery of welfare and to better welfare outcomes, and concludes by discussing the potential impact a four-nation UK has on the idea of multicultural welfare delivery.

'It's different here' – race and racism on the 'Celtic rim'

45 per cent of the entire minority ethnic population of the UK lives in London. Beyond the metropolis there are large concentrations of ethnic minorities in urban centres across the UK such as the West Midlands (13 per cent), the South East (8 per cent), the North West (8 per cent) and Yorkshire and Humber (7 per cent). These concentrations reflect historical migration and settlement patterns, in particular those from the former Commonwealth countries in the post-war period. By contrast migrations to Wales, Scotland and Northern Ireland are more a product of a variety of pre-war social and economic exchanges. For example, the settlement of Black people in Butetown, Cardiff during the mid-nineteenth century reflects the industrial history of coal mining in Wales. The boom in the coal industry and merchant shipping led to Black sailors from Africa, the West Indies and America staying to take advantage of newly available jobs. In Scotland the activities of the East India Company prompted migrations to particular port cities (Dundee, for example, grew wealthy through the jute trade and connections to present-day Bangladesh), and the presence of prestigious universities led to some of the earliest settlement of Black students (Dabydeen *et al.* 2007). In Northern Ireland the presence of Gypsy/Travellers and early Chinese entrepreneurs marks out early encounters with difference (Lentin and McVeigh 2002). Elsewhere in these nations there are scattered histories of individuals finding

a home as slaves, domestic servants and even landowners (Green 1998; Llwyd 2005).

The contemporary settlement pattern for the so-called Celtic countries is consequently of small, diverse and largely scattered populations. By contrast with the national percentage (8 per cent), the ethnic minority population of Scotland is 2 per cent (100,000), Wales 2.1 per cent (62,000) and Northern Ireland just under 1 per cent (14,279). In all of these countries the largest concentrations of minorities are located in the major cities such as Cardiff, Swansea and Newport in Wales, Glasgow and Edinburgh in Scotland and Belfast in Northern Ireland. In Wales the largest ethnic minority groups are Asian and those of mixed ethnicities, in Scotland the larger groups are Pakistanis, Chinese and Indians and in Northern Ireland the Chinese ethnicities predominate among the ethnic groupings alongside Gypsy/Travellers who are a recognized ethnic group in the province, as they are in the south of the island, in the Republic of Ireland, where they have a particular protected legal status. These ethnic minority populations are rapidly being augmented as a result of policies such as asylum dispersal, the opening up of labour mobility across Europe and de-urbanization and the migration of minorities to new social contexts. Some of the most rapid transformations of the ethnic profile of communities are happening in more rural areas of the UK (LGA 2007; De Lima and Wright 2009) and ethnic minority migration to suburban, small town and small community living is notably rising (Ratcliffe 2004). Where you live, and the sense of attachment and belonging that you have to a locality or place, clearly has important implications for well-being and indeed for access to welfare goods.

The nature of minority settlement in the Celtic countries gives rise to a number of particular issues that have been identified most usually by research on 'rural racism' (see Chapter 7). The geo-politics of low numbers and low visibility has led to considerable inequalities for ethnic minorities in these areas in terms of banal and direct racial harassment and violence, lack of access

Table 3.1   Ethnicity in the 2001 Census

	England %	Wales %	Scotland %	N. Ireland %
White	91.0	97.9	98.0	99.3
Mixed	1.3	0.6	0.3	0.2
South Asian	4.6	0.9	1.1	0.2
Black groups	2.3	0.2	0.2	<0.1
Chinese/Other	0.9	0.4	0.5	0.3
All Minority Ethnic	**9.1**	**2.1**	**2.0**	**0.7**

Note: Minority ethnic groups were not subdivided in Census data except in England.

to services and exclusions from participation in social and civic life. Much of this discussion of racialized minorities in such areas has, however, had as its focus the rural community and largely neglected to consider the way in which these localities reflect the wider national context. More recently conceptual and empirical research has sought to connect the micro politics of the village community with wider ideologies of race and place that are mediated through political discourses of nationhood (Williams 1995 and 2007a; Neal and Agyeman 2006). Such theorizing illustrates how specific racist practices as well as anti-racist responses and multiculturalist policies are a product of particular political and cultural contexts and reflect wider ideologies of nation and national identity.

The notion of the Celtic countries is itself a homogenizing misnomer as the Celts historically were a broad confederation of peoples bound by a particular language. The diversity of social and cultural life between Scotland, Wales and Ireland is as great as between each of these countries and England. What this term does signal, however, is the particular positioning of these countries in relation to England as they were in fact the first colonies of English imperialism (Hechter 1999). The struggle of nationalist political parties for recognition of their distinctive cultures, traditions and histories and for political independence has been ongoing since the 1500s. These struggles have taken different trajectories in each of the nations and political commentators and historians such as Tom Nairn (1977) long predicted the 'The Break-up of Britain', a scenario in which these national minorities would gain self-rule. Devolution in this respect is nothing short of an historic triumph and its antecedents remain important to an understanding of the way in which race relations have evolved and been configured in these countries. This legacy, however, has produced the distinctive character of race relations within the countries of the 'Celtic Rim' and has been the subject of some considerable theorizing both pre- and post-devolution (see, for example, Miles and Dunlop 1987 on Scotland, Williams 1995 on Wales, McVeigh 1998 on Northern Ireland). Comparative and associated analysis comes from the Republic of Ireland (Lentin and McVeigh 2002; Fanning 2002; Garner 2004; Dwyer and Bressey 2008). What these accounts establish is that a particular constellation of factors – historical, political, social and cultural – produces the very specific nature of racisms and racialized relations in these territories.

These are countries with relatively low concentrations of minorities and they display very distinct differences in the way in which ethnic minorities from the Commonwealth countries arrived and settled. The overall small size, dispersal and low visibility of these populations meant that they posed no perceptible threat to the national collective and as such were not seen to constitute a social problem. The relative absence of inter-racial disorder lent itself to an empirically supported proposition that 'race' was only significant in areas of Britain with high ethnic minority settlement. In addition these countries are characterized by a political agenda where other forms of ethno-national conflict distract attention away from 'race' as a political issue. For example, in Northern Ireland and indeed Scotland issues of 'race' were largely displaced by a focus on religious and political conflict. In Wales, Williams (1995) demonstrates how a focus on the politics of Welsh language activism and a national narrative of community-mindedness and internationalism, underpinned by a strong rhetoric of Wales as a tolerant nation, effectively kept an acknowledgement of 'race' out of political discourse. There has been a characteristic lethargy therefore in terms of multiculturalist policy making.

The marking out of Welshness, Irishness and Scottishness from English-ness and indeed Britishness has been important to the struggles for self-rule. It is clear that the ethnic mesh in these societies is coarser and a more keenly felt part of the lived experiences of the populations. These identity constructions, however, are often based on exclusive ideas about the essential characteristics of these identities, tied to factors of history, heritage and particular cultural symbols. For example, writing in the Welsh context, Williams (1995) argued that constructions of authentic Welsh national identity became closely associ-ated with the Welsh language and particular cultural inscriptions that effect-ively cast Welshness as Whiteness. Connolly (2006: 23) argues that 'a timeless depiction of Irishness and the continued evocation of an ancient and mythical past' have ensured that Irish identity remains essentially white. Such exclusive definitions of national identity operate subtly to deny 'substantive citizenship' to ethnic minorities by limiting the exercise of formal citizenship rights. They are significant in that they can in very benign ways operate to ring-fence ser-vices and deny access to services for those who are seen as not belonging, or outsiders.

Taken together, this combination of factors perpetuates a 'no problem here' discourse that has meant in that the pre-devolution period the ethnic minority presence and issues of 'race' barely featured on the policy landscape of these countries. As a result racially inscribed animosities and exclusions have become airbrushed out of the collective memory and contemporary manifestations of racism are explained away as individual aberrations. Jarman and Monaghan (2003) report on the scale and nature of racial harassment and violence in Northern Ireland and confirm the ongoing and rising presence of racial hostility in the province (Hainsworth 1998; Connolly and Keenan 2001; Jarman 2002) affecting all the various minority communities, across a broad range of towns in Northern Ireland. Their detailed account illustrates that, for many people, 'harassment is a repetitive and persistent fact of life, in which the harassers are people they recognize or who live locally' (2003: 6). In an associated study of racism among youth they find public agencies slow to respond to racism and conclude that racism and racist bullying is not simply a problem of the education system but part of a 'wider problem of intolerance and hostility towards the "other" within Northern Irish society' (2003: 138). In a high-profile case in Northern Ireland in 2009 more than 100 Romanians were forced to flee their homes and take refuge in a church in the face of violence from local residents (Guardian, 17 June 2009). Singularly few politicians were bold enough to stand up in their favour.

Evidence of overt racisms and institutional discrimination from Scotland and from Wales is no less troubling. A survey by the Scottish Executive in 2002 showed that in 2000, 67 per cent of those surveyed had heard of between one and ten racist incidents and the same number knew someone who had experienced at least one racist incident (Scottish Executive 2002). In a comprehensive research review across all the social policy domains produced for the Scottish Executive, Netto *et al.* (2001) evidence widespread racial harassment, disadvantage in access to services and inflexible and inappropriate service delivery. Wales is no exception. The historian Neil Evans documented over 150 years of racial animosities and some of the most vicious racial conflicts in British history (Evans 2003), and animosities in contemporary life in areas of Wales have been consistently highlighted in research by Robinson and Garner (2006).

It is not that the nature of racisms is any different in these countries but that the politics of 'race' and race relations have been substantively different from areas where there are greater concentrations of minorities. A legacy of neglect and complacency about 'race' issues dictated a largely *laissez faire* politics in these nations prior to devolution. At the same time, lack of political clout among minorities led to an inability to push their concerns onto the political agenda. Factors of diversity, dispersal and isolation militated against minority groups establishing any kind of strong collective political identity able to forge change. What grassroots activity existed was poorly coordinated and focused much more on social support than political lobbying. Effectively minorities in the territories remained largely disenfranchized, powerless and hidden.

Transformations in multicultural citizenship: race policy in the devolved nations

There is little doubting that equality issues generally and race equality have been afforded a higher profile in Scotland, Wales and Northern Ireland since devolution. The nature of the constitutional settlement provided a robust legislative and policy context for pursuing equalities. Equality of opportunity was one of the underpinning imperatives of the New Labour government in 1997 and devolution was seen as an opportunity to design a proactive equality agenda and mark a radical departure from the past. It was a disappointment to many, therefore, that the newly constituted seats of government included not one elected member from an ethnic minority background. At the time the then head of the Commission for Racial Equality, Trevor Phillips, commented on the devolved bodies as being 'ethnically cleansed', a situation that has remained largely unaltered (Phillips 2000). To date Wales has one member of its 60-strong Assembly from an ethnic minority background, Scotland similarly has one member in a 129-strong Parliament and in Northern Ireland there are no ethnic minority members of an assembly of 108.

Devolution was never an even process; in effect the settlement produced an asymmetrical devolution, with each of the three countries being afforded different degrees of power and slightly different remits. The core social policy areas – health, housing, education, social services and associated areas of well-being such as the environment – were devolved in all cases. However, the New Labour agenda on equalities has been variously adopted in the different nation states (Chaney 2002). The EU concept of 'mainstreaming' provided the overarching frame of reference for the development of equality policies in all countries. Mainstreaming is an approach that signals the systematic integration of an equalities perspective in all aspects of the work of government, from policy making to delivery, and not simply as an add-on set of activities. While this approach has its limitations it is considered a major advance in terms of embedding equality practices in public sector organizations (Rees and Parken 2003). Hot on the tail of the enshrinement of equality duties under the devolution Acts came the duties set out in the Race Relations (Amendment) Act of 2000, which provided a further impetus for change. The power to enact anti-discrimination legislation is, however, reserved to Westminster, although Northern Ireland can enact its own equality law, the Fair Employment Act 1976, which outlaws discrimination on the basis of religion, and has its own Equality Commission (www.equalityni.org). Matters of immigration and asylum, so central to an understanding of 'race' and welfare, are also not devolved, nor are matters of adult criminal justice and policing. Despite extensive similarities in response to the refreshed equalities mandate, there are particular differences in the policy machinery and legislation between the countries and the trajectories and initiatives taken on race equality in the respective administrations that deserve some detailed consideration. McLaughlin (2007: 111) refers to equality regimes as made up of a specific country's equality law and the total redistributive and equalizing impact of its social welfare system. Accordingly, she argues, the four countries of the UK differ from each other in significant respects in relation to their legislation.

Northern Ireland

Northern Ireland is perhaps the most distinctive of the three newly constituted bodies because devolution and equal opportunities were inextricably linked to the peace process established under the Good Friday Agreement of 1997. The story here is much more protracted and difficult. The history of deep-seated religious and political animosities forms a very particular context for a consideration of equalities issues. The central issue of peace negotiations shaped the establishment and progress of the equality mandate under what has been described as on again/off again devolution (E. McLaughlin 2005). The Northern Ireland (Election) Act 1998 established an Assembly and an Equality Commission for Northern Ireland. The Assembly was suspended in 2002, only to be reinstated in 2007 under a coalition between the Democratic Unionist Party and Sinn Fein. This has continued to be an 'on–off' process into 2010.

The Northern Ireland Act confers a statutory duty on its Assembly to have due regard to the need to promote equality of opportunity between persons of different religious belief, political opinion, racial group, age, marital status or sexual orientation. These equality duties contained in Section 75 of the Act were the first 'positive duties' to be introduced in the UK. Positive duties established for the first time the requirement for public bodies to undertake anticipatory and not simply reactive interventions. These duties, now enshrined in all UK anti-discrimination law, seek to pre-empt inequalities through strategies of encouraging or promoting preventative practices and behaviours (see Chapter 2). They would include activities such as consultative and participative policy making, monitoring for inequalities, creating a strong ethos of equalities practice through good guidance and undertaking anticipatory impact assessments. Thus the second equality duty, Section 75(2), provided that as a public authority the Northern Ireland Assembly would have 'regard for the desirability of promoting good relations between persons of different religious belief, political opinion or racial group'. Promoting good relations requirements were not new to Northern Ireland. These duties were also embedded in the Race Relations (Northern Ireland) Order of 1997, which prior to the Race Relations (Amendment) Act required District Councils to have due regard to the elimination of racial discrimination and promote good relations between people of different racial groups. In several respects, therefore, the pre-devolution Northern Ireland arrangements provided a stronger legislative basis for promoting race equality than elsewhere in the UK and set the example that was taken up UK-wide. In addition, well ahead of the rest of the UK, the generic body, the Equality Commission for Northern Ireland, took over the duties and responsibilities that were formerly under the aegis of the separate Commission for Racial Equality Northern Ireland, the Equal Opportunities Commission for NI, the Fair Employment Commission and the Northern Ireland Disability Council. The new Commission comprised separate directorates for each of the equality strands and was required to provide a public report accounting for how resources were distributed between its four main functions. Osborne (2003) suggests that this exemplar of integrating staff with strong commitments to specific areas of equality work and illustrating working practices that did not produce a hierarchy of equalities paved the way for the establishment of a single equality body UK-wide.

The Equality Commission NI has published a range of good practice guides to benchmark race equality standards in the province. Guidance in health, education and housing were published in the early 2000s and in 2002 *A Wake Up Call on Race* was published, which addressed the issue of racial harassment in the province (McGill and Oliver 2002). In 2003 the Assembly launched a package of measures aimed at tackling race equality and promoting the social inclusion of Gypsy/Travellers. It launched the Northern Ireland Race Forum, a partnership aimed at tackling racial harassment and violence and its Race Equality Strategy, a five-year plan published in 2005 which stipulated six primary strategic aims. Launching the measures, the Minister Des Browne said:

> This package of measures gives a clear signal to everyone that we are committed to taking forward the work already commenced in tackling inequalities faced by people from so-called ethnic communities . . . I am determined that suspension will not delay further the realization of the vision developed by the Executive.
> (www.equalityni.org/index.cfm/section/News/Key/
> 954ABB52-B0D0-7815-0)

Jarman and Monoghan, writing in 2003, when that document was in the consultation stage, bemoaned the lack of data and hard evidence to drive policy. They suggested that in large part agencies could not quantify the scale of the issues they presumed to address and as a result policies would remain ineffective and lack the potential for good evaluation (2003: 83). The NI government, in line with its Strategy, publishes yearly annual implementation plans (www.ofmdfmni.gov.uk) and has also undertaken a major public awareness campaign entitled: 'KNOW Racism'.

In common with the other countries of the UK, the establishment of the Assembly with its extensive consultative reach acted to prompt a mobilization of groups within civil society. The Northern Ireland Council for Ethnic Minorities (NICEM) was established as an umbrella organization working on behalf of ethnic minority communities in providing advocacy, legal advice and support to victims of racial harassment and facilitating policy consultations. Similarly the Multicultural Resource Centre (MCRC) operates as a multi-ethnic umbrella organization supporting community development work, undertaking modest research and offering support to smaller groupings of minorities and those in rural areas. Work has been done to foster inter-community relationships, work with refugees and asylum seekers and with Gypsy/Travellers. In addition a plethora of single ethnicity groups such as the Chinese Welfare Association, the Indian Community Centre and the Belfast Islamic Centre have been brought into new relationships with the Assembly as part of its Race Equality Strategy.

Despite these developments Osborne (2003) finds evidence to suggest public bodies have been slow to change, making little progress on the 'good relations' provisions and not taking mainstreaming to the heart of policy initiatives. He argues that public officials may have grasped the more procedural requirements of the statutory obligations but there is little evidence of a more wholesale transformation of how they work. He suggests the language of the 'burden of equality' is still pervasive in public service agencies (2003: 356). The case of the Roma families driven from their homes in the summer of 2009 by teenage boys reflected the triple whammy of Belfast prejudice but also the sluggishness of statutory agencies. These families were outsiders, Catholic and akin to Irish Travellers, which surveys have shown to be one of the most despised ethnic groupings in Northern Ireland. They were easy targets for the working-class Protestant youth who attacked them as local resentment over the fact that over 100 Roma people were living in three or four houses spilled over into violence. These housing conditions, however, and the fact that the Romanian families have no rights of access to welfare provision, are a product of political decisions and reflect the tension between those powers that are within the ambit of the Northern Ireland government and those that are reserved at Westminster. The limits of devolved powers and the tension this throws up over issues such as asylum, deportation and immigration have also been played out in Scotland and in Wales.

Wales

Scepticism of the nationalist movement's designs on self-rule led to a reluctant start to devolution in Wales. The referendum in 1997 was won with a very slim margin and the incoming National Assembly for Wales had a lot of ground to cover in its aspirations to create an inclusive civic nationalism against a key driver of devolution, ethnic nationalism. The equality powers enshrined in the newly established Assembly were extensive. Chaney (2004) has argued that the Welsh powers are no less than unique in the whole of Europe in that they were non-prescriptive, applying to *all* citizens of Wales, rather than being restricted to the traditional equality strands, and applying to *all* of the Assembly's functions. Section 48 of the Government of Wales Act 1998 makes the provision that 'The Assembly shall make appropriate arrangements with a view to securing that its business is conducted with due regard to the principle that there should be equality of opportunity for all people'. As such the equality mandate in Wales would incorporate distributive interventions as well as conferring on the people of Wales a series of positive rights to exercise, unparalleled in the rest of the UK. Section 120 of the Government of Wales Act 1998 imposes an 'absolute duty' on the Assembly to exercise equality of opportunity which could be enforced in the courts if necessary. Equality of opportunity has been given a high priority in the work of the Assembly, being established as one of three cross-cutting themes that underpin all its work. To take forward implementation, a standing Committee on Equal Opportunities was established within the Assembly, an Equality Policy Unit to stimulate action on equality issues across government, and structures for consultation with key stakeholders, including the creation and funding of the All Wales Ethnic Minority Association (AWEMA) to facilitate policy dialogue between the Assembly and ethnic minorities across Wales.

This institutional framework itself represented a radical departure from the past. It was coupled with a high degree of political rhetoric from all the major parties. On being appointed to First Minister, Rhodri Morgan, addressing minority ethnic audiences, refuted an old stalwart of Welsh egalitarianism by saying:

> I do not think we ever want to revert back to the famous line of complacency about race relations in Wales: 'We are all black underground aren't we?' This complacent line can mean that all is well and good in race relations in Wales, which is not the case.
>
> (Morgan 2003)

By the second term of Welsh devolution, the engine room was gearing up for a long ride. The universal and extensive nature of the equality duties in Wales produces at one and the same time a strength in the Welsh response and an inherent flaw (Williams 2004b). To move from a standing start in a scenario where 'race' had barely appeared on the public agenda to one in which it formed a small part of the wider mainstreaming agenda of the Assembly would inevitably lead to difficulty. Monitoring the impact of the new Assembly on Wales's ethnic minorities as part of that wider study, Williams and Chaney (2001b) note the emphasis of the early Assembly interventions on getting its own house in order in terms of increasing the representation of staff from minority backgrounds, providing equalities training for staff and developing systems for equality-proofing policies and for undertaking impact assessments across its directorates. The Assembly also showed itself willing to utilize contract compliance to institute race equality considerations and a range of levers were deployed to drive improved equality performance with local government partners and associated public bodies. The new Assembly committed funding to initiatives such as a Gypsy and Traveller Strategy, a strategy on refugees and asylum seekers, a Black and Ethnic Minority Housing Strategy and support for a number of consultative bodies in addition to AWEMA, such as the Refugee and Asylum Forum and the Inter Faith Council. Williams and Chaney's assessment of the first term of the Assembly concluded that overall it had failed to engage significantly with ethnic minority individuals and groups beyond a small and well-known cohort of people, with a large degree of expressed disenchantment and scepticism on the part of minority groups about the Assembly's ability to secure change (Williams and Chaney 2001b).

When surveyed in the second term, members of ethnic minority voluntary organizations did attest to a greater sense of access to policy making but were cautious about any claims that this translated into direct influence on policy outcomes (Williams 2004b). AWEMA, the main vehicle of communication between the Assembly and the minority ethnic population, suggested there was little evidence of its recommendations shaping or making policy and strategy (Williams and De Lima 2006).

In the longer run, the course set in the second term of office for greater egalitarianism and increased citizen involvement focused on the redistributive potential of the Assembly and on the assumption of greater mainstreaming equality. A piece of research commissioned by the newly established Equalities and Human Rights Commission provides an overview of the Welsh Assembly government's progress on its equalities agenda (Chaney 2009). This study indicates a number of major developments that have taken place including the establishment of an equalities infrastructure, the development of a more participatory and inclusive approach to policy making and policy scrutiny and the establishment of a number of cross-Wales strategies tackling issues such as asylum, Gypsy/Traveller issues, forced marriages and inter-faith dialogue. It also evidences the commitment of resources to equalities work. However, the report notes that, while there have been a number of policy initiatives, many of these can be characterized as declaratory, few policies having detailed targets and implementation plans, and fewer being able to evidence impacts. It concludes that a clear implementation gap exists between policy development and delivery. Devolution has resulted in some efforts being made to tackle the paucity of detailed data that had marred earlier policy making, to clearly demonstrate need and to stimulate research on issues impacting on minority groups and on equality issues (Williams *et al.* 2007). The new collectivism to which the Morgan administration and latterly the coalition government have aspired has, however, smacked of the old style universalist post-war welfarism that so spectacularly failed to adequately meet ethnic minority need (Williams and De Lima 2006). While the shifts in public awareness of a multicultural Wales have been profound, the tangible impacts on racial inequality remain more elusive (Winckler 2009).

Scotland

The Scotland Act 1998 (Schedule 5) empowers the Scottish Parliament 'to encourage' equal opportunities and to impose duties on public authorities to ensure that their functions are carried out with due regard to equal opportunities requirements. As such the Scottish legislation is more voluntaristic than in Wales or Northern Ireland. The Scottish legislative mandate also differs from Wales in its prescription of nine specific fields of equality, such as race, gender and disability. However, many of the infrastructural arrangements between the two countries are similar. A standing Committee on Equal Opportunities was established which guides the work of an Equality Unit set up as the primary driver for change within the policy machinery. Equality is seen as part of a much wider agenda of social inclusion in the Scottish context, rather than being confined to equality of opportunity. A long history of high expenditure per capita on public services and a social justice tradition provides for a political culture conducive to the incorporation of equality principles (McLaughlin 2007). Despite this, there was early recognition of widespread ambivalent attitudes towards ethnic minorities which stood counter to the image of Scotland as a welcoming country. A number of high-profile anti-racist campaigns aimed at raising awareness of the issues characterized the Scottish approach in the early days of devolution. The particular demographic issues and skills gaps and shortages recognized by the Scottish government provided a key driver to presenting Scotland as a welcoming and diverse country open to in-migration. The 'One Scotland Many Cultures' campaign' (2002) was one of many campaigns and surveys aimed at shaping public attitudes to issues of immigration and paving the way for the 'Fresh Talent' initiative, which sought to attract skilled workers and students from overseas to stay and work in Scotland. The 'Fresh Talent' initiative, although highly debated and contested within Scotland, demonstrated pivotally that Scotland was prepared at least to generate an alternative discourse on immigration to that of Westminster even within the context of its limited powers (Mooney and Williams 2006). This policy brought into sharp relief some of the tensions that exist around the relationship between reserved and devolved powers. In 2005 the Scottish Parliament was lobbied hard to take a stand on the forced detainment of asylum seekers at the Dungavel detention centre, near Glasgow, and forced to respond in particular to the detention of children in this way. Despite the proclamations, however, it is by no means the case that the 'Fresh Talent' initiative was a call for open borders or that Scottish devolution works to produce a climate more conducive to asylum seekers and their families (Mooney and Williams 2006).

As in Wales, investment in race equality initiatives has been evident. The Black and Ethnic Minority Infrastructure (BEMIS) and Council for Ethnic Minority Voluntary Organizations (CEMVO) in Scotland were set up to build capacity and facilitate coordination and consultation with the Black voluntary sector and with minority ethnic groups and individuals. The Scottish Executive committed significant funding to large-scale audits of the state of play in its first term (e.g. Netto *et al.* 2001) and subsequently embarked on a wide-ranging review of race equality work in Scotland in 2004 (Scottish Executive 2005). The outcome of extensive consultation indicated a high degree of concern about lack of priority accorded to race equality work among public service agencies, poor funding and resources to take forward interventions and a notable lack of capacity among minority ethnic groups to engage effectively in the new governance. Williams and De Lima (2006) suggest these organizations have been dogged by internal organizational difficulties, confusion and lack of clarity over their roles and consequently are largely weak in coordinating strong democratic involvement in the new politics of Scotland. A package of measures aimed at tackling this state of affairs was put forward in a review document which set out a National Action plan for a more coordinated approach (Scottish Executive 2005). More recently efforts have been made to bolster the evidence base for practice. The health sector in particular, led initially by developments in Glasgow by the Health Board, and more recently by the Scottish national health service, made significant investments in support for multicultural health care, such as the Equality and Diversity Information Programme (EDIP) and the National Resource Centre for Ethnic Minority Health, both of which have now been absorbed into mainstream activity, which continues to place a high priority on equality and diversity activity. A new research strategy aimed at improving the health of ethnic minority groups in Scotland has been launched with the aim of making available reliable and robust health information. The report *Health in our Multi-ethnic Scotland* (NHS Health Scotland 2009) recommends better data collection as a top priority, indicating how little is known about the health of ethnic minority groups in Scotland and setting out proposals for good ethnic coding and for making the best use of data linkage methods so that ethnic status can be linked more accurately to health-related databases. The report calls for a health survey of ethnic minorities in Scotland and for a more coordinated research on major health problems and issues (www.healthscotland.com). Attention has been paid also to the needs of asylum seekers and refugees, and 'new' European migrants, and the Black Leadership Network has been created to work with Health Boards to review their equality schemes. All of this tends to belie the relatively small numbers of Black and minority ethnic citizens living in Scotland.

Impacts, issues and challenges

It would be easy to overstate the case of clear policy divergence from Westminster or between the three devolved administrations in respect of equalities. Factors of path dependency in policy making, where traditional customs and practices determine current ways of doing things, the historical cast of race relations and neo-liberalism as the overarching policy frame of reference ensure a certain amount of continuity between 'West'-minster and the *Rest*. Anti-discrimination legislation is not devolved and the shape of equality policies across the UK has been largely dictated by the European Union and ambitions for greater harmonization across nation states. The current shift to a Single Equality Act and a single equality regulating body, the Equality and

Human Rights Commission (see Chapter 2) is indicative of this trend. Race equality, whether pushed by the wider UK policy under the Race Relations (Amendment) Act 2000 or by the substantive clauses in the devolution legislative architecture, or both, or simply by labour market and local political imperatives, is now explicitly on the political agenda in the four nations.

Legislative drivers alone, however, do not ensure race equality. Where devolved bodies have been able to flex their wings is in relation to the redistributive potential of their broader social policies and in shaping public attitudes. The responsibility for taking the temperature gauge on race relations is now closer to home. Gradually public opinion has warmed to the idea of increased self-rule and there is a growing recognition of community as well as state responsibility for issues of racial tolerance and racial equality. Incidents such as the animosities towards the Romanians in Belfast (2009), or the deaths of an asylum seeker in Swansea in 2004 (http://www.hafan.org/) or Firsat Dag, a 'dispersed' asylum seeker in the Gorbals in 2001, seem more proximate and confront more acutely idealized views of the national character. There is little doubting that the climate change on race equality in the three nations has been significant. McLaughlin (2007) cites evidence from the Northern Ireland context to suggest social attitudinal change has accompanied the development of the equality provisions with non-discrimination being a value now held by significantly higher proportions of the population than previously.

The redistributive potential of social policies is also beginning to be evident. Policies such as free personal care in Scotland, the establishment of an Older Person's Commissioner and free swimming and free breakfasts for disadvantaged children in Wales are all social justice measures that will impact on ethnic minorities' well-being. The devolved administrations have clearly upped their game and have been keen to mark out a departure with the past and indeed a departure from the Westminster approach. It is often argued that the strong social democratic tradition in Welsh and Scottish politics has determined a more egalitarian and inclusive approach than that of Westminster, based on social justice principles. This is perhaps more aspirational than actual given the wider context of New Labour retrenchment and modernization projects but nevertheless signals some level of resistance to the neo-liberal agenda (Mooney *et al.* 2006). What is more questionable is whether the old style collectivist/universalist welfare regime they are fashioning will serve ethnic minorities any better than its post-war counterpart.

Policy initiatives on race equality issues are apparent and plentiful and the recognized data dearth is being gradually addressed. Difficulties with the lack of fine-tuned data on minority ethnic need have confounded policy efforts and, while still very patchy in substantive policy areas, efforts are being made to plug the gaps (Scottish Executive 2005; Winckler 2009). There is, however, a huge gulf between policy making and policy implementation. Concerns remain that progress has been slow in terms of public services gearing up to diversity. There are doubts about the efficacy of the mainstreaming approach as the framework for addressing equality issues in the devolved administrations. McLaughlin (2007: 119), for example, suggests mainstreaming acts as a cloak hiding the limited capacities of public bodies and services to promote equality and reduce inequality. She refers to 'proliferation and distraction', indicating the way in which policy proliferation acts to distract attention away from achieving real outcomes. Mainstreaming, she suggests, implies an emphasis on process and the duty to demonstrate involvement in decision making rather than showing how these equality considerations actually affect the decisions made. Requirements dictate the need to consider equalities in decision making but do not determine outcomes. Osborne (2003) concurs and bemoans the tick box mentality that policy proliferation engenders. He suggests public servants are kept well within their comfort zone and not challenged to tackle the less tangible processes of change towards equality. The administrations may have grasped the nettle of equality of opportunity in their deliberations but this is far from producing demonstrable equality of outcomes.

The issue of lack of representation in the major organs of governance and in public life remains a major problematic to advancing race equality if only because of the symbolic value of changing the portrait of the nation as a demonstration of inclusion. In Wales, for example, there are currently no Welsh MPs from a minority ethnic background and the Assembly only acquired its first ethnic minority member in 2007. Only 0.8 per cent of councillors are from minority ethnic groups and among the Assembly's 800 public appointments to some 70 or so public bodies just 1.3 per cent of these appointments were to people from minority ethnic backgrounds in 2006/07 (Winckler 2009). It is apparent that the politics of Wales is a very white affair. The ability to hold and retain positions of power and to participate widely in the governance of welfare is still very limited in these new welfare regimes.

That said, there is no small amount of evidence to suggest greater engagement in matters of welfare on the part of ethnic minorities under devolution. Williams and Chaney's (2001b) study, for example, indicated both aspirational and actual involvement on the part of ethnic minorities in the new governance arrangements in Wales. New structures developed under devolution have to a degree opened up access to policy making and provided opportunities to voice concerns in ways not previously possible. Politicians have become more proximate to their constituents and more conscious of their responsibilities to consult and communicate closely with members of minority ethnic groups. There has been increased learning on both sides of service delivery and experiential encounters in the small countries which enable more fine-tuned policy making. Additionally, local activist voluntary sector groups such as the Newport-based MECHAN:IC (Minority Ethnic Communities Health Association for Newport: Initiating Change), or Gwent Association for the Blind, have made great efforts to ensure that there is also grassroots pressure for change. The question remains, however, how effective are these new partnerships, who benefits from them, and how? Writers have questioned the extent to which the new dialogic and decision-making arenas in the devolved nations favour minority participants (*inter alia* Hodgson 2004; Day 2006). The Black voluntary sector is traditionally a very weak player, too often underfunded and lacking in capacity to meet the new demands of consultation (see Chapter 4). Political mobilization among minority groups in areas where they are diverse, isolated and lacking critical mass will inevitably be weak and the efforts of the devolved governments to orchestrate a dialogue through umbrella bodies such as NICEM, AWEMA and BEMIS has proved largely ineffective (Williams and De Lima 2006). Consultation is often cursory, tokenistic and undertaken with a few prominent 'well-known' partners. Such partial consultation does not incorporate dissenting voices and too easily becomes tokenistic (Williams and Hong Baker 2009).

Perhaps more sceptically, it could be suggested that this new close to home governance represents part of an increasing corporatist state surveillance of minority groups. The new-style engagement facilitates closer control of minority lifestyles and makes possible extending the arm of the state into the private arena of civic association and family life. What can be regarded as effectively a 'racist state' rather than an anti-racist state are mechanisms of governance that shore up involvement through a semblance of care and interest in multiculturalism in order to effect greater control of diverse groups. Minority groups in turn become guarded in the face of this deeply suspicious neo-liberal state and cautious about the loss of autonomy greater involvement brings. Craig and Taylor (2002) have referred to the 'dangerous liaisons' that characterize these new relationships between voluntary sector bodies and the state where their autonomy is compromised by the nature of contractual arrangements. This may well be one of the downsides of the more intimate relations established under devolved administration.

Where there has been a noted impact post-devolution is on the politics of identity. A number of studies have illustrated the significant effect devolution has had in reformulating national identity and in the vocalization of hybrid identities such as Scottish–Pakistani, Black–Welsh and others (Saeed *et al.* 1999; Scourfield and Davies 2005; Condor *et al.* 2006; Hussein and Millar 2006; Netto 2008). There is a greater confidence in asserting what Saeed *et al.* have called 'new chemistries of identity' (1999: 840). Saeed *et al.*'s study among Scottish Pakistani teenagers noted a complex combination of religious, ethnic and nationality labels adopted by the respondents, with dual ethnicity labels being preferred. A study by Scourfield and Davies (2005) among school children in Wales similarly found strong identifications with Welshness among some minority ethnic children. What these studies illustrate is the contested character of national identity and the constant shifts and renegotiations of identities in particular contexts that make problematic the notion of an inclusive 'civic' identity. Clayton (2005: 99) uses the term 'amibivalences of belonging' to mark out the complex positioning of ethnic minority individuals' relationship to places of settlement. These identity shifts are interesting sociologically but they are also important to an understanding of welfare. Issues of identity, and the sense of belonging or otherwise they communicate, form a critical intersection with issues of welfare. A sense of belonging affects beliefs about entitlement to services, affects access to welfare services and impacts on the individual's willingness and ability to participate in policy making. People from minority ethnic backgrounds too often withdraw from involvement or take-up of services because they believe they are 'not for them'.

What can we conclude about the new relationship of some of Britain's ethnic minorities to the new constitutional arrangements? There is ample evidence to suggest that from a position of 'no problem here', governments in the Celtic countries have beat a path towards the recognition of multiculturalism, if not as yet substantive race equality. Policy discourses and debates have been developed that interrogate the assumptions of the so-called cultural majority as a way of forging a new sense of civic inclusion. Multiculture is celebrated and welcomed and this has had a consequent effect on constructions of national identity and on people's willingness to assert claims to belonging. Multicultural imagery and symbolism grasps the imagination of what are changing societies. At the same time, however, this semblance of multiculturalism conveniently provides ideological legitimation to notions of Scottish/Welsh/Irish egalitarianism without substantive shifts in the power base of these societies. For many this new universalism reflects little more than the renewed assimilationism so familiar to wider contemporary British race relations narratives.

In the light of the 'renationalization' of the constituent parts of the UK, it must always be a postscript that the neat ordering of the world into nation states in any contemporary sense is increasingly untenable (as in Europe, a new politics of a 'Europe of the regions' has emerged: Borras-Alomar *et al.* 1994). Economic and geo-political restructuring, global networks of exchange and welfare reciprocities, increased international migrations, hybridity and admixture challenge the idea of nations as the organizing unit for the distribution of welfare goods. We are left, therefore, with deep questions about the search for distinctiveness and difference that devolution implies and the ways in which it politically disaggregates the minority ethnic constituency of the UK. Is this indeed a useful way of considering minority ethnic citizenship? What is significant in terms of considering regional devolution is not so much to regard it as a technical response towards finding the one best way to structure the governance of welfare but to see it as a profoundly political set of processes in which new forms of social solidarity and new claims of citizenship will be expressed that contribute to the notion of a welfare society.

PART 2
The Mixed Economy of Welfare

4 The 'Black' voluntary sector

Introduction

Public sector reform has dictated a stronger role for the third sector in providing services and determined higher levels of user involvement in all aspects of service delivery. Profiling the importance of voluntary sector activity, New Labour protagonists have argued for its potential to foster social solidarity and to provide the basis for responsive and accountable public service delivery. For example, a former Home Secretary has gone on record as saying:

> Voluntary activity is the cornerstone of any civilized society. It is the glue that binds people together and fosters a sense of common purpose. It is an essential building block in our work to create a more inclusive society. It contains the principles of commitment and engagement that are the foundations of democracy. A strong culture of volunteering brings with it confident individuals, empowered communities which are safe and friendly places to live, better services, local and national government which is more responsive and a more vibrant economy.
>
> (Blunkett 2001)

The Labour government committed itself to achieving a greater role for the third sector in service provision, as an important medium for providing supplier diversity at local level in order to create the conditions for greater choice and user involvement. Although the sector has a long tradition of active lobbying and alternative provisioning, it is essentially commissioning bodies across the range of public services that determine whether this objective is achieved. To this end a number of initiatives have been developed at local level: the establishment of COMPACTs in 1998 with their associated Codes of Good Practice (www.thecompact.org.uk), Local Strategic Partnerships (LSPs) and Local Area Agreements (LAAs), as well as direct funding schemes such as the Faith Communities Capacity Building Fund and the new Tackling Racial Intolerance Fund (TRIF: DCLG 2009). Variants of similar local partnership agreements and voluntary sector schemes have been set up in Wales and in Scotland but without the same emphasis on commissioning (see Chapter 3). Civic participation has been a major strand of the Labour government's modernization agenda. Across all the nations of the UK efforts have been focused on empowering community groups and building capacity in civil society for fruitful engagement. Strong, well-integrated communities are the cornerstone of public service delivery as detailed in policy guidance for England (HMSO 2008b), Wales (WAG 2004) and Scotland, for example under the Communities Scotland initiative. They are also an important barometer of social cohesion and integration, and thus vital to the promotion of social justice aspirations, to well-being and avoiding social unrest (Spratt and James 2008).

The government has been particularly concerned to ensure that those community groups and organizations that are too often seen as 'hard to reach', overlooked or marginalized by state sector providers are now more fully engaged in the policy and welfare delivery processes. Accordingly strategies for improved consultation and engagement have become a contemporary preoccupation. As part of the wider Compact with the third sector, the government adopted a BME Code of Practice in 2001 (Home Office 2001), which emphasized the role Black and minority ethnic organizations can have in filling the gaps in service provision and even in direct service delivery.

But the 'modernization' project is not the only project of government vis-à-vis minority community groups. In the post-9/11 and post-7/7 context the activities of this sector have become the subject of increasing suspicion and a number of implied and explicit charges have been levelled at particular Black and minority ethnic groups within civil society, in particular faith groups, ranging from the undermining of solidarities through processes of ethnic exclusivity and self-segregation, to being seen as harbouring terrorist activity. As a consequence these organizations have been co-opted by the state machinery not simply for the purposes of securing greater race equality and more responsiveness in service delivery but also for the purposes of greater surveillance and to act as a key vehicle for promoting social or community cohesion (DCLG 2007; Boeck *et al.* 2009).

An immediate conceptual question arises when considering the patterning of civil society in relation to Black and minority ethnic groups. Would a healthy civil society be one in which there existed a distinct, autonomous and vibrant network of minority group association, or would it be a civil society in which voluntary effort and association reflected cross-cultural diversity? This begs the critical policy question: should ethnicity be the basis on which to sponsor associational life at all? Should governments be in the business of funding and supporting discrete co-ethnic voluntary organizations? In this chapter we consider the development of the 'Black voluntary sector' and 'Black volunteering' as an alternative source of welfare provisioning and meeting minority needs; its constraints and its possibilities. We illustrate how this development provides a counter story to the master narrative of the welfare state. At the same time we note the tensions posed for Black and minority ethnic groups by the notion of civil society as it is popularly conceived and consider the ways in which Black and minority ethnic collective mobilization has been variously positioned under the policy lens.

Policy conundrums

Civil society is a pivotal arena for the satisfaction of welfare needs, and for political activity – lobbying and protest – and it serves as a source of sanctuary and solidarity beyond mainstream institutions. Traditionally, non-governmental organizations (NGOs) have been the main medium for voicing and influencing the race equality agenda and an important site of resistance and protest against oppressive regimes. The radical potential of this terrain inevitably makes it a key site for coercion and control of minority communities. Thus in policy terms this arena can be seen as a locale of mutuality, security, investment and civility but at the same time the terrain for the consolidation of exclusive ethnicities, elites, tribal or caste groupings, bodies (such as the BNP) based on intolerance and the discrete interests of faith-based groups (such as, perhaps, *Hizb ut Tahrir*). In this respect, association on the basis of ethnicity, faith or belief becomes somewhat problematic in relation to ideas of social integration. From this viewpoint, civil society is characterized not only by disagreement and conflict, but also by lack of trust, lack of tolerance, lack of reciprocity and consequently alienation. In recent policy debates this has led to greater consideration of the limits of policies of multiculturalism that have been focused on discrete ethnic groupings. The dilemma is therefore how to accommodate and nurture diversity and the articulation of specific interests while at the same time promoting allegiances and universalizing values and norms that transcend the basis of these groupings. Arguments in favour of ethnically based organizations cite their importance in terms of the assertion of difference, identity, the 'politics of recognition' and the lobbying of common interests. Opponents point to the detrimental effects of 'self-segregation'. Neither view provides the whole story, of course, because one powerful rationale for ethnically based affiliation is the historical and sustained exclusion from mainstream institutions. Their evolution and development has often been a response to marginalization and exclusion within the institutions of civil society in situations where the bonds of civil society – trust, reciprocity, mutual concern, security and participation – have not been extended to everyone (Williams 2006).

A further problematic for policy makers relates to the definition of ethnic minority association. What constitutes the 'Black' voluntary sector, as it is often called, or 'ethnic minority community groups'? These terms are bandied around in policy discourse as if these were homogeneous groupings. However, within migrant communities individuals may associate on the basis of a shared region, a caste or religion, as do tribal associations among African migrants, or on the basis of age, gender or some other social status or interest (such as 'West Indian' domino clubs). Not only are ethnic communities internally differentiated but these associations exist alongside other networks of association which may or may not have an ethnic basis – work-based, sport-based, trade unions, women's groups, political groups, and so on. Neither do they respect national boundaries with associations that cross nation state borders, near and far. The cultural limits of such groups are inevitably fluid and permeable in a way that defies their categorization for the purposes of policy intervention. In rural areas or other areas of low minority concentration, virtual or internet-based associational life flourishes – for example social networking among Chinese youth or cultural and associated advice for the Islamic population. Ethnic association in and of itself may become a narrow basis on which to organize and carries the risks of exclusion and segregation. Accordingly, many people recognize their interests are not well served by ethnic exclusivity, for example their business interests (see Chapter 6).

Carving out a niche: the development of the 'Black' voluntary sector

It is perhaps a characteristic of all migrant communities, whether refugees or economic settlers, that they seek to take something of 'home' with them to their new abode, and that they very rapidly start to create social networks and organizations in their new homelands. British colonial settlers in Africa, Asia and the Pacific often began by creating a club, whether around a bar or a sporting activity, and, of course, religious and cultural activities all required some form of organization to ensure that key festivals and events like the Queen's birthday and St George's day were marked. In the same way, minority ethnic groups in Europe (and elsewhere) seek to create support networks, that will reproduce social networks, form a basis for self-help and welfare, provide in due course education and socialization for children into their parents' valued traditions and cultures (including, for example, language classes as well as religious instruction) and in general provide a shelter from the social exclusion or incomprehension faced among members of the majority community(ies). The core of these has often been religious – as illustrated by the strength of contemporary Muslim organizations, and also by Busia's treatise on urban churches:

A city church must be seen in the context of numerous and diverse groups often pulling apart in the pursuit of their separate goals and interests. They all aim at providing substitutes for the primary relations and neighbourhood associations of the small community which city life tends to destroy . . .

(Busia 1966: 19)

Other support groups are often very largely focused around the problems of migration and coping with an alien legal system – for example, giving advice and assistance on negotiating the immigration regulations and bringing family members to join the original migrant(s). Many 'Advice Centres', like the Asian Resource Centre created on the Lozells road in Birmingham's Handsworth district by Ranjit Sondhi in 1976, began on this pattern. These then developed to provide language-competent counselling and advice on form filling – often in a very 'culturally familiar' milieu, where community members gathered around a table to share problems and advice like the traditional village 'panchayat', rather than the austere and characterless but 'confidential' approach of the Citizens Advice Bureaux and council offices. A history of the ARC, published on its twenty-fifth anniversary, suggests how it came about, and the importance of ideology and idealism among 'professional' members of the community in creating it – as in all communities, such organizations stem from a sense of altruism and community solidarity:

The ARC emerge(d) to meet the slightly different demands of the Asian communities – and provides a safe space and linguistically appropriate services. In this, the ARC represents an offshoot of the community activism movement and a chance for those who could have become 'professionals' and 'gate-keepers' to use their education and skills for the benefit of the wider community. 'One of the things that came out of that student movement was the desire to give up what our destinations were [as] prescribed, as it were, as physicists, as engineers, as teachers, and actually to go out of that cycle and go back into neighbourhoods and to try and work on the principle of getting people to have power – to have some control over their lives' . . . for many there was a sense that community service and activism could provide an alternative outlet for the skills gained from education. 'The idea was that we would come into a community, we would be there only for a temporary period. We would try to do ourselves out of a job. The success of our venture would be the extent to which we were no longer required by local people. They would themselves decide what they wanted to do.'

(Ranjit Sondhi cited by Bhattacharya 2003)

Ranjit Sondhi was a founder member of the Birmingham Asian Resource Centre and went on to play a leading role in Birmingham's local politics and governance, taking on such roles as Chair of the Primary Care Trust and chairing the local mainstream charity for visually impaired people, 'Birmingham Focus'. In interview, he explained the process that led to the birth of the Asian Resource Centre at that time:

> A group of friends … all felt that we should do something. That we should have advice sessions, loosely, and we should encourage women to learn English, have a library. Try and do everything from the cradle to the grave and provide something for everybody and we set up the Asian Resource Centre. We didn't get any funding from government or any statutory body, it came from the charitable grantmaking bodies, it came from Cadbury's. And I think it was very significant at that time that it was only those types of institutions [charitable trusts] who were prepared to take that risk, to invest in new projects working around the notion of race and ethnicity, using race and ethnicity as a basis of radical grouping inside the wider community. They took a risk and they were proved successful.
>
> (Bhattacharya 2003 :12)

As the Asian community became more settled in Birmingham, it became clear that the growing numbers of Asian elders required a whole set of culturally sensitive services that were not being met by any mainstream service provider (Bhalla and Blakemore 1981). The Asian Resource Centre, like many such groups in other cities, and agencies founded by other migrants and religions, was led by the need to improve the services received by members of those communities. The setting up of the centre was, in this, both a critique of, and a form of engagement with, the statutory agencies of the local and national state and 'host society', but, equally, remained outside the cosy consensus or 'gentleman's club' (the implicit sexism of this phrase is perhaps appropriate here) of the relationship often demonstrated between local or national government and 'mainstream' charities. Had they not engaged in such a political way, it is of course possible that they might have been accepted into that consensus. Equally, it is as likely that they would not, and then, as now, mainstream, majority-white oriented associations and 'third sector organizations' would have continued to scoop the pool of available funding. Indeed, they might well have obtained special funding, such as support from the 'traditional' Urban Programme, on the basis that they were providing 'additional' services for the benefit of minority migrant-descended populations, over and above their normal remit while Black-led groups would be criticized for being 'specialized and not serving the wider community' (see, for evidence of this tendency, Johnson 1991 or PSMG 1985). Nevertheless, in Birmingham and elsewhere, local authorities ('city councils') were subsequently prepared to subsidize these minority-led centres and to provide social support through them since this was a cheaper and more effective form of provision than bureaucratically run council departments could offer.

Other such bodies – particularly among the 'New Commonwealth' – descended population of Britain – were more overtly political, and related to issues such as the struggle for independence. The League of Coloured Peoples, set up in 1931, is one such early example. Another of this type was the Indian Workers Association (IWA), established in Coventry in 1938. IWA's main aim (before the Second World War) was to further the cause of Indian independence, and membership was predominantly male, made up of itinerant tradesmen, students and professionals. At that time there were few families of minority origin, and less concern about welfare issues. These early foundations, however, were ready to be revived when post-war migration began to create settlements of concentration of newly arrived Indian migrants. The Coventry and London IWAs were revived in 1953 and 1955 respectively, and associations were formed in Wolverhampton in 1956, Birmingham in 1958 and Southall. In 1958, Avtar Jouhl became instrumental in setting up the Birmingham branch of the IWA. The Association's initial role was to support local workers, helping them to write letters and supporting any claims of unfair dismissal. During the 1960s the IWA became increasingly allied to the Trade Union movement, and became involved in more widespread campaigns against the unfair treatment of immigrant workers as well as challenging the wider colour bar present in Birmingham at that time.

With the passage of race relations legislation (see Chapter 2), and the decline of the original political interest, these bodies have declined in significance, but the issue of political engagement and approach among minority and migrant-led organizations remains a real concern and, in the case of newer migrant groups and religious ones, has become again a matter for controversy that may have adverse effects in terms of their role in promoting welfare. Equally, under the 'post-7/7' dispensation, it has been found that some Muslim-led organizations have been able to obtain 'community cohesion' funding, while other faith-based groups find themselves marginalized (Boeck *et al.* 2009). Overall, therefore, it can be observed that the popular (or, at least, often stated) misconception expressed by politicians and 'voices in the pub', that 'immigrants come over here and then they take our jobs and consume all the welfare', is strikingly misconceived. Such evidence as exists, however, fails to support the accusation that 'migrants cost welfare states more than they contribute' (see Chapter 1). Indeed, it can be legitimately argued that the more common outcome is that Black and minority and religious or cultural minorities have over the years done more to create and contribute to the national welfare system – creatively, as well as in terms of their contribution as employees (see Chapter 8) – than to consume it.

It is hard, however, to find concrete evidence to substantiate this contention. Indeed, there exist in print several statements that suggest that members of the ethnic minority communities are seriously under-represented in voluntary action. We shall attempt to explore this, and suggest why this is a misguided belief. In particular, we need to examine the statistics that are available on the role and size of the voluntary or 'third sector' organizations and the volunteer workforce.

What is known about Black and ethnic minority voluntarism and how it operates?

Craig, in a report for the Carnegie Trust on the future of 'civil society', reports that:

> The third sector (what have characteristically been known as voluntary and community organizations), according to the 2007 Voluntary Sector Almanac, covers as many as 400,000 voluntary and community sector organizations in England and Wales alone, including, according to an earlier estimate, at least 250,000 general charities. It has an annual income of £28bn, a paid workforce of some 611,000 (38 per cent of them part-time), representing 2.2 per cent of the total UK workforce. Fifty per cent of the population of England and Wales volunteered in the period covered by the 2005 Home Office Citizenship survey –11.6 million people volunteering at least once a month – while 78 per cent gave to charity over a four week period – figures which have steadily increased in recent years, as has the number of general charities.
>
> (Craig 2009)

However, it seems from some reports that ethnic minority faces and activity are conspicuously absent from this picture. There are many references in the literature to the apparent absence of Black and minority ethnic people from the world of volunteering (Machin 2005), and at one stage in the 1990s, the Home Office funded a unit to encourage greater involvement in charity activity among ethnic minority groups (Obaze 2000). This finding was supported by the 1997 National Survey of Volunteering – and a smaller study in Luton by Foster and Mirza, which also found that 96 per cent of volunteers in 'mainstream' organizations were white (Foster and Mirza 1997). Another study, by the National Coalition of Black Volunteering, found that 41 per cent of charities had no Black volunteers and 43 per cent of charities had no Black trustees (Obaze 2000). It has to be noted, at the same time, that people with disabilities, despite the focus of many charities on the needs of such groups, were also significantly under-represented in their staff, volunteers and trustees (Boeck *et al.* 2009). That said, more recently there have been strong moves among such charities to ensure that 'users', in line with the growing 'user-led' movement in health care, are playing a more significant part in their activities, as managers, trustees and employees (although not necessarily as volunteers). There may also be a move to include larger numbers of people from Black and Asian backgrounds in the work and management of major 'mainstream' charities – if only because of the pragmatic recognition that this is a donor population which may have more disposable wealth than hitherto recognized.

While a number of studies highlight rates or levels of civic participation among minority ethnic groups, or barriers to civic participation (DCLG 2006), the focus on broader non-political community-based participation of ethnic minorities has been slower to develop (Campbell and McLean 2002). The *Home Office Citizenship 2001* study (Attwood *et al.* 2003), asking individuals about their own activity rather than approaching recognized third sector (charity) organizations, reported that adults of Black and minority ethnic origin were probably as likely to take part in formal volunteering of some sort as white people (42 per cent of Black groups, 35 per cent of Asian groups and 39 per cent of the white population). Similarly, Smith *et al.* (2004) noted that although 62 per cent of organizations approached stated that Black and minority ethnic people were under-represented as volunteers (compared to only 52 per cent noting a lack of 'disabled' volunteers), minority ethnic interviewees stated that volunteering was common but was undertaken on an informal basis, and that they had encountered significant barriers to participation in more organized groups. Aspects of volunteering, neighbourhood activities and engagement in social networks among different minority ethnic groups formed the focus of Ahmad *et al.*'s study (2007). Interestingly, this study pursued diversity among ethnic groups to illustrate differences in participation activity by ethnic grouping. They found major motivations for participation to be making friends, helping, being part of the community, interest and personal development. The major barriers were lack of time, family commitments, work commitments, crime and victimization and racism and religious hatred. They conclude that a common theme raised by people of all ethnic groups was the lack of opportunities to participate for people living in deprived areas because of the lack of community facilities, coupled with concerns for safety. It is also apparent that there are differing conceptualizations of volunteering among respective minority communities.

Some reinforcement for this explanation can be found in the work of Lukka and Ellis (2001), who contend that the concept of volunteering itself is culturally grounded and that current policy debates merely reflect the dominant Western construct of volunteering. They argue that 'as a cultural construct or an ethical proposition, one word does not fit all cases because the activities and specifics that constitute volunteering vary so dramatically across cultures'

(Lukka and Ellis 2001: 87). Their overriding observation suggests that ethnic minority people do not see these activities as volunteering but rather as a normal part of self-reliance, everyday community support and helping each other. We could equally describe this as an underlying norm of caring and responsibility among Black and minority ethnic communities that is culturally endorsed and expressed as a preference for volunteering within their own communities. This is supported by Leigh's study of Black elders (2000), which concludes that members of minority ethnic groups do not use the notion of volunteering or the word volunteer to describe their activities. In South Asian cultures, there is a normalized expectation that members will undertake such 'charitable' works as an expression of the *Sewa* (Hindu/Sikh) or *Zakat* (Muslim) duties within their faith community – without that duty being confined to serving members of their own faiths. As the national Hindu Students Forum explains:

> It is commonly accepted . . . that the term *sewa* translates to 'selfless service' . . . We define the terms 'selfless' as that which is not performed primarily for one's own benefit and 'work' analogous to 'useful service' simply as any physical act resulting in gain. Hence we derive a basic definition of 'sewa' as: 'any physical act performed for and resulting in the gain of others' . . . The motives that inspire human beings to do an act of Sewa have been varied and many. The feelings of compassion, feeling of humanity, and sympathy are usually mentioned as reasons why human beings do Sewa. The cardinal principle is that God is residing in all beings, human, animal, bird or plant. The same God who is present in me is also present in other beings. Therefore serving man and other beings is serving God.
>
> (NHSF 2009)

It may, of course, be that such involvement by Black and ethnic minorities is more likely to be found in Black-led groups and agencies than in the mainstream large white-led bodies which have traditionally dominated thinking about the third sector. This, at least, was one finding of the National Black Carers and Carer Workers Network, when reviewing and responding to the agenda of the Prime Minister's Carers Initiative (Johnson and NBCCWN 2008). Certainly, Smith *et al.* (2004) noted that there was some reported reluctance among mainstream organizations to recruit from minority ethnic communities, and a failure to use targeted or appropriate channels to seek them, in some cases even arguing that this would be discriminatory in itself. Other barriers reported to participation include, as might be expected in older groups, a problem of language ability, but also a failure among some mainstream bodies to recognize that volunteers from minority ethnic backgrounds may have religious or cultural needs that have to be accommodated, such as the requirement to pray at set times, or to fast – and even to abstain from attending meetings in places where alcohol is served or tobacco smoked. These might interrupt their ability to provide a service to white majority clients – and some of these service users are also reportedly unwilling to accept help from Black volunteers.

In fact, Black and minority ethnic would-be volunteers have many such opportunities for service within their own sector, since the Black voluntary sector has a long tradition, characterized by a high degree of civil autonomy and radicalism and the development of alternative forms of welfare provision beyond the mainstream. These cover almost the whole spectrum of civil society and welfare need, including faith schools and Saturday ('supplementary') schools, advice centres as noted above, the Black Housing Association movement and even health centres such as that set up for the Chinese and similar communities to accommodate their different patterns of working and free time. The so-called 'hidden' Chinese community created the Chinese National Healthy Living Centre (www.cnhlc.org.uk), which is now very active in London and Manchester in campaigning, supporting research, and developing alternative, appropriate and accessible services. Central to these has been supplying primary health care on a Sunday (in London, at least) when all other services are shut but Chinese restaurants are also relatively quiet (Lynn 1982; Li & Logan 1999). As Chan and colleagues (2007) have noted, Chinese people, both where their population is dispersed and where it is concentrated, have actively formed organizations to meet their social and cultural needs. However, Chinese organizations were weakened by inadequate resources and the diverse needs of different Chinese groups. Thus, their review concludes, UK Chinese people were neither self-sufficient nor isolated from each other (Chan *et al.* 2007). The experiences of Chinese organizations further show that in spite of government expectations of community organizations, state input has been mainly in terms of regulation and control. The state and other 'mainstream' bodies conveniently perceive the Chinese people as a silent and self-sufficient community, which, as stated in a Home Affairs Committee report, prefers 'self-reliance and mutual aid within the family and community' (Runnymede Trust 1986: 6). As a Home Office minister pointed out: 'There is a great desire among the Chinese to sort out their problems for themselves and not ask others for help' (National Children's Centre 1982: 3). As a result, Chinese people have always been perceived by statutory bodies as having sufficient resources to meet their needs (cited by Chan *et al.* 2007: 510); similar experiences have been noted by the Vietnamese community (Tomlins *et al.* 2002; Shieh 2006).

The 'Black' voluntary sector

All over Britain, whether in areas of concentration or dispersal, Black and minority ethnic groups, like the Jewish diaspora before them (Harris *et al.*

2003), have been active in creating self-help and community-focused third sector bodies. The first large-scale study of Black and minority ethnic-led voluntary organizations was conducted by McCleod, Owen and Kahamis in 2001. Their findings suggested that there were at least 5500 identifiable organizations in England and Wales serving a variety of minority ethnic communities. The Council for Ethnic Minority Voluntary Organizations (CEMVO) has more recently suggested a figure of 10,000 (CEMVO 2005). The McCleod *et al.* study challenged the perception of minority organizations as being small, informal and short-lived bodies, finding in the majority of cases a degree of sustainability and formal legal status. Chouhan and Lusane (2004) found in their review for Joseph Rowntree Foundation that there were more than 3000 Black non-government organizations in London and they also located approximately 700 in a small city such as Leicester, with a population of about 300,000 – although, it has to be said, about 40 per cent of its population is of south Asian origin, and such a vibrancy might be expected. A common finding of this study and others (Davis and Cooke 2002; Craig *et al.* 2002; CEMVO 2005), however, is a continuing concern about levels of core funding, overstretched services and a marked lack of 'joined-up' approaches to capacity building and strategic development. CEMVO, for example, argue that in terms of funding, Black and minority ethnic organizations capture only 2 per cent of the total funded grants from leading charitable trusts and foundations.

That is to say, Black third sector bodies, like Black and minority ethnic people, are marginalized and dependent on their own resources for much of the time, not benefiting from the common pot of support available to 'mainstream' bodies that equally fail to reach their needs. Too often funding favours particular types of organization, usually the larger and more professional bodies to the exclusion of smaller interests groups, such as women's groups (see Davis and Cooke 2002) or groups in areas with low ethnic minority populations. Davis and Cooke found differences in local authorities' approaches to different ethnic groupings of Black women, suggesting that they do not understand issues of race, gender, faith and nationality within their area and the complex interaction between these factors. They found Black women's organizations across the country did not feel that they were sufficiently engaged with local and regional strategic partnership schemes. This was reflected in the limited funding given to Black women's groups by regeneration programmes like New Deal for Communities and Health Action Zones. This can perhaps be attributed to conflicts in policy priorities between race equality and pro-feminist agendas. Interviews with local authority officers revealed considerable confusion in understanding of Black women's organizations. For example, one officer explained the absence of funding for African Caribbean women's groups as due to her view that women themselves placed more emphasis on 'race' issues than on gender issues. There was also a lack of funding for

Black women's organizations with religious affiliations and those from Black migrant and refugee communities.

As the Commission for Racial Equality have noted:

> Central government funding of community organizations has increased in recent years, but there is little evaluation of how much has reached different ethnic groups or the effects of funding particular projects on community cohesion. Historically the Neighbourhood Renewal Unit has refused to collect data which would allow it to measure the effects of its funding on different ethnic groups.
>
> (CRE 2007: 53)

This reflects the traditionally poor quality of the relationship between the state sector and the Black voluntary sector, mirroring that between the state and the communities in political and service delivery terms, being characterized by poor methodologies of engagement, short-term funding initiatives, poor consultation and the existence of inflexible or inappropriate structures – which might be recognized as the symptoms of the 'institutional racism' identified in the Macpherson report (1999). An evaluation of the experience of Compacts and the BME Code of Practice found its effect had been very limited. Many minority ethnic groups remained unaware of it and many public bodies did not actively engage with it (Syed *et al.* 2002). As Ellis and Latif (2006) noted in their report for the Joseph Rowntree Foundation:

> Despite the BME sector's ability to provide culturally appropriate services and to play an active and key role in civic engagement and social inclusion, BME organizations are often marginal to local policy debates and feel 'used by mainstream and statutory agencies to deliver the latter's goals and targets rather than being fully involved in strategic policy discussion' (Craig *et al.* 2002). Many BME groups experienced exclusion from the traditional structures of the voluntary and community sector, and from different levels of government decision making combined with a more stringent level of funding scrutiny.
>
> (Ellis and Latif 2006)

The ambivalence felt or expressed by central funders and supporters of the third sector is, in this case, complicated by the consideration of whether Black and minority ethnic service providers are catering for ethnically specific services or providing generic services that are highly used by people from minority backgrounds because of their appropriateness to their needs. This has led government – at both national and local levels – to recognize the value of these services for their own agendas, while maintaining the separate and marginal position which characterizes the 'BME' world. Thus, in recent years the national political interest in Black and minority ethnic third sector organizations has grown exponentially, even if its attention in policy documentation has not been reflected in a concomitant amount of resource and support.

All small voluntary organizations, but most particularly Black and minority ethnic groups, find it difficult to access funding, particularly core funding. Many of their leaders and trustees complain that the pursuit of grants takes up a disproportionate amount of their time. Black and minority ethnic organizations certainly perceive that they are treated unfairly by some funders, through over-scrutiny, stereotyping and inaccurate perceptions of the way in which they work. This is often also exacerbated by a lack of awareness of the specific challenges facing the sector, particularly with regard to organizational capacity.

> The Black voluntary and community sector plays an important role in capacity-building, civic engagement and social inclusion of Black and Minority Ethnic communities. This was not recognized by many funders, which focus primarily on service delivery; it has important implications for the building of social and civic capital.
>
> (Chouhan and Lusane 2004)

As that study noted, many of those whose role is to fund the third sector were unaware of the main organizational, managerial and administrative challenges and issues facing the Black voluntary sector. Several respondents cited groups' lack of management and organizational infrastructure as a barrier to offers of funding.

> We were asked what guarantees we could offer for proper financial management, as another African Caribbean group in our area had fallen down on this. We felt that because of the 'sins' of one Black group, others were unduly scrutinized as if we are all the same. Many white groups must also falter, but are others compared to them? It would have been fine if the question had stopped at quality assurance and proper financial and monitoring systems, that we understand, but to put it into the framework of another African group highlighted the funders' propensity not to distinguish between one Black group and another.
>
> (A representative of an African Caribbean community group, cited by Chouhan and Lusane 2004)

In another recent evaluation of an NHS-funded initiative, members of an African community complained that their project had been terminated without consultation, implying that their agency was not capable of meeting the organizational requirements – an assertion they rebutted:

We are not unfamiliar – we have delivered projects before . . . they seem not to trust us to do something – you cannot fool someone again: are we going to beg and sacrifice one of our community to apply for something like this again? . . . we are very vulnerable and we are just fed up with 'hard to reach communities' – we are here, we are not hard to reach . . . we've just taken all the negative things and cannot develop a track record of being trusted even though we meet all the quality assurance of PQASSO (Charities Evaluation Services, 2008).

(Community Member)

The role of minority ethnic voluntary organizations is now under scrutiny in relation to their ability to support cohesion, rather than simply providing advocacy for and services to particular groups. However, it is the area of capacity building that remains most controversial. Single identity groups have now been receiving such funding for several decades, which may not only have helped to legitimize unacceptable patterns of service delivery, but also to create a group of community leaders who feel obliged to cling to separate funding in order to safeguard their position as much as to protect their community's interests. The statutory and voluntary sectors have also been complicit in the separate funding arrangements, actively encouraging them on occasion, as part of local political negotiations in which support from one community or another has been solicited in exchange for the provision of specific services or funding of particular facilities. In defence of Black and minority ethnic community organizations, it has been argued that so much time, energy and resources have to be put in to challenging and combating racism that stigma, discrimination, disempowerment and oppression faced by service users cannot be tackled, or become a low priority. There has to come a point (hopefully very soon) when community groups and services can no longer justify a lack of action around service user involvement at a variety of levels. Arguments that Black and minority ethnic community organizations and services are too busy tackling racism do not hold water. Participation has to be at the forefront of shaping the design and delivery of campaigns, policy development and services (Begum 2006: 17).

The most recent waves of government interest in such organizations have been traceable to the events of 9/11 and 7/7, the urban disturbances in the 'northern cities' such as Burnley and Oldham, and the policy focus on community cohesion thus engendered (Cantle 2005). The sector has been in the policy spotlight as the core vehicle to provide closer surveillance of the activities of minority groups as well as being the point of intervention for policies of community cohesion. The Black and minority ethnic community sector is somehow both in and out of fashion. We have already noted (see Chapter 1) a certain policy ambivalence in relation to the Black and minority ethnic voluntary sector, as a necessary partner in addressing social inequality but at the same time a source of suspicion, fear and threat to social stability and social cohesion. While government is in clear retreat from the language of 'race', and accentuating the politics of difference around 'faith', the agenda of minority organizations has shifted away from prioritizing race equality to prioritizing social cohesion, to respond to the given funding priorities of government (Dinham *et al.* 2009), as made very clear by Cantle:

> Those organizations that provide services may do so in ways that reinforce separate interests rather than cross divides. Given that such groups are often established to fill particular gaps in public services, their single-minded approach is hardly surprising, but it can result in further separation, and the opportunity to work across boundaries and to develop commonalities may well be missed . . . The role of voluntary organizations therefore needs to be reviewed in relation to their ability to support cohesion, rather than simply provide advocacy and services to particular groups, valuable though this may be.
>
> (Cantle 2005:6)

This more recent move has, however, also highlighted the potential that faith-based groups have to play in welfare, since they bring to the table resources such as buildings, staff and networks as well as credibility and a source of independent financial support to underwrite some of their costs (Harris *et al.* 2003). In addition, they also provide relatively accessible and simple 'one stop shops' for the state and other agencies to 'engage' with communities for the Community Cohesion agenda, via apparently legitimate representatives, possibly ignoring the very different positions and roles of priesthoods and congregational leaders in different faith communities.

We should note, before concluding, that most of our examples have been drawn from the field of providing health and social care support. It is important to note that, in addition, most Black and minority ethnic grassroots-based third sector bodies, including the faith-based organizations, are concerned with many more issues. Indeed, as Dinham *et al.* 2009 and Boeck *et al.* 2009 demonstrate, they tend to take a much more holistic approach. Education has traditionally been regarded as a charitable activity, and the traditional strength of the Christian churches in supporting faith schools has been controversial at times – there is now growing state support for faith schools with a religious ethos that reflects a Jewish, Muslim, Sikh or Black-majority Christian denominational influence. Equally, and more specific to the sector, the prevention of racial attacks, and support for their victims, has also been seen as significant role for the Black third sector, and a part of the well-being of the community (see also DCLG 2010: para 3.32). There are also housing-oriented activities (although many of the former 'Black-led' housing associations have now been absorbed into larger generic associations), some of which also support welfare agendas, and, of course, the recreation of social and cultural milieux was always a key role for any expatriate organization. In fact, all of these play a significant role in supporting welfare, in its most broad definition, and very few have been exclusive in their welcome to members of the majority population either as users of their services, or to enjoy their cultural richness.

Conclusion

There can be little doubt that the current rationale for the increased governmental interest in civil society lies not so much in the critical evaluation of its nature and organization than in harnessing its potential towards specific political and social policy agendas. Empowering and capacity building in the voluntary sector is high on the government agenda for a number of reasons. The ambitions of New Labour in relation to the third sector extended well beyond a reaction to the individualism of right wing politics, to mobilizing this sphere in the interests of equal opportunity, social inclusion, social stability, trust, active citizenship and accountability in the provision of welfare. Yet this must be achieved against value for money objectives, which have perhaps been behind other agendas. A number of developments reflect this refocused relationship between the state and civil society. Commissioning practices have been engineered to become more third sector friendly and to manipulate compliance to wider social objectives such as regeneration or cohesion; consultative fora have been set up to maximize user engagement; and local area partnerships between the sectors have been established to promote community planning (see Cabinet Office 2006; HM Treasury 2007). In addition to this the wider impact of the European Union's Race Directive and the Race Relations (Amendment) Act 2000 demands meaningful dialogue between public bodies and NGOs serving 'BME' interests. For all these reasons the 'Black' voluntary sector has been launched suddenly and forcefully into the new policy framework.

The policy agenda for the third sector inevitably creates opportunities to radically change services, to maximize user involvement, to avoid gaps in service delivery and to produce real choice and better outcomes for minority groups. Concerns persist, however, about the relative powerlessness Black and minority ethnic organizations experience in these new-found relationships. The idea of fostering greater dialogue between groups fails to grasp the core of unequal power relations within society and the inevitable tensions and conflicts of interests between groups. In addition, civil society itself reflects unequal power relations both within and between organizations. The better resourced, better connected and better networked organizations can command greater positions of power and a louder voice. Recognition of this politics of difference gives rise to the very difficult issues of how links can effectively be made across communities of interest and of how to engage with and stimulate activism in minority communities without disregarding the essence of their constituency. Institutionalization within the machinery of the state of the Black and minority ethnic constituency is necessarily a deradicalizing force and organizations struggle with loss of autonomy as formalization brings with it co-option and the suppression of diverse voices.

The new consultative arrangements driven by these requirements have had a significant impact on ethnic minority networks. Expectations have been raised both among the minority communities and from policy makers. This has brought in its wake both progressive and regressive developments for the voluntary sector. Consultative and participatory mechanisms have been put in place to ensure a two-way dialogue and there are dedicated funding flows to support infrastructure capacity building. The impacts are, however, differential. Skills deficits and lack of capacity hinder meaningful engagement between the policy makers and minority communities. Consultation overload and elite burnout are commonly reported. In addition, no small amount of conflict has been created between Black and minority ethnic groups as they grapple for secure funding and attention from the powerful (Williams 2004a, b). A small number of policy entrepreneurs too often command the field and gate-keep the voice of minority groups and the autonomy of many groups and their agenda is compromised by political funders (Craig and Taylor 2002). The internal workings of organizations too frequently produce oligarchies far removed from the rank and file of the constituencies they purport to serve. A number of writers have pointed to the potential distortions produced by such government orchestration of minority association (*inter alia*, Vertovec 1999; Hodgson 2004) and its potential to damage spontaneous relationships of trust and voluntarism (Harris *et al.* 2003).

Despite these hazards, this arena is critical to the development of appropriate and responsive services for minority ethnic populations and what we have termed the 'welfare society', and it will continue to close the gap created by the shortfall of mainstream services. The move towards greater engagement and more sophisticated engagements in the public arena has transformative potential in terms of shifts in delivery mechanisms and at the level of public service values.

5   Informal care and carers' support

Introduction

Chapter 4 explored the locating of welfare provision at the level of community organizations. In this chapter the focus is on care giving and reciprocities in the private sphere, primarily within the family and informal networks of social life, where it is likely that the majority of care giving actually takes place. The chapter brings together and reviews research studies, reports from community and campaigning groups, and evidence about official policy and practice in relation to the informal sector, as they apply to the needs of the UK's Black and minority ethnic populations, and considers how their situation may differ from that of the majority population, as well as the ways in which this has been manipulated or exploited by the state. It argues that policy makers and practitioners have consistently misunderstood the nature and functioning of minority ethnic communities and families, and avoided responsibility with the famous (and inaccurate) assumption that 'they prefer to look after their own'.

'Carers' were defined in the 1995 General Household Survey as 'people who were looking after, or providing some regular service for a sick, handi-capped or elderly person living in their own or another household'. That is, in this definition, care is provided on an informal basis by families or friends as distinguished from formal care provided on an organized and paid basis. Informal care is commonly associated with feelings of love, obligation and duty, and can refer to a range of caring activities and relationships. The term became more common during the 1980s due to research examining the experience of carers (Glendinning 1983; Lewis and Meredith 1988) and the feminist critique of community care (Finch and Groves 1983; Ungerson 1987), which examined the role of women as unpaid carers and the subsequent impact in both public and family policy. National policy on community care and the closure of long-stay hospitals because of their impact on the NHS budget has encouraged the tendency for dependent people to be cared for at home, with the role of statutory services being to support informal carers to continue in their caring role. This applies to the needs of both dependent adults and children and, increasingly, to the care of older people. It is also increasingly being noted, however, that in some cases the care is provided by children as young carers of family members (as noted explicitly by the Carers (Recognition and Services) Act 1995), as well as the more traditional position where parents are carers of dependent children with long-term conditions. In the current context the shift in the nature of the relationship between the state and the individual implies even greater reliance on the informal sector in terms of negotiating and sustaining independent care arrangements. These factors, coupled with considerable demographic change among the ethnic minority population of the UK, highlight the informal sector as worthy of closer consideration in terms of future policy challenges (see also HM Government 2008a).

Despite a growing number of insights into the nature of care, caring and family obligations and reciprocities in minority communities, albeit as what Ahmad (1996: 51) called a 'by-product of researchers' substantive interests in migration', this remains an area of study still to be fruitfully researched. Patterns of inter- and intra-generational care relationships within families reflect people's economic resources as well as their cultural and moral positioning. These are inevitably dynamic and changing within the context of migration, settlement and integration, such that they are not determinative but in constant process of being actively shaped and reshaped. Ahmad's (1996) early overview of the literature on kinship obligations is instructive, as is his caution that the realities of social norms and behaviours are complex, contested and constantly in flux (1996: 71). While obligations in specific ethnic minority communities provide useful insights to guide policy and practice (Chau and Yu 2001), practitioners and policy makers' attempts to establish authentic or prescriptive versions of ethnic minority traditions and values will ultimately be misplaced.

Black and minority ethnic carers

The 2001 Census reported that around one in ten of the UK population (i.e. over 5.2 million people) was a carer, and in response to the estimate by CSCI (2009a) that local authorities were spending around £20 billion per annum on social care, the charity Carers UK retorted (press release, 28 January 2008: Carersuk 2008) that carers save the nation an estimated £57 billion per year. The census also demonstrated that the 'carer burden' (i.e. proportion of the population acting in carer roles) was actually proportionately higher in the Black and minority ethnic population than in the majority white population. It is estimated there are about 6 million carers in Great Britain who can be categorized either by the caring activities they perform (Parker and Lawton 1994; Twigg and Atkin 1994) or by the relationship between carer and the person requiring care. Glendinning (1983) concentrated on parents caring for children with disabilities; Lewis and Meredith (1988) considered specifically daughters caring for mothers, while Parker (1992) studied spouses caring for partners. There is also a growing body of literature looking at the needs of young carers (Aldridge and Becker 1996; Becker *et al.* 1998), defined as children under the age of 16 years who are giving some form of care to family members who are sick or disabled. However, information about young carers is limited as there has been little analysis or consideration of factors such as class, income, gender or race upon caring activities, which could mean that some groups of children may not be recognized as carers. Most research studies concentrate on the white population, so inadequate national data is available on the care needs and provision of care among Black and minority ethnic communities. Although more recent research is now addressing this issue, especially in respect of carer burden (Yeandle *et al.* 2007) and perhaps in relation to the care of older people and those living with disabilities (Begum 1992; Netto 1999; Katbamna *et al.* 2004; Ali *et al.* 2006), there remains little consideration of minority ethnic children as carers, which could add another dimension to the issue generally and provide fresh challenges to services who support carers (Shah and Hatton 1999; Mills 2003).

Most of our information in the UK about the levels of care being provided comes from the decennial Census, which asked in 2001 whether people were providing care. Overall, one in five households said they were doing so, and 5.5 per cent were providing over 20 hours of care per week. Over one million were providing in excess of 50 hours per week. The figures show that almost the same proportions of Black and minority ethnic households were providing care for someone, despite their much younger age profile. Indeed, a quarter of South Asian households said that they provided this sort of care, and were providing much the same level of support. Against the stereotype of a male-oriented, gender-separated society, it can also be seen from these data that young Bangladeshi and Pakistani men and women were three times more likely than white younger people to combine paid work and caring. One in eight young Pakistani and Bangladeshi men (aged 16–29) who were in employment also provided unpaid care compared with just one in 25 young white British men. One in seven young British Pakistani and Bangladeshi women who had a paid job were also carers, compared with just one in twenty young white British women. Among people who might be regarded as more mature (between age 30 and state pension age), rates of caring were highest among Indian men (15 per cent) and Pakistani women (19 per cent) and lowest among Chinese men (6 per cent) and women (9 per cent). While African–Caribbean informants were also less likely to report that they provided care to a member of the household, their family sizes were much smaller. It would seem likely that carers in these communities are more likely to provide care for someone living in an independent household – i.e. on their own, which was not counted by the Census question.

It is also important to note that while Black and minority ethnic elders are still a relatively small proportion of the population, this population also carries a high health care burden. Children in minority ethnic households also have higher rates of need: 6 per cent of British Pakistani and Black Caribbean children and children from mixed groups have a 'long-term limiting illness', compared with just 4 per cent of white British children. Many early migrants were employed in arduous and poorly paid or risky jobs, and a high proportion of the older generations still suffer from industrial illnesses, or diseases associated with poverty and poor housing. For various other reasons, there are very high levels of diabetes and cardiovascular disease in Black and Asian populations, which mean that they have high risks of developing disabling conditions. Since there is little knowledge or awareness of services, or familiarity with what can be done for those growing old in Britain, uptake of rehabilitation services and of preventive care (such as eye checks, physiotherapy, mental health counselling) is low, and many disabilities are believed to be the natural and inevitable effect of ageing. This places additional burdens on the family carers, who may not know of, or be too proud to seek, assistance that is taken for granted in the majority white population. Black and minority ethnic carers also face additional barriers of ethnocentrism and racism and this forms part of their experience with services. For minority ethnic carers there are two relationships at play: the general relationship between carers and service provision and the relationship between minority ethnic communities and service provision. Racism (whether it emerges at individual or institutional level) may therefore be at the heart of the issue of underuse of some services by minority ethnic communities.

In an analysis of carers' situations based on longitudinal data from the British Household Survey, Hirst (2004) demonstrates that the adverse effects of caring are not something that necessarily affects all carers. These bad outcomes are associated with particular circumstances and relationships, and may be made worse by belonging to specific groups, whether defined by gender or some other social category – including ethnicity. It follows that a failure to distinguish between sub-groups of carers will give inaccurate and misleading results which cannot be used for policy formulation. Hirst (2004: 31) concludes that 'much more needs to be known about health inequalities among minority ethnic carers to inform policy thinking and service development'. The issue is urgent as the current demographic trends show that Black and minority ethnic communities are ageing faster than society at large (but that they and service providers have had little experience of looking after an older population from these groups in the UK). In particular, an age 'bulge' is working its way through the system of those who entered the UK in the late 1950s and early to mid-1960s, settled as UK citizens and had families, which means we are looking at a significant increase in the population of older people from Black and minority ethnic communities who will need care.

Lack of access to, or provision of, information about available support services is frequently reported as an issue which particularly has an adverse effect on the health and care of minority ethnic people. There are a number of reasons why ethnic minority groups may have a particular information deficit. Some people may not seek information about support because care giving is perceived as the family's responsibility; information may not be given in a culturally appropriate way or may contain images and advice which conflict with cherished cultural traditions; we know that often there are language barriers between service providers and care givers, which go beyond translation to include literacy (in whatever language); there are also issues of social isolation, which may be due to cultural pressures and fears – including avoidance of racism; and some research suggests that there are carers who avoid seeking information as part of a strategy of concealment of illness due to stigma. Further, as highlighted above, the term 'carer' itself is a relatively new term in social policy which may not have resonance in minority languages, as the National Black Carers Network points out:

> . . . most communities use 'spoons' for eating and cooking. There is in most languages a word for spoon and correct translation will conjure up the image of the same thing; maybe different shapes or sizes or materials, but essentially the same thing. The concept of a spoon exists. However in Gujarati or Urdu there is no word for 'table fork', as forks are not used for cooking or eating, but only in gardening! Equally, there are some words which exist in other languages but do not translate easily into English. The use of 'family' to translate *Biradari* (Punjabi/Mirpuri) or *Kutumb/Parivar* (the word for family in Gujarati) really does not conjure up the same thing: the 'English' nuclear family of two adults and 2.4 children. The Asian conception is the extended family of all those people who are related to you.

> . . . British communities are brought up with this social care system and are beginning to understand the concept of a 'family carer' as an attached concept based on an understanding of social care . . . In addition to this we have yet to find a word in Gujarati, Urdu, Punjabi, Bengali which translates to 'a carer'. Therefore if the word does not exist, the concept cannot exist either
>
> (Johnson and NBCCWN 2008: 5)

There are, of course, other barriers to the use of services and entitlements, apart from information. It is certain that caring is associated with extra costs and restricted opportunities for education, employment and promotions. We already know that people from Black and minority ethnic backgrounds have lower average incomes compared to others and the quality of housing among minority communities is considerably worse than that of the rest of the population (Modood *et al.* 1997; Winckler 2009). This is bound to have an impact on their ability to care and their needs, since it is more common for people from ethnic minorities to live in extended families and at higher housing densities. This could also means that there are more stresses and also possibly fewer opportunities for respite in everyday life.

'They look after their own': policy assumptions and care giving

In policy circles, it has often been presumed that the implementation of community care would pose few problems in South Asian communities, due to a perception that strong networks of extended families would be available to provide support. Research has shown that care givers in these communities are generally unassisted by those outside their immediate family, apart from through community organizations and activities such as the provision of food (such as the '*langar*' of the Sikh Gurdwara) and social/religious or spiritual support and opportunities for association in religious community centres (Morjaria-Keval and Johnson 2005; Johnson and NBCCWN 2008). A range of other issues have an adverse impact on the capacity of the traditional family organization to provide the anticipated levels of care, including housing problems springing from the low value of homes in inner city areas and the availability of larger buildings suitable for multiple-family occupation (Johnson 1987; Tomlins *et al.* 2000.) Other issues include strict immigration laws preventing easy movement or even visiting by overseas relatives, and the question of 'modernization' or 'assimilation', whereby increasingly subsequent generations born and educated in Britain are adopting 'Western' ideals, including a growing preference for living in nuclear families and more occupational and geographical mobility. Fragmentation of family networks impacts on where carers are available and issues such as gender, class, employment status of the carer and their integration into such networks impact on the support they are receiving. Negative attitudes and stigma may also influence help-seeking behaviour.

The most recent research commenting on the situation of Black and minority ethnic carers was commissioned by Carers UK (Yeandle *et al.* 2007). In their survey of around 2000 carers in England, Scotland and Wales, nearly 10 per cent were from minority ethnic backgrounds. This research found that, compared with other carers, carers from minority ethnic communities were:

- more likely to report that they struggled to make ends meet;
- more likely to be caring for their children, particularly children aged 20–25;
- less likely to be caring for someone over the age of 85;
- more likely to be caring for someone with a mental health problem;
- more likely to say they were using Direct Payment arrangements to pay for services.

Black and minority ethnic carers were also more likely than other carers to say that they were unaware of local services, that services were not sensitive to their needs and that their use of services was limited due to cost or a lack of flexibility. A number of people made comments about a lack of culturally appropriate support and services, although, when present, it was much appreciated, even if things did not always run smoothly. Very similar findings arose from the survey of Black and minority ethnic carers undertaken by Afiya Trust and the NBCCWN as part of their response to the consultation leading to the new Carer's Charter (Johnson and NBCCWN 2008). This found that voluntary sector organizations, mostly from 'within' the minority communities, played a key role as gateways to information, support and services. Carers from Black and minority ethnic communities expressed a clear preference to be contacted in a personal, face-to-face way. It is possible that carers who responded to that study were in some respects untypical in that most were already in contact with voluntary agencies working in Black and minority ethnic communities, since that was the only available framework to distribute the survey. However, it became apparent that the information organizations gave could only be as good as the information they were given, which was reduced by the perception among official bodies that Black and minority ethnic people and groups were 'hard to reach' (rather than, as the report suggests, 'easy to ignore'). It was apparent that carer organizations and those experienced in carer work could have provided comprehensive information about carers' rights and the latest government policy initiatives on carers, but that they were often ignorant of the specific needs and concerns of Black and minority ethnic people, and of ways to locate agencies working with them. By contrast, Black and minority ethnic community organizations, many of which did not have expertise in carer work, were unable to offer anything like adequate information on carer or disability issues (see also Morjaria-Keval and Johnson 2005) and in many cases seemed unable to offer basic information about accessing community care services.

The NBCCWN research (Johnson and NBCCWN 2008), as others have also suggested, found that Black carers wanted the personal care services delivered to the person they supported to be more culturally relevant, and were loath to accept help if they felt that it would compromise the cultural values and expectations of their loved ones. The carers in the research highlighted many situations where personal care services failed to take into account specific needs, beginning with language but also extending to dietary needs, especially in regard to 'meals on wheels' and food supplied to in-patients in general and psychiatric hospitals or respite settings or day centres. There seemed to be problems for providers in meeting both religious and cultural aspects of such provision and preference, such as the use of spice, or a need for vegetarian or other 'halal' (religiously permitted) options. There were also many personal care needs which required cultural knowledge, such as the timing of baths (as well as a preference for showers and running water), which were linked to prayer observance, and issues such as dressing (assisting someone to put on a sari for example) and hair and skin care (in particular for African–Caribbean people). Social activities among Black and minority ethnic communities were also not as easily provided by participation in 'bingo', theatre trips or other such traditional 'day centre' activities. They and their cared-for people expressed strong preferences for participation in community and spiritual events. Many carers, especially from the South Asian communities, wanted services to support them in playing an active part in their communities by attending religious festivals and places of worship such as mosque, church or temple. The ability to perform religious duties including prayer was seldom recognized or supported by existing services. Even in 'secular' activities there were marked cultural differences, such as the preference among African and African–Caribbean people for culturally relevant activities with others within their community such as competitive (and noisy) games of dominoes or sewing traditional clothes, while South Asian women enjoyed poetry events, usually in south Asian languages. In all cases, Black and minority ethnic carers and cared-for people emphasized how important it was for them to feel part of their cultural and linguistic/religious community and consistently described their preference to spend their time participating in shared culturally relevant activities rather than pursuing 'leisure' activities such as clothes shopping, going to the gym or library, walking, or hobbies such as train spotting and bird watching. This is not to say that Black and minority ethnic carers do not enjoy such activities: it is simply that they expressed a strong preference for services to enable them and the person they cared for to play an active part in events and functions within their own cultural communities, both for their sense of belonging and as a way of keeping their cultural traditions alive.

Developments in carer policy

Until the formation of the national welfare state in Britain, and still in many societies across the world today, all 'care' – that is, provision for people who are ill, in poverty or infirm, or otherwise unable to look after their own welfare – was provided by members of their family and their local community. The introduction of support structures through religious organizations and communities has also a very long history: the Christian New Testament records the creation of a cadre of deacons under the leadership of Stephen to manage the distribution of food and care of widows (Acts 6: 2–6), and similar traditions can be found in the holy books of other religions including Islam, Sikhism and Hinduism. However, even in post-war Britain, following the establishment of the NHS and national insurance provision, there was very little formal attention given to the needs of those people – mostly female – who suffered social isolation, financial hardship and challenges to their own health in looking after dependent relatives. A key change took place in 1965 when the National Council for the Single Woman and her Dependents was set up, and created pressure for the provision of tax concessions and pension credits to recognize the sacrifices of those who gave up work in order to take on caring responsibilities. In the 1970s, these were supplemented by the creation of payments to carers such as Attendance Allowance and Invalid Care Allowance (ICA). A second lobbying body, the Association of Carers, was founded in 1981, and in 1988 these two groups merged to create 'Carers UK'. It was not until the twenty-first century that carers were given more direct access to government policy, and that the concerns of Black and minority ethnic groups began to be found within this.

Gradually, public opinion and the work of the charities did mean that government policy began to take on board the needs of carers, and to give them specific rights as well as entitlements to support. The Disabled Persons Act 1986, for example, gave carers the right to be consulted as the legal representative of the cared-for person under certain circumstances, and in Section 8 of the Act, the legislation placed a duty on the local authority to establish the abilities of carers to perform their role, and make appropriate provision. The NHS and Community Care Act 1990, in addition to making regulations relating to the local authorities' duties to carry out needs assessments, required them to take account of the representations of voluntary sector bodies representing carers in making plans for community care services (Section 46). Even so, there was little effective support or recognition of the needs of carers given at this time, and few sources of specific information, so that even the term 'carer' (defined in the latter Act) was not commonly understood or used in any formal sense. However, these campaigning organizations, during the latter part of the twentieth century, led to a groundswell of change, including the formation of the Princess Royal Trust for Carers on the initiative of Princess Anne, HRH The Princess Royal, in 1991. At that time, their website reports, people caring at home for family members or friends with disabilities and chronic illnesses were scarcely recognized as requiring support. This charity has now created a network of comprehensive carers' support services including 144 Carers' Centres, 85 young carers services and interactive websites, www.carers.org and www.youngcarers.net, to provide quality information, advice and support services to almost 354,000 carers, including over 20,000 young carers.

In 1995, the first legislation that was focused specifically on carers was passed (the Carers Recognition and Services Act 1995), giving carers the right to request a personal needs assessment at the same time as the cared-for person. The focus of this assessment was to be the ability of the carer to provide care and, as necessary, to provide them with support to perform this role. However, as there was no duty to publicize this, and little attention was paid to it in the media, few carers knew of this right and were able to take advantage of it. Others, also, viewed the assessment as more of a 'test' of their ability to care and were understandably reluctant to engage with it. However, the legislation laid the foundations for the production of a national strategy document (DH 1999). The launch of this document was widely circulated and supported by the Prime Minister, and included announcement of a proposed new special grant for local authorities specifically to enhance and diversify the provision of breaks for carers. It noted specifically that, as was to be revealed by the Census, one in eight people in Britain at the time was a carer. The government observed that without this unpaid informal support many more elderly, frail, sick or disabled people would need the support of the statutory services, or might enter a residential or nursing home or hospital at considerable cost to the taxpayer. However, despite an extensive consultation phase during autumn 1998, there was little consideration of the specific needs and provision of care in Black and minority ethnic communities. The report did note that 'There remain many areas where we have insufficient information. These include the numbers of carers from black and ethnic minorities . . .' (1999: 21) and it promised that a question in the forthcoming Census would seek to resolve this. Similarly it noted that there were expected to be specific needs in these groups:

> Carers from minority groups have some additional needs that health and local authorities need to pay particular attention to. They may need information about services in appropriate languages. Health and local authorities should consider employing support workers who understand the needs, cultural traditions and religious practices of carers from minority groups. People from ethnic minorities may also have particular health problems, such as sickle cell disease.
>
> (DH 1999: 42 – para.18)

Unusually, the report made several other references to the needs of Black and minority ethnic groups, and was particularly sensitive to the needs of young carers from these communities:

Young carers from minority groups

As well as sharing the specific experiences of all young carers, those from ethnic minority groups face other issues:

- minority families may be less likely to contact social services departments for fear that their children will be taken away;
- children from ethnic groups are more likely to be excluded from school. The Government is already taking action through initiatives to reduce school exclusion and through behaviour support plans to combat such problems. Increased awareness training of teachers will also help;
- children from minority groups are often expected to take responsibility for interpreting for the person they are caring for, regardless of whether or not they understand the issue or it is appropriate to their age.

(DH 1999: 78)

The policy imperative of this strategy led to the passage of legislation which provided rights not only for independent assessment of carers and provision of services to meet their needs, but also to vouchers and other direct payments (Carers and Disabled Children Act 2000). However, there was at the time no opportunity given to seek comments from, or to consult directly with, Black and minority ethnic community representative groups. Consequently, Black and minority ethnic community organizations and workers, under the umbrella of the National Black Carers network and Afiya Trust, met to develop and launch a national Black and minority ethnic Carers' Manifesto (Black Carers Manifesto 2000) and subsequently a report whose title insisted on parity of esteem: *We Care Too* (NBCWN 2000). The former identified a number of key concerns about current provision, and stated in unequivocal terms a demand for Black and minority ethnic voices to be heard, while noting the lack of (cultural or diversity) competence that was perceived to characterize existing professional approaches.

Major problems identified in the Black Carers' Manifesto 2000 included:

- Colour-blind approach to service provision and assessment.
- Myth that black people are 'looking after their own'.
- Lack of information about services in community languages.
- Individual and institutional racism – overt and inadvertent.
- Services provided in a non-culturally specific manner.
- Language barriers between service users and providers.
- Geographical isolation, social exclusion and lack of outreach work.
- Poor uptake of services due to lack of information and knowledge.

- Financial hardship due to lack of awareness about benefits.
- Lack of faith in organizations' ability to deliver culturally appropriate services.
- Failure to involve black communities in consultation from the outset, including setting the agenda.
- Local authorities failing in their statutory duty to plan and purchase culturally appropriate care.

The primary concern was that the distinctiveness of Black and minority ethnic cultures and needs was being ignored, possibly on the basis that 'one size fits all' and that some normative assessment of need and provision would be adequate for everyone irrespective of religious or cultural needs – and also ignoring the facts of existing racialized exclusion from economic and social aspects of life revealed in countless studies of employment, housing and lifeworlds (Modood *et al.* 1997). The so-called 'colour-blind' approach, when providers state that they do not discriminate but provide a broad, generic service without exceptions, ignores the fact that the majority of services were designed by, and for the needs of, 'majority white' (and frequently male, also 'middle-class') people, rather than taking into account the fact that there are many diverse needs in British society. Indeed, regional and religious distinctions within the majority white community are also, it is true, often ignored and sometimes cause complaint (neglecting to address the needs of Welsh language speakers might be one example of this) – but local 'work-rounds' are often put in place or these issues quietly managed using the implicit knowledge of the local situation by workers coming from those local (majority) backgrounds. For minority ethnic or religious cultures, this implicit or even explicit knowledge is often lacking among professionals, and adaptations to meet their needs may be seen as 'special provision' or 'additional expense'. The lack of even basic adaptations of health care to meet the needs of minority users – famously in one case, provision of a white prosthetic ear for a black youth, or recognition of the religious imperatives of Ramadan (the Muslim fasting month) – leads to a lack of trust in the ability of services to meet needs, and acts as a positive discouragement to access services.

Support services for carers, like other health and care services, are also not taken up, or are not known about, because information about them is not provided in formats or languages that can be easily accessed by minority ethnic communities. Images of typical white families and majority activities may be less likely to attract Black and minority ethnic users – for example, reference to respite care holiday opportunities at seaside resorts where traditionally few Black and minority ethnic people are to be seen – do not portray an inclusive approach. Similarly, there is some evidence that many people from culturally distinctive communities make less use of mainstream media, whether print, broadcast or even 'community' posters, but shop and otherwise engage in recreational pursuits in distinctive spaces: using shops run by 'ethnic entre-preneurs' and religious activities rather than the majority marketplaces (Ogenyi *et al.* 2004). If information about a service or a form of support is not available to a community, then the concept of freedom of (informed) choice is a fantasy, and absence of use cannot be taken as absence of need. Should this be compounded by an impression (real or imagined) that the services that are known about are inappropriate or insensitive to culturally specific needs, then less effort will be made to search out further information about the services offered by providers that are known.

An alternative explanation also proffered by those responsible for care support is that Black and minority ethnic populations were seen as not want-ing to engage in, or avail themselves of, the generic services of the state, not because these services were exclusionary or inappropriate, but because of a cultural preference to 'look after their own'. This is an explanation which conveniently might have allowed service providers to ignore these groups and fail to adapt their provision. However, and unfortunately for them, there is a very substantial literature, including authoritative reports from the Social Services Inspectorate, which contradicts this long-standing (and still prevalent) perception or excuse (Murray and Brown 1998; Chan *et al.* 2007). Managers unwilling to alter their services or to extend them to take in new client groups, whether because of a desire to defend services for the majority, a lack of resources or competence, or failure of imagination to see Black and Asian cit-izens as equally worthy of support, are in essence acting in a discriminatory and illegal way. It is also, perhaps, possible that the much discussed concept of the 'extended family' or *biraderi* (see for example Ballard 1979, Anwar 1979, or Werbner 1990), which had been proposed by early social researchers as an underutilized resource, has been adopted over-enthusiastically by the state. However, these formulations fail to take into account the other well-established feature of Black and minority ethnic households, which is that they are relatively under-resourced in terms of income (Winckler 2009). Low rates of pay for stigmatized jobs, large families and also the direct operation of racist exclusion has meant that, for many minority families, both personal and household income has been well below average (Nazroo 2003) and there is therefore less to share around this extended group.

A further feature highlighted by the Manifesto (NBCWN 2000), and by countless studies of health and social care, is the relative lack of knowledge about services that exists across Black and minority ethnic communities. For the majority community, growing up over time in a society where one of the major points of conversation and debate has been the growth, maintenance and funding of the welfare state, there is a high level of awareness and know-ledge about the various elements that make up its benefits, whether financial or practical. It remains true that not everyone in the majority white com-munity knows all about their entitlements and the complexities of services, but there is a considerable 'folk knowledge' about these resources, and a high level of discussion and passing on of suggestions about services ('my Gran got this benefit'; 'so-and-so was able to get their bathroom rebuilt'; 'the social worker arranged a holiday for her: it's called "respite care" . . .' and so on). We might term this propensity a 'lay referral system', whereby non-professionals are able to pass on advice and information about useful resources to friends and family, and, through the operation of 'common knowledge', to ensure free flow of information and better uptake of these resources. However, for those who are socially excluded, for whatever reason (but primarily by language, social networks and opportunity to join in discussions, through being part of other networks, places of work and recreation or worship), lay referral networks are missing. It is only by assertive outreach that care services and others seeking to penetrate or offer services to the minority can make their offerings known and attract users from these communities.

While this suggests that there is a need for action to be taken in increasing awareness and encouraging minority ethnic carers to take up services, change cannot be confined to the community and advertising or information giving. If the services on offer are not appropriate, and the cultural competence of staff is not assured, then inviting users to a service that cannot meet their needs will be a sham, and create greater disillusion and future barriers to uptake and engagement in use and consultation processes.

> Before policies affecting carers are produced, professionals require in-depth training regarding both black carers' and white carers' issues. Policies and directives should not be based on assumptions, they should reflect clearly the real needs of carers.
>
> (Black Carers Manifesto 2000)

While we address issues of training and professional competence in a later chapter (Chapter 9), the question of a culturally competent and anti-racist stance also applies to organizations, resources and policies. Staff need access to appropriate equipment and support materials – as it is now (for example) assumed that a hospice will have copies of the holy books and other impedimenta associated with end-of-life rituals (such as tulsi leaves, and Ganges water for Hindu patients (Gaffin *et al.* 1996; Firth 2001; Randhawa *et al.* 2003), and that hospital chaplaincies will be able to refer people to a faith leader from their own tradition. Regrettably, this is an expectation still often unmet (Johnson and McGee 2006). Similarly, it is essential that any new policies and the consultations associated with them should also be 'culturally competent' by taking into account the likelihood that they will affect minority ethnic groups differentially. Indeed, this is now formally an expectation or requirement, insofar as the Equality and Human Rights legislation demands that equality impact assessments should be prepared for all new policies and developments (http://www.equalities.gov.uk/ or see, for example, the Scottish Government's Equality and Diversity Impact Assessment Toolkit: http://www.scotland.gov.uk/Publications/2005/02/20687/52421).

Strong expectations were aroused by the introduction of new approaches to personal and social care, especially the potential of 'personalization' and personal budgets to respond to the need of minority carers and cared-for people to obtain tailored and flexible care, rather than being reliant on 'mainstream' services. It has been noted, in briefings issued by the Social Care Institute for Excellence (SCIE 2009a and b), that the traditional service-led approach had often meant people not receiving the right help at the right time, and thus being unable to shape the kind of support they need. It was (and is) expected that 'personalization' should be about giving people much more choice and control over their lives, going beyond simply allocating personal budgets to those who are eligible for council funding. In SCIE's view, the agenda would go beyond the mechanical distribution of funds to those who claim, by ensuring that everyone in the community should have access to the information, advice and advocacy they need to make decisions about their support (and thus, indeed, be enabled to claim for the support to which they are entitled).

> It means ensuring that people have wider choice in how their needs are met and are able to access universal services such as transport, leisure and education, housing, health and opportunities for employment regardless of age or disability ... Personalization is not just about what social services can provide, it is also about what and how other public services can help – for example, through providing health, housing, transport, leisure services. What personalization is supposed to do is find the solution that is right for you and meets your and your family's needs.
>
> (SCIE 2009b)

On reading the briefings issued by the Institute relating to the reforms and development of the social care system more recently, it is apparent that while 'ethnicity' and diversity issues are often not specifically addressed in most of these documents, the examples and case studies are clearly designed to send messages about inclusiveness, using Black and minority ethnic names and images and, in guidance to commissioners of services, referring to the fact that there may be an under-representation of older people from Black and minority ethnic groups in all services (see for example, SCIE 2009a). However, we are unable to locate and point to properly researched evidence on which to found such policies or impact assessments. On the other hand, there is plenty of evidence that previous schemes, despite their potential, have so far failed to deliver equally to Black and minority ethnic service users and carers. Indeed, the NBCCWN research already referred to (Johnson and NBCCWN 2008), enquired of carers about their use and knowledge of the new Direct Payments scheme and the personalization agenda. However, a very small proportion, 9 per cent of the carers in that study, indicated that the people they supported were in receipt of Direct Payments to purchase services. Nearly all (84 per cent) reported that the people they cared for were not and 5 per cent said they were either unsure or didn't know. It was clear that the operation of the Direct Payments scheme was confusing for both service users and carers and especially so for people with little experience of the community care services they were designed to replace. The carers in the survey, in common with many others, were unsure whether the Carer's Allowance and other welfare benefits were Direct Payments. The researchers therefore tried to distinguish between those carers who regularly used Direct Payments to purchase carer support services and those who were given a one-off payment for a holiday or breaks service which would be classified by their local authority as a 'Direct Payment'. They discovered that 13 per cent of the carers in their survey reported receiving one-off payments while 6 per cent said they were regularly in receipt of Direct Payments in lieu of services (Johnson and NBCCWN 2008).

Ossie Stuart, in a paper specially commissioned by SCIE (Stuart 2006), notes that although the Direct Payments scheme has been seen as an important step towards the goal of achieving independent living, one group has failed to benefit from the choice and flexibility offered by Direct Payments: Black and minority ethnic communities. As he notes, and as we have suggested already, local authorities have a history of consistently failing to provide Black and minority ethnic communities equal access to direct services. It is therefore suggested that a growing body of evidence will demonstrate that Black and minority ethnic service users will also be under-represented in Direct Payments schemes and personalized budget programmes. In fact, there is already some evidence that Black and minority ethnic communities are the least likely to be offered the Direct Payments option by local authorities, despite their mandatory duty to do so (Hussain *et al.* 2002). Part of the problem, Stuart suggests, is that voluntary organizations were expected to bid for local authority projects to support the expansion of access to Direct Payments. The DH had assumed that this would be a key part of the delivery of Direct Payments, expecting community-based support and advocacy services to overcome the one major weakness of Direct Payments – its complexity. With this in mind, in 2002 the DH did announce that it would provide a Direct Payments development fund of £3 million a year for the next three financial years to support such community-based support schemes. However, it does not appear that many (if any) of these went to minority ethnic-led groups, perhaps because of the problems already noted in this sector (Chapter 4) of survival, capacity and the ability to satisfy centrally imposed audit requirements to be eligible for funding.

On the other hand, this approach would fit very closely to the findings of the Barnado's study of young carers (Mills 2003), that existing carer support groups were failing to reach carers among the minority groups, and that partnerships should be generated with organizations already working within the minority ethnic communities:

> The literature suggests the key to successful engagement of BME families is allaying fears that the service will have a negative impact on the family. One way this can potentially be done is through improving links with the local BME community. For example, Barnardo's 'Care Free' Young Carer service in Leicester encountered problems identifying young Asian carers. This was rectified by the service joining forces with a local Asian voluntary organization, which was the main source of support for Asian families in the area. Similarly, the referral rate of black young carers in Southwark increased when training was given to local black voluntary organizations. Other suggestions for appropriate links to BME families include community shops, mosques, temples, churches, community centres, libraries and GP surgeries. This was seen as important because it gave confidence to those families using the service that their culture would be understood and valued.
>
> (Mills 2003: 11)

It would not be unreasonable to suggest that this approach would fall within the newest proposed development in health and social care, of 'co-production' (Needham and Carr 2009). This is not, clearly, a totally original idea or policy: public services have always relied on input from their users and the term co-production itself dates from the 1970s, a time when movements to challenge professional power and increase citizen participation in community affairs coincided with efforts to reduce public spending. This fashion lapsed for a while, especially during the early 1980s, when UK policy makers favoured market approaches and a managerialist culture which highlighted the separate interests of service producers and consumers, rather than the value of collaboration. However, the co-productive insight – that the people who use services have expertise and assets – continued to be evident in a range of reform movements and the development of the consumer's movement as a pressure group in relation to NHS-funded research (www.involve.org.uk). The return of co-production as a mainstream idea in public policy in the last few years has coincided with various pressures for reform, which not surprisingly include pressures to increase service efficiency and reduce public spending as well as evidence that target-based and process-driven models of service delivery have failed to deliver the expected benefits, and have in many cases increased inequality. It must be remembered that 'equality' and reduction in health inequalities is, at present, a prime aim of the NHS and allied services (NHS 2000). It also fits the arguments for subsidiarity and local decision making, as long as that does not appear to threaten other agendas and government priorities.

The term 'co-production' is increasingly being applied to new types of public service delivery in the UK, including new approaches to adult social care. It refers here to active input by service users, as well as – or instead of – those who have traditionally provided them and provides a contrast to approaches that treat people as passive recipients of services designed and delivered by someone else. The fit with the 'Black and minority ethnic' agenda is patent, and it is also congruent with the move towards a model of 'empowerment' argued by the 'disability lobby', which emphasizes that the people who use services can help to improve those services, rather than simply being represented as having needs which must be met. It is, however, important to recognize that these assets are not usually financial, but are the skills, expertise and mutual support that service users can bring into the equation. However, there is small evidence of evaluation or prior testing of the model, and there is very little in the literature that seems to refer explicitly to the risks or potential of this model to affect the situation of Black and minority ethnic groups. Consequently, issues of power remain central and need to be addressed. Even in the majority white population, in many cases service users lack full information and power and are therefore are still reliant on 'expert' providers who define what the service shall be and who gains access to it. Needham and Carr observe that:

> When employing this model of co-production, adult social care services should not lose sight of their role in promoting social justice and should 'aim to achieve a fair distribution of outcomes, paying particular attention to the narrowing of unjust inequalities (such as between people from different social class backgrounds, or of different gender, ethnicity or sexuality)'.
>
> (Needham and Carr 2009)

Evidence for the fact that this will require additional inputs comes also from Australia, where Bartnik and Chalmers (2007) found that people from culturally diverse backgrounds may require extra support to participate in the scheme of co-production. It seems that cutting and sharing costs also costs money but, as stated throughout this volume, that is no reason why the needs and rights of diverse, minority citizens, should be rated less highly than those of the majority, particularly in a welfare society.

Conclusion

We have recognized in this chapter that the majority of care is actually a private, largely family-based activity. Voluntary care giving, which does not always only involve family members, of course, has become increasingly recognized and the role that informal caring plays in saving the state very large costs has been reciprocated by increased rights given to carers. The role and needs of carers in the Black and minority ethnic communities is also, belatedly, becoming recognized, although it is still under-researched and under-resourced by support services. The new Carers Strategy promoted by the Prime Minister (HM Government 2009a, b) has raised expectations significantly, and has also, for the first time, given a raised profile to the needs of Black and minority ethnic communities and carers in them. However, there is a long history of suspicion and neglect to be overcome, and a gap in ability to care that has widened along with other inequalities in society (Hills *et al.* 2010; Marmot 2010).

On the other hand, it is still probable that many social care providers and carer support agencies continue conveniently to regard low uptake by minority ethnic service users as reflecting the misleading belief that 'they prefer to look after their own'. However, third sector agencies and faith-based organizations are beginning to change the awareness of entitlements, and UK-born and educated minorities have begun to make more proportionate demands for support as the older generation's needs have increased beyond the capacity of the communities to care for them. New developments such as personalization and Direct Payments have, however, not apparently been subjected to equality impact assessment in relation to their impact on Black and minority ethnic communities, and there remain concerns as well as some potential opportunities in relation to them. The principle of co-production, on the other hand, seems very likely to have implications for the well-developed Black and minority ethnic third sector which we have already discussed (Chapter 4), and may also fall under the 'privatization' agenda, to which we now turn.

6 The privatization of welfare

Introduction

Ethnic minorities make a substantial contribution to the delivery of private welfare services in the UK through their direct labour and through entrepreneurship. They make up a significant and growing proportion of the army of social care workers within the private sector and without them the care system would collapse. Their entrepreneurial activity contributes significantly to the UK economy, as does their spending power. In this, of course, their existence, activity and contribution resemble the impact that migration and cultural diversification has had on the wider market, in terms of the creation of both 'niche' markets and services and also of alternatives widening choice for all consumers. They are inextricably linked to the private sector both as providers and consumers of public services which are now increasingly privatized. Arguably a growing private sector means increased opportunity to improve their market position. There is also considerable potential for the private sector to be harnessed as a vehicle for regeneration and combating disadvantage. At the same time they are among those most vulnerable to some of the more negative impacts of the increased privatization of welfare services and to the potential exacerbation of inequalities it portends.

The private sector and the commercialization of welfare has grown exponentially since the Thatcher era, moving from what was initially a marginal place within the compendium of services used by the state to being a mainstream provider and stakeholder in the provision of welfare services. Between a quarter and a third of all spend on public services is committed to what has been dubbed the 'public service industry', commanding an annual turnover of £79 billion and estimated to grow steadily to £100bn by 2012 (Kable 2007). This private provision of services can range from something as straightforward as the contracting out of cleaning or laundry services within the NHS, providing a transport service to schools or running a home care service, to projects where the state finances the private sector to build and run a service (Private Finance Initiative [PFI]), such as a prison, hospital or social housing or where a partnership (Private Public Partnership [PPP]) is developed between public and private funders for the delivery of a service, such as the City Academy Schools initiative. Direct services to the public, such as social care, health care, school support and insurance and pension services, are now dominated by the private market provider and the private sector now plays a direct and influential role in policy making and policy guidance to government.

This widespread expansion of the private sector has a number of social and economic implications and has been subject to considerable debate and commentary (Drakeford 2007; Unison 2008). Some would argue it offers greater flexibility and choice to the consumer or user of services and drives up standards through vibrant competition. Others suggest this is not a reality for most, that markets in welfare effectively compound inequalities by leading to a two-tier system and that the values and principles of profit-orientated organizations clash with a care-driven, needs-led priorities approach (Unison 2008). As a political directive privatization is differentially embraced by the devolved nations (see Chapter 2), with these administrations seeking to buck the trend of the more overt tendencies of neo-liberal politics and signal alternative values in the delivery of their public services. The reality is, however, that private sector provision of public services is 'here to stay' and is likely to be sustained by successive governments of whatever political persuasion. Governments simply cannot afford to fund the upgrading of the outdated infrastructure of the welfare state on their own, or to meet the projected demand placed on welfare services by an increasingly older population, and particularly so in the face of economic recession. What is more debatable, however, is the relative role this sector will command, the nature and degree of regulation it will be subject to, and whether it can be engaged in more public sector ambitions such as the pursuit of equality aims, combating discrimination and enhancing social and economic inclusion.

This chapter considers some of the implications of the extension of privatization and marketization in welfare delivery for ethnic minorities. It seeks to explore whether these groups and individuals have benefited or been able to take advantage of opportunities opened up by this enlargement of business in welfare. What is their role and experience as providers or as users of private sector services? And what is the wider social and economic impact when public services are handed over to private sector operators? Given that it is increasingly recognized that the large-scale procurement of private sector services can be used as a lever for the social justice ambitions of the state, to regenerate areas and to enhance equality practice, what is the evidence that ethnic minority businesses are benefiting from this form of positive action or that private sector providers contracted by the state are becoming any more equality proficient?

Ethnic minorities, the private sector and employment

The private sector is by far the largest employer of British workers. Over 80 per cent of the workforce is engaged in the private sector. Despite this, ethnic minorities are more likely to be working in the public sector or to be self-employed than their white counterparts (Walby *et al.* 2008). Post-war migration was a direct response to the demands for labour in certain industries, including the then newly established welfare system, and this fact has in part contributed to certain minority groups favouring public sector organizations. The 'West Indian' nurse, hospital cleaner or porter and the Indian doctor are perhaps the stereotypical manifestations of this slice of British history (see Chapter 8). Outright exclusions from the labour market have also gone some way to explaining the preponderance of some ethnic groups in self-employment. The often grudging acceptance of the need for their labour resulted in widespread discriminations and the denial of access to appropriate job opportunities. What is perhaps surprising is the fact that this labour market stratification, both vertical and horizontal, has remained so static over time. A recent Cabinet Office report (2003) indicates that while Black and Asian communities figured prominently in the post-war migrations to Britain, many ethnic groups have experienced persistent labour market disadvantage ever since, in terms of employment and unemployment rates, earnings, occupational attainment and progression within the workplace, resulting in the so-called 'ethnic penalty'. Ethnic penalties are a measure of the extent to which ethnic minorities are disadvantaged by comparison with those in the majority population of the same age and educational qualifications. Recent research by Cheung and Heath (2007) indicates that all the major visible minorities still find it more difficult to obtain jobs commensurate with their qualifications than white groups and this pertains for the second generation.

The exclusion from private sector occupations is at least in part attributable to racism and discrimination in private sector employment practices. When ethnic minorities do attain jobs within this sector their progression is limited. There is a clear pattern for ethnic minorities to be under-represented in professional and managerial occupations and over-represented in semi-routine and routine occupations within the private sector (Cheung and Heath 2007). Ethnic minority men also tend to have lower earnings than white men in the private sector, patterns not found in the public sector where ethnic penalties tend to be markedly lower than the private sector (Cheung and Heath 2007). Furthermore, there are pay differentials even when they do attain commensurate jobs. In a comparison of pay between Britain's public and private sector, a study by Chatterji and Mumford (2008) found public sector employment more beneficial for ethnic minority workers. Chatterji and Mumford show that ethnic minority workers earn a 9.3 per cent premium in the public sector whereas they experience wage discrimination of 7.5 per cent in the private sector (2008: 19). They demonstrate that a larger proportion of public sector workers are in elite, high-skill, white collar occupations than in the private sector, which may go part way to explaining this differential.

A report for the CRE by the Policy Studies Institute (Hudson and Parry 2004) indicated that while the private sector is the largest employer of workers, a high proportion of employers are inactive in race equality and diversity work, suggesting working environments not conducive to the recruitment or retention of ethnic minorities. Trade unions have proved largely ineffective in protecting their minority ethnic members from the impacts of workplace discriminations (see Chapter 8), with the Trades Union Congress (TUC 2009) recognizing the persistence of racism and subtle forms of discrimination. This broad brush picture has not, however, been complemented by detailed qualitative research into why such discriminations persist and what can be done to address them. Hudson and Parry (2004) draw together existing statistical information to map out the context, challenges and opportunities for advancing race equality in this sector but ongoing research work is needed to explore the nature of minority ethnic experiences in private sector employment, looking at what private sector agencies can do to facilitate the integration of ethnic minorities into private sector employment, and looking at the role of legal regulation and the role of the trade unions in promoting race equality in the workplace (see ESRC DTI/PSI 2005). The overall picture of private sector employment is that ethnic minorities are concentrated in low-skill, low-paid and insecure jobs with poor working conditions. The 3 Cs – Cleaning, Cooking Caring – typifies the labour market enclave of ethnic minorities in the production of welfare, with newly migrated people or undocumented migrants desperate for work stepping into the care gap opened up by growing demand for carers in an already small labour pool, and, as we show in Chapter 8, there seems no prospect of an end to the recruitment of such workers from abroad, whether 'overseas' (i.e. non-EU) or from Europe.

The care industry

The widespread privatization of services is now a reality across all areas of welfare delivery, but the sector where the increased impact of government spend on private services has been particularly dramatic is in social care. The care industry alone is a large employer, with care workers now numbering some 1.5 million workers in England (CSCI 2009b). Since the 1993 NHS and Community Care Act opened the way for the privatization of residential and nursing care services this provision has grown apace, with the private sector now providing 74 per cent of care homes against 14 per cent in the not-for-profit sector and 12 per cent in the public sector (Laing and Buisson 2007). Within the private sector there are a great variety of providers, ranging from the small family-run enterprise to large chains which encompass a number of care homes across the UK. These major providers now command 48 per cent of the provision, 52 per cent remaining in the hands of small independent businesses (Laing and Buisson 2007). An indication of the extent of these business interests is that the current share of the market in long-term care is £5.7 billion and this is expected to rise to £7 billion by 2012 (Laing and Buisson 2007). Home Care Services similarly have been increasingly privatized, with home and day care services amounting to £3 billion of spend on private sector providers, estimated to rise to £4 billion by 2012 (CSCI 2009). Some local authorities now have no direct home care service at all. These largely privatized domiciliary services are engaged by individuals using the Direct Payment system or private funding to hire and fire home care workers from a pool of what is increasingly casualized labour.

The use of migrant labour within the contemporary care industry has attracted a substantial amount of academic research (Hochschild 2003; Raghuram 2004; McGregor 2007). The care labour market now operates along 'global care chains', with the powerful nations of the global north recruiting care workers from poorer parts of the world, in particular women. Nurses, nannies, care workers, cleaners and other ancillary workers move across nations in search of employment opportunities provided by the care needs of the affluent, in particular in response to ageing populations of the affluent world (see, for example, Palese *et al.* 2004). These workers provide a vital resource to the developed nations. Yet far from being rewarded for undertaking socially necessary but undesirable work, migrant workers are stigmatized and demeaned by the work they undertake in the receiving countries (Dyer *et al.* 2008). In addition there are knock-on social and economic implications for the sending countries who are left with a care deficit as parents leave children or other dependents behind with friends and family and doctors, nurses, social workers and other professionals leave the vulnerable of their own societies to cope in the face of a wholesale skill attrition. Hochschild (2003) has likened this extraction of 'love' from the global south to the exploitative economic relationships of the colonial powers of the past.

Whether an individual is seeking to pay for someone to provide them or a family member with care, running a small family-run business or a large corporate player, the issue of the supply of care staff has driven the recruitment of ethnic minority and migrant workers apace (Anderson 2007; McGregor 2007). McGregor's study of Zimbabwean migrants and the UK care industry is illustrative. She examines the narratives of Zimbabwean men and women working as carers in the UK, a highly educated middle-class group who have had to use care work in the UK as a means of supporting themselves and others in their home land. So substantial is the recruitment of care workers from Zimbabwe that the process of migration to Britain and being subject to demeaning, dirty and feminized work has become part of a national stereotype, with compatriots joking about 'joining the BBC' (British Bottom Cleaners) (McGregor 2007). Zimbabwe provides the highest percentage of the non-UK born social care workforce (12 per cent), closely followed by workers from the Philippines (10 per cent). McGregor's study finds that transformations to the care sector have opened up opportunities for newly arrived migrants both as workers and as entrepreneurs who have opportunistically set up care agencies providing work for their co-nationals and others. Despite their skills, however, these workers have become concentrated in insecure, low paid and stressful care and cleaning jobs where they are subject to exploitation and to racism and discrimination. This work, in a sector subject to increased pressure to reduce costs and reduced regulation, is increasingly precarious, casualized and characterized by atypical employment relations, making the care jobs that are so unattractive to many people available to migrants (TUC 2003).

While the opportunity structure of the welfare market is clearly a pull factor for migrants, a study by Anderson suggests that migrants may be desirable household workers precisely because they are migrants rather than simply by virtue of their availability to do the work. Anderson's work (2007) focuses on workers within private households, such as *au pairs*, domestic helpers and personal carers. She notes how the nationality and the immigration status of migrants themselves can lead to exploitative relationships, with particular migrant groups being attractive to employers because they are more likely to live in, be more flexible in terms of the tasks they are prepared to undertake (cleaning as well as personal caring) and in terms of the hours worked. It is not therefore simply because they are available to undertake these tasks but their flexibility that makes them attractive to employers. Further, Anderson argues, these migrants may be easier to retain if they are bound into some formalized arrangement with the employer through their immigration status (Anderson 2007). They effectively become tied into an potentially exploitative relationship by virtue of the agreements under which they entered the country. Anderson shows how the gendered nature of this work is also augmented by racial dimensions, as workers become subject to racial categorization in selection and potential racism within the workplace. Private households in the UK are exempt from the Race Relations Amendment Act 2000 and this means that it is legal for a person to employ someone (or not) on the grounds of their colour, nationality or religion. Anderson's study highlights a racial and ethnic selection in operation via the care agencies, with potential employees masking their intent by using the more neutral language of national origin to reject or select applicants. Workers in these situations have little protection against employer prejudices and discrimination. For those who are tied to household employment, especially to families operating with diplomatic passports, or who employ unregistered labour and retain passports, an effective form of modern domestic slavery develops, with a 'Damoclean sword' of illegality hanging over those who choose to complain to the authorities about their lot.

The experiences of these care workers overall is characterized by the insecure nature of their work, the long hours, hardship and low status which often bears no relation to their educational qualifications or status prior to entering the country. They care for some of the most vulnerable citizens in Britain but paradoxically are subject to some of the worst prejudice. Many endure these difficult circumstances in order to send remittances to family and kin back home and to fund part-time study in the UK. According to 2006 figures some 105,000 care assistants, 16 per cent of the registered care sector workforce, are from overseas. Sixty-eight per cent of care workers in London are born overseas (ONS 2006, cited in Rawles 2008). Another 23,000 work as childminders, making up 19 per cent of all childminders, with others working as nursing assistants, house parents and wardens, nursery nurses and play group leaders among other care sector work. In total non-UK workers make up 12 per cent of the social care workforce (Rawles 2008). Without them the care system would collapse. Data on the contribution of these non-UK carers to the UK economy is sadly lacking but qualitative surveys on the impact of their contribution attest to their value, both formal and informal, to the care sector (Rawles 2008). Interestingly, Dyer *et al.*'s work (2008) illustrates how caring work in hospitals is undertaken by migrant worker cleaners and porters as well as by those in formal care roles, for example by providing interpreting or translation or through emotional tendering work offered informally while cleaning. Dyer *et al.* argue that this provides valuable 'emotional labour' that is largely hidden within the formal data, a contribution that acts to enrich greatly the quality of care (Dyer *et al.* 2008: 2031).

Entrepreneurship

Self-employment rates have been traditionally high for some minority ethnic groups. There are many examples of the successful development of this entrepreneurship in the welfare arena: the Indian doctor on Harley Street, the Nigerian private landlord, the Filipina au pair agency, the African–Caribbean home care manager, the Zimbabwean care agency owner, the Chinese medicines shop and, perhaps less visible, the Pakistani housewife operating a pharmaceutical business on the internet. In addition, successful ethnic minority businesses such as catering and laundry services, construction or IT services are intricately bound up with state and private welfare provision. However, entrepreneurial underdevelopment among these groups has been more the norm. As far back as the Scarman Report in the 1980s the recommendation that enterprise be promoted as a way of redressing the deep alienation and underemployment among African–Caribbeans was put on the policy agenda and this issue has been the subject of a number of government initiatives ever since (Ram and Smallbone 2003; see also http://www.fbrn.org.uk/). In an increasingly privatized market of welfare, opportunities for the self-employed, for small businesses and for the start-up of new businesses quickly expand. The position of the singleton self-employed professional or the small business contractor may be strengthened by the current volume of work contracted out by the state and governments have recognized this as a potential lever for fostering upward mobility and combating disadvantage and exclusion among these groups.

Labour market discrimination has long been regarded as one of the key factors driving higher self-employment rates among minority ethnic groups. The Asian shopkeeper and his (sic) corner shop evolved, it has been argued, as an alternative to paid employment and as a significant cultural resource to the newly settled ethnic minority community (Ram 1992; Modood *et al.* 1996). By and large ethnic minority businesses emerged very much along the lines of what Ram and Jones (2008) call the 'ethnic resources model', with high levels of entrepreneurial self-employment being a manifestation of the communal pooling of resources among newly migrated groups in inner city areas. Business would emerge in areas of settlement where capital and risks could be shared, flexible labour could be available and customers in need of ethnic resources or the succour of communal solidarity would guarantee loyal custom. Often, it would also be based on the professional skills of members of the family – which in African–Caribbean households may include nursing, and in the Asian community drawing upon the specific requirements of faiths such as Islam and Hinduism, for services such as funeral care. Overall, the 'ethnic', family-owned, family-run business became the stereotypical norm for many minority communities.

This axiom has, however, been revisited more recently (see Ram and Jones 2008: 353), with a more refined view of the diversity of drivers shaping ethnic minority entrepreneurship. Migration to Britain involved a large variety of groups with very different educational, skill, class and wealth backgrounds as well as religious, linguistic and cultural backgrounds and these factors all have a bearing on the geographic and labour market locations they occupy, providing a complex picture explaining labour market differentials (Ratcliffe 2004; Clark and Drinkwater 2006; Cheung and Heath 2007). Clark and Drinkwater (2006), for example, find evidence that paid labour market discrimination does lead to higher self-employment for some discriminated-against groups but at the same time some aspects of minority ethnic culture, in particular religious orientation, act to shape the choice towards entrepreneurship. They note that particular religious beliefs can serve to actively enhance entrepreneurial ambitions, and for some the nature of self-employment itself provides the necessary flexibility and exclusivity to facilitate religious observance. Furthermore, as Ram and Jones (2008) point out, continued transformations are occurring in this sector, in particular in relation to the expansion of women's self-employment, for example in personal and medical services and following the impact of new migrant groups from the Eastern European countries. Younger, better educated second generation ethnic minorities are now less likely to be in self-employment than their parents as aspirations change inter-generationally. The picture is not static and while self-employment might have brought social mobility for some groups, co-ethnic concentration in relatively deprived areas can serve to depress self-employment and curtail the expansion and development of small businesses.

Almost one in ten employing businesses in England are owned or primarily led by people from minority ethnic groups (Whitehead *et al.* 2006). Throughout the UK there are more than a quarter of a million small and medium minority ethnic enterprises which contribute some £15 billion to the UK economy each year (Whitehead *et al.* 2006). Many employ staff and this sector is growing significantly, with start-ups estimated to be double that of total business start-ups. There are some clearly identifiable issues for ethnic minority-led business that relate to ethnicity specifically and there are differences apparent between particular ethnic groups in the operation of their businesses. In general, by contrast with white-led small businesses, minority ethnic businesses tend to be in the service sector and located in urban areas, with almost half (40 per cent) based in the most deprived wards of the UK. They experience greater difficulty in terms of start-up and growth and are more likely to have difficulties accessing finance. Black-led businesses in particular are more likely to mention obstacles to gaining finance and to growth and expansion than other ethnic groups. Many report experiencing discrimination (Whitehead *et al.* 2006) either in the form of customer resistance or vulnerability to violence and criminality (Ram and Jones 2008).

The nature of these businesses varies considerably, with different ethnic groups concentrated in different sectors of the economy. Black Caribbean groups, for example, are thought to favour the construction sector, while south Asian and Chinese groups have greater representation in distribution and catering. There is some evidence of ethnic minority-led businesses as direct providers in health and social care (McGregor 2007; Ram and Jones 2008), taking advantage of the new opportunity structure in welfare delivery and particularly among women. Owning and running care homes, running care employment agencies and pharmaceuticals and other forms of private practice, including medicine or dentistry, may be a feature of this development, and one of the growth sectors of the twenty-first century has been 'Chinese medicine' outlets, tapping into the demand for alternative or complementary medicines. A number of publicly funded initiatives have been aimed at promoting enterprise and supporting minority ethnic small businesses (Ram and Smallbone 2003). This begs the question as to whether they have been successful in achieving the social justice objective of combating disadvantage and in generating jobs and business competitiveness. Ram and Jones's (2008) brief assessment suggests minority ethnic self-employment is undoubtedly an important ladder out of disadvantage. However, businesses often struggle to take advantage of government support initiatives despite engagement strategies aimed at boosting self-employment among under-represented minority groups. As a consequence many minority ethnic entrepreneurs are stuck in lower order market niches, have to work long hours, have lower turnover and rely heavily on family or co-ethnic labour (Whitehead *et al.* 2006). Deakins *et al.*'s (2007) study indicates that while this community social capital has traditionally been seen as a positive factor for entrepreneurial development it can also act as a considerable constraint, particularly for second and third generation entrepreneurs who may need to develop wider relationships beyond the bonds of the co-ethnic community and capitalize on wider networks and on institutional sources of advice and finance.

Despite optimism about minority ethnic entrepreneurship, all the evidence suggests that even self-employed minority ethnic people are by and large still in fairly discrete areas of the labour market and over-represented in low paid jobs that are casual, insecure, unhealthy and dangerous, or indeed unemployed (Clark and Drinkwater 2007). Efforts by the former Commission for Racial Equality to stimulate better diversity and equality employment practices within the private sector through policy guidance and high-profile naming and shaming tribunal discrimination cases met with limited success largely because of their permissive and voluntary nature. The new Equality and Human Rights Commission has recognized that procurement remains a major mechanism to achieving an overhaul in the for-profit sector and has called for statutory force to underpin procurement practices under the terms of the proposed new Equality Act. To this end the commissioning and purchasing power of the state sector as a level for sponsoring minority ethnic businesses and promoting equality in the workplace deserves closer inspection.

Procurement

Local authorities have huge budgets dedicated to private sector contracts. This purchasing power has been recognized at least since the initiatives of Ken Livingstone's GLC in the 1970s as a lever to pursue social justice aims, whether it be directed towards regeneration in a disadvantaged area by sponsoring the development of businesses and sustaining entrepreneurship among disadvantaged groups or when used as a mechanism of contract compliance to ensure private services engage with the ethos and values of public sector services in tackling discrimination. Supplier diversity initiatives refer to mechanisms aimed at increasing the number of ethnic minority-owned businesses that supply goods and services to public and private organizations and contract compliance refers to the use of public sector procurement to achieve wider social and economic goals. In recent years these initiatives have grown apace, driven by legislative stimulus.

In the United States procurement has been actively deployed as a mechanism for affirmative action and social justice, with programmes like Set Aside (Theodore 1995) realizing considerable success. There are several reasons why such strategies have not developed in the same way in the UK as in the States. Many would argue that demographics alone make the direct transfer of a quota system like Set Aside unworkable in anything other than areas of minority ethnic concentration in the UK. But there are also legislative constraints on utilizing such radical positive discrimination approaches to managing equal opportunities in the UK as they are proscribed by EC regulations (Orton and Ratcliffe 2005; Ram and Jones 2008). EC procurement rules aim to open up the market to competition and the free movement of goods and services across the EU and therefore purchasers often cannot give preference to target localities or target groups (PAMECUS 2009).

Under the 1988 Local Government Act, Compulsory Competitive Tendering (CCT) was introduced, bestowing a legal duty on local authorities to put certain services out to competitive tender. They could not, however, take into account any 'non-commercial considerations' in the awarding of contracts that might confuse judgements about value for money. Nevertheless, they did have scope to ask potential contractors six questions relating to race equality in employment and require associated documentation. Thus the notion of achieving wider social objectives through contractual arrangements was given a policy lever. Local authorities were at least able to give a nod to issues of promoting equality but they were severely constrained in utilizing procurement to stimulate local regeneration as their overriding considerations in selecting contractors had to be economic stringency. The 1999 Local Government Act introduced Best Value, which opened up the narrow practices of CCT, allowing both value for money and quality issues such as equal opportunity, health and safety and the encouragement of new suppliers to be considerations in the awarding of contracts.

Orton and Ratcliffe's (2005) examination of the policy on procurement demonstrates the ongoing tension between neo-liberal ambitions to serve the interests of the free market and the rhetoric of observing the social justice potential of procurement policy. They argue that the Byatt review (DTLR 2001) of local government procurement, which provided extensive recommendations for change, gave but minimal consideration to the use of procurement to promote racial equality in employment and gave maximum emphasis to the issues of value for money (Orton and Ratcliffe 2005). The question of whose values, and whose money, were not raised.

The Race Relations (Amendment) Act 2000 represented a step change and provided a new stimulus for diversity in public sector procurement. Procurement is a function to which the statutory duties to promote race equality apply and the contractor acting on behalf of a public authority becomes liable under the Act if guilty of racial discrimination. Alongside this the Local Government Act 2000 established the principle that local authorities have a responsibility to promote local well-being, which necessarily includes social and economic development. Taken together, these two pieces of legislation open up considerable supply opportunities for local businesses.

Despite the more conducive policy environment there remain considerable barriers to minority ethnic businesses in securing public sector contracts. A major hurdle is the bureaucratic process itself. There are a number of pre-qualification stages in the process that must be completed prior to getting onto the lists of recognized suppliers. These include the completion of detailed documentation outlining the financial position of the organization, making available audited accounts, policies on equal opportunity and health and safety, outlining relevant experience and making available references. To many small firms this can be off-putting. Firms may struggle to find information about potential contracts and despite being on supplier lists they may not be invited to tender because of perceptions about their size and capacity and turnover. The bidding process itself may be time-consuming and demand too much from a small supplier (Ram and Jones 2008), while language barriers and lack of experience of dealing with bureaucracy, and the perception that the tendering process is a closed shop, deter their involvement (Steele and Sodhi 2004). Many minority ethnic businesses are very small in size, engaged in a narrow range of activities, and the majority are involved in relatively low added value activities. As a result providers may be sceptical of their ability to respond to procurement opportunities. Steele and Sodhi's study (2004) of UK Housing Associations' contracting power for construction and maintenance work found that despite the potential for positive action in this area few housing associations recognized the potential of their purchasing power in promoting equality or the business benefits of doing so. Their study found that particular emphasis was given to inviting 'known' or 'recommended' contractors and consultants, which militated against equal opportunities or being proactive in including new providers. Furthermore, the location of many small businesses, often in poor and deprived urban areas, may make them ineligible for some locally focused purchasing initiatives. More recently researchers have signalled some caution about the nature of the policy focus on minority ethnic businesses, arguing that such policies can lead to a distorted over-emphasis on ethnic determinants and ethnic culture rather than seeing these small businesses as sharing many of the difficulties of small businesses *per se* (Ram and Jones 2008: 364).

The EHRC recognizes that public authorities have underutilized the potential of procurement strategies. In 2005 only 40 per cent of local authorities in England specifically addressed equality and diversity with examples or targets in their procurement strategies. Many lack understanding of how the concept of value for money includes social considerations, and in particular how equality can be seen as an essential component of quality, and there is insufficient training for those in authorities responsible for making procurement decisions (EHRC 2009). Nor, as yet, has the considerable potential of the growing notion of 'social enterprise businesses' made much headway or impact on this sector (see www.socialenterprise.org.uk/).

In June 2008 the pamphlet *Buy and Make a Difference: How to Address Social Issues in Public Procurement* (OGC 2008) attempted to clarify that equality duties do apply to procurement processes and make clear that candidates for contracts could be rejected 'on grounds of grave professional misconduct', which might include breaches of equality legislation, such as having been subject to an adverse tribunal finding. However, the guidance stopped short of condoning any approach that allowed a public authority to require tendering firms to meet such criteria as identifying and addressing imbalances among job applicants and employees according to their gender, ethnicity and disability or adopting an explicit equality strategy. There remains therefore considerable confusion about how far public authorities should apply the existing equality duties to public procurement, what criteria they are allowed to apply and at what stage, what information they are allowed to ask for, and how they can legitimately make equality criteria relevant to the contracting process in a way that protects them from legal challenge (EHRC 2009). It is to be hoped that the anticipated Equality Act will make equality in procurement an explicit statutory obligation, sending a clear and unequivocal message to public authorities as purchasers and to prospective private sector suppliers.

Consuming private welfare

The movement between public and private forms of welfare is multidimensional and has involved significant shifts not only in the transfer of ownership of public services and the creation of competitive markets in welfare but in the reallocation of responsibilities from the public to the private sphere (Land 2004). Responsibility for sourcing, choosing and reviewing a service has moved beyond state towards the individual consumer, for example in the shift toward personalized care budgets (see Chapter 5). Drakeford suggests that, in any system that regards the individual as consumer rather than a rights-bearing citizen, those who are well placed to exercise their advantage as 'market actors' inevitably benefit over others who are less so (Drakeford 2007: 65). The most vulnerable, marginalized or excluded of society or those without economic clout are those most often unable to mobilize good quality services. The supply of public services through the 'public service industry' means service users may become more vulnerable to market changes, such as change of ownership of a provision, rise in prices or withdrawal of a provision or the curtailment of quality as for-profit organizations seek to square the circle of rising costs. For example, evidence from the Federation of Black Housing Associations indicates that ethnic minorities are three times more likely to be statutorily homeless than their white counterparts and one of the key factors explaining this is being forced to leave private rented accommodation (Chahal 1999).

The general rule of thumb is that the more economically secure can take advantage of the choice and flexibility offered by private sector services; those in less advantaged positions, for example on low incomes or marginalized for other reasons in society, will be far less likely to benefit. Poverty among minority ethnic groups must be a determining factor in accessing and utilizing private sector services and not just based on their ability to pay. People from ethnic minorities are concentrated in urban areas, with over 70 per cent of ethnic minorities living in the most disadvantaged wards in Britain. Such disadvantage is highly linked with poor health chances and with poor access to a range of beneficial services (Johnson 2003a, 2003b). Workers from ethnic minorities are more likely to be unemployed and to have lower earnings than white people when in full-time employment. Overall 12 per cent of people from minority ethnic groups are unemployed compared to 5 per cent for white people. In work, poverty is high among ethnic minorities. The average pay gap between white men in full-time employment and minority ethnic men is 4.5 per cent but this rises starkly for some groups, such as Bangladeshi men (39 per cent) and Pakistani men (19 per cent) (Steventon and Sanchez 2008: 38). The combination of low earnings and high levels of worklessness means that many people from ethnic minorities live in low-income households. For example 77 per cent of households headed by a Pakistani or Bangladeshi adult of working age and 46 per cent of those headed by a Black adult of working age live on incomes in the bottom 40 per cent of the income distribution (Steventon and Sanchez 2008: 39). Hardship, debt, financial exclusion and all the associated factors of poverty including ill-health are linked to the difficulties of living on a low income (Runnymede Trust 2007: 8). Exercising choice in accessing services may be constrained by ability to pay but other factors – of language, culture, know-how of the system – make utilizing the services of the private sector unlikely for many people from ethnic minority backgrounds. The case of private pensions illustrates this differential.

Relatively few people from ethnic minorities are in the retirement age group (at the time of writing) but this proportion is set to increase rapidly in the near future as the cohorts of migrants who came to the UK in the 1950s reach state retirement age. Other sources of income and in particular private pensions are becoming more and more significant in protecting against poverty in later life. Ethnic minorities tend to have lower income in later life from private pensions, partly as a result of their shorter employment records in Britain since migration. Yet this is not the whole explanation and cannot explain the persistence of ethnic variation in private pension acquisition. While minority ethnic groups are extremely diverse, taken overall their circumstances suggest that they are more likely to have the characteristics associated with lower pension incomes than the rest of the population (Ginn and Arber 2001). Because they are more likely to work part-time, be self-employed or indeed unemployed, they are considerably more likely not to qualify for full state pension or to have accrued savings towards a private pension. They are more likely than those in the general population to have opted out of saving for a private pension due to higher rates of in-work poverty or lower levels of financial know-how, and there are perhaps cultural and institutional reasons for lower private pension participation, including language barriers or lack of experience and confidence in dealing with financial institutions (Steventon and Sanchez 2008). The types of job and types of employer are also determining factors as ethnic minorities are less likely than white people to be employed in well-pensioned industries. Ginn and Arber's (2001) study shows that gender and ethnicity interact in terms of private pension coverage. While both men and women are less likely to have private pensions than their white peers, Ginn and Arber's study shows particular disadvantage for women and especially for Pakistani and Bangladeshi women.

Private pension provisioning is an increasingly significant factor potentially contributing to the widening of inequality in later life. As policy shifts towards private provisioning, it may well be that ethnic minorities and particularly women from minority ethnic backgrounds will be disproportionately dependent on means-tested benefits in later life as access to private pension provisioning is denied to them (Ginn and Arber 2001). The Labour government planned pension reforms which include all employees being auto-enrolled into saving into a work-based private pension from 2012, with the right to opt out if they choose. In addition a new national saving scheme called 'personal accounts' will be introduced for those earning over £5000 who do not have access to a good quality in-work pension scheme. Steventon and Sanchez (2008) estimate that ethnic minorities will form a disproportionately large portion of the target group for these personal accounts. However, the extent to which ethnic minorities will benefit from these reforms is challenged by those who suggest that ethnic minorities are more likely to opt out of these schemes due to high rates of in-work poverty, lower levels of proficiency in English and lack of familiarity with pensions terminology (Runnymede Trust 2007). It is uncertain, therefore, that they will benefit from the proposed reforms.

Another facet of consuming private welfare causes in social care, were the impact of the extension of private provisioning is an under-researched area. The evidence in relation to Direct Payments, for example, is thin. Clark, Gough and McFarlane's (2004) discussion provides some evidence to suggest that the extension of choice, control and flexibility and innovation offered by the Direct Payments system has positive advantages for ethnic minorities (see also Stuart 2006). They provide examples to illustrate the ability of individuals from minority ethnic backgrounds to employ culturally sensitive workers to assist with their care needs. In this way issues of safety, language, and respect for cultural norms are overcome and a relevant service secured. Ethnic minority organizations and outreach workers were also identified as important mediators of information about Direct Payments and facilitating access to Direct Payments for ethnic minority individuals.

> Direct Payments were undoubtedly the sole means by which the Somali participants could find workers who spoke their language. Statutory and independent agencies in the City simply didn't have Somali speaking care assistants. However, it was expected that this might change as some younger Somali women working as PAs had expressed an interest in also working in home care agencies.
>
> (Clark *et al.* 2004: 14)

Using Direct Payments, however, involves a range of tasks including recruiting, employing and managing a personal assistant, keeping financial records, a separate bank account, making financial returns and demonstrating compliance with employment law. Further research is clearly needed on how people from ethnic minorities engage with and manage such a system. The restriction on the use of relatives as Personal Assistants may be an inhibiting factor for some but Clark *et al.* (2004) found the older Somali participants in their sample emphatically opposed to employing relatives on the grounds that it may produce unwanted tensions or them thinking they were the boss instead of being employees. They found a high degree of satisfaction with being able to purchase their own support among the Somali participants and a sense that family relationships improved, that they were able to secure a more culturally relevant service and that having their own workers enhanced their feelings of safety (2004: 32). Yeandle and Stiell's study of a northern English city (2007: 125) also reports some evidence of the Direct Payments scheme enabling older people to receive culturally appropriate support, although the experiences recounted to them were not so straightforwardly positive. Take-up of Direct Payments by the general population is reportedly low (Yeandle and Stiell 2007: 120) and there are clearly additional barriers to be encountered for ethnic minority older people. Most local authorities expect users to have separate bank accounts for their Direct Payments, with payments made by cheque, and to keep clear records for auditing purposes. These factors alone may inhibit take-up by those whose first language is not English. The expansion of opportunities for minority ethnic care workers' that schemes such as this provide has been discussed earlier in this chapter. The potential, however, for exploitation and compromised employment rights can be apparent even within a highly regulated scheme such as this and the variable quality of relationships between provider and user is a perennial concern. The less well-off will need to rely on publicly funded support and it is likely that the more affluent will benefit from the Direct Payments system.

The experience of ethnic minorities in residential care is similarly under-researched, whether within the statutory or independent sector (Mold *et al.* 2005). The notion of ethnically segregated or ethnically specific provision for this age group does not feature in the UK literature in the way that it does in the US, for example. Specific attitudes to ageing and care of older people among particular minority groups, lack of concentrations and sustainable numbers have frustrated such a development in the UK. There may be some (religious) provision of this kind (most notably in the Jewish community) but beyond this minority ethnic elders make up the random composition of residential and nursing home residents largely within a privately run care sector. The lack of specific data must raise questions about care standards and the development of appropriate long-term care provision for this group. The issue of access to residential care, including respite care, has consistently been raised as a concern (Age Concern 2001; Jewson *et al.* 2003); however, Mold *et al.*'s review estimated some 25,000 ethnic minority adults in care homes in England and Wales and this is expected to increase as minority-origin older people make up a greater proportion of those retired. The majority of these individuals will find themselves serviced by private sector care provision. Low uptake of care services is related to the perception of culturally inappropriate care, particularly for services such as respite and hospice care (Jewson *et al.* 2003; Johnson 2009). The overarching theme identified in Mold *et al.*'s review was the challenge of tailoring care to the cultural needs of individuals within these settings, either through the development of staff training or greater engagement of the resident themselves and their family and of minority ethnic organizations in order to ensure an appropriate service to elders (see Chapter 5). Whether current service delivery in the private sector within nursing home and residential home settings in this respect can be assured by the new Care Quality Commission is still moot.

However, the issue of their vulnerabilities within a largely privatized care system extend far beyond this. The lack of ability to pay and exercise choice of provision because of poverty among minority ethnic elders must be of concern. For this reason they are acutely exposed to vulnerabilities within this sector, including high staff turnover, the use of unskilled workers, reliance on over-burdened and underpaid workers and the push for greater and greater savings.

The care home sector is undoubtedly struggling to meet the demands of the Care Standards Act (Vernon 2009). In areas of specialized care concerns about standards have steadily mounted and this includes responsiveness to the needs of minority ethnic elders and to equality issues. Increasingly standards of care are being regarded as a human rights issue. The new Care Quality Commission, operative from April 2009, has undertaken to work closely with the Equality and Human Rights Commission (EHRC) in the strategic development of service delivery in respect of rights and equality. The EHRC has developed a series of proposals and actions in relation to the delivery of a more effective approach to care and support, including instilling an equality and human rights culture across care and support based on a national rights-focused framework of outcomes (EHRC 2009). The regulatory levers available to these two Commissions in bringing the private sector providers into line are substantial if enforcement powers are effective. It is too early to say whether this is mere rhetoric or will lead to a major transformation in approaches to the delivery of care.

Conclusions

The expansion of private sector provision in welfare delivery inevitably produces both potential gains and losses for ethnic minorities. While growth in this sector has ostensibly opened up opportunities for minority ethnic workers and for minority ethnic enterprise, concerns remain about worker exploitation in this sector and the extent to which ethnic minority-run businesses are able genuinely to capitalize on contracts from the state. Strategies to promote the use of levers of contract compliance are still permissive, voluntary and woefully weak. Overall the contributions of the minority ethnic labour force remain largely under-recognized. The evidence suggests the need for better data on the distribution and contribution of minority ethnic enterprise and their contribution to GNP. The importance of their contribution in terms of the added value and quality of care delivery and in building social capital is underestimated in markets of care that stress purely economic factors. The emotional labour expended by migrant workers and the enhancement and enrichment of care practices they bring are not factored into the cash for care transactions of the market economy.

At the same time, concerns about discriminations and racisms by private sector employers persist. Legislative and policy levers against discrimination in the workplace (see Chapters 2 and 8) to guard against exploitation of workers have proved ineffective and too many still work for pay below the minimum wage. In the care sector, even where wage rates have traditionally been poor, there is evidence of pressure to cut wages, working hours and staff numbers and employers are relying on workers from other countries who are willing to work at minimum wage or below (Unison 2008). Care UK's annual report, 2007 for example, cited over 62 per cent of employed health care professionals being recruited from overseas to avoid recruitment from within the NHS. In the largely outsourced home care sector, increased pressures mean employers failing to train, support and develop workers, which undermines the quality of care delivery.

Above all, however, this major shift to private sector provision raises broader issues about inequality in welfare that does and will further impact on ethnic minorities. The rise of the 'public services industry' poses a number of potential threats to service quality and to the values inherent in public services. The recent trend has been towards the consolidation and concentration of providers into increasingly large businesses. For example, many care homes that started off as small family-run enterprises found regulatory demands undermined their viability so they were relatively quickly subject to merger or takeover by large care companies. This has had implications for continuity of care and other aspects of service quality as providers are driven to prioritize cost cutting over investment, especially in the context of the current economic climate. The additional costs incurred by private providers or the transaction costs they generate through the complex processes of tendering, bidding and administering contracts are often passed on to the users by way of higher fees and charges for services. Further, the contracting-out of services has been shown to lead to poorer monitoring on the part of public bodies, undermining public service accountability. This in turn inevitably excludes those most vulnerable, the complex service user or those who cannot afford to pay or have few resources to exercise choice, thus reinforcing a two-tier system.

The widespread privatization of services is a contemporary reality and it is a trend that is unlikely to be reversed by future governments. Commitment to utilizing the diversity of provision offered by a mixed economy within a state-funded and state-regulated control is one way of looking at privatization. The residualization of state services and the uncontrolled and unregulated private sector expansion in which vulnerable groups, including ethnic minorities, are increasingly left to the vagaries of market forces is another.

7   Rural communities

Introduction

Much of the focus for exploring issues of race and ethnicity and public policy has been on areas of the UK with ethnic minority concentrations. Such is the geographic distribution of ethnic minorities across the country that 'non-white' ethnic groups are considerably more likely to live in England than in Wales, Scotland or Northern Ireland (see Chapter 3), and in each of these nations they are more likely to live in major cities. Nearly half (45 per cent) of all non-white minorities in the UK live in London where they comprise 29 per cent of all residents (ONS 2010). Beyond the metropolis, however, what can be called 'predominantly white areas' make up the vast majority of local authorities, areas typified by low concentrations of minority ethnic groups. A high proportion of local authorities have ethnic minority populations of less than 2 per cent, including areas as varied as Great Yarmouth, Caerphilly and Dover.

Overall, while around one in five of the white British population lives in suburban or rural England, less than 3 per cent of the 'visible' minority ethnic population of England lives outside urban areas of more than 10,000. Indeed, the majority are to be found in the metropolitan counties of London, West Midlands, Yorkshire and the North West. Similarly, in Wales (Table 7.1), applying a looser definition of 'urban', there is a huge discrepancy in the probability of finding minority ethnic people outside larger urban settlements. That said, visible minority ethnic people, of south Asian, African–Caribbean and Chinese backgrounds, are fully citizens of the United Kingdom, the majority born in these islands, and still they have less access to the relatively higher quality of life associated with suburban and rural living.

Characteristically, however, these rural, semi-rural or small town places have largely been marginal to the dominant discourse of race relations and have been neglected in terms of attracting sustained policy attention. It is also, perhaps, true to say that the whole debate on inequality has been slow to

Table 7.1   Distribution of ethnic groups by type of settlement, England and Wales (2001)

Census ethnic group	White British %	South Asian/British %	Black/British %	Chinese/Other %
England				
Urban (>10 k)	78.7	97.65	97.6	93.4
Town/Urban fringe	9.1	1.1	1.1	3.2
Village/Rural	11.4	1.2	1.3	3.5
Wales				
Proportion Urban (>1,500)	81.7	94.8	93.7	92.1

Source: Office for National Statistics 'Key Statistics' KS06, recalculated by authors

Data following similar breakdown not available for Scotland or N. Ireland.

Note: Minority ethnic groups include 'mixed' categories. Urban in England refers to settlements over 10,000; in Wales to settlements over 1500 (ONS definitions).

consider factors of rurality as a disadvantage. While definitions of rural vary considerably, including subjective interpretations (Craig and Manthorpe 2000), it is true to say that where minorities have lacked a visible presence as a specific concentration they have also lacked a policy presence, with local authorities exercising a 'blind spot' in relation to their needs based on the misguided assumption that low numbers equals low need. At the same time, minorities themselves living in such areas have lacked the political clout to draw attention to their experiences as being qualitatively different to their urban counterparts. While factors of place and locality have long figured in sociological analysis of 'race' and race relations, up until relatively recently a paucity of analysis has been available for what can broadly be called rural localities. Gradually the spectre of issues such as rural racism has received policy recognition, not least because of growing awareness of the flux and change to rural communities as a result of new migrations (de Lima and Wright 2009) and especially from the so-called A8 states of eastern and central Europe. Renewed concerns about freedom of movement for work and the community cohesion agenda led Trevor Phillips, former Chair of the Commission for Racial Equality (CRE) and now head of the Equality and Human Rights Commission, to identify the countryside as implicated in a form of 'passive apartheid' (Phillips 2004b) in which Black and Asian incomers do not feel welcome. Phillips suggested the countryside as the 'last bastion for black people to say "we are here" ' (Phillips 2004b), and in doing so located the rural phenomenon within the context of wider British race relations debates and, more specifically, within issues of contemporary multiculturalism and of national identity.

Since 2000 the race imperative has been indiscriminate of place, in marked distinction to the earlier focus on 'hotspots' of diversity, such as the 'Section 11' funding awarded to places where there was a concentration of 'New Commonwealth' immigrants of 'distinctive' cultural and linguistic backgrounds (Johnson *et al.* 1989). The Race Relations (Amendment) Act 2000 made it mandatory on all public authorities across the UK to undertake appropriate monitoring of their communities, to design and deliver services in consultation with their communities and takes steps to actively promote good race relations. For these 'elsewhere' places this set of duties represented a step nothing short of revolutionary but the impact of ten years of race equality legislation has not been so startling. While increased migration to rural and remote areas of Britain has served to crystallize media and political attention on the existence of minority populations, this has not always been matched by increased competence in responding to diversity. This chapter explores the specificities of racial and ethnic diversity in rural and semi-rural settings and seeks to raise questions about the challenges posed for welfare delivery in such a milieu. Factors of nation (as discussed in Chapter 1 and 3 of this book) and factors of rurality and locality act as powerful mediating factors in addressing issues of racial equality as they impinge on welfare policy and practices. We are concerned here to demonstrate how the localized infrastructure for equality practice should be understood as part of the situations to which they are a response, and to speak to 'street level' influence on welfare policy and practice in addressing the needs of ethnic minorities and race equality ambitions in rural areas.

'Out of place, out of mind': the topography of difference

The settlement of ethnic minorities in rural areas is not a new phenomenon. In the Edwardian era it was not uncommon to find Black and Asian domestic servants, wards or even country gentlemen living comfortable lives in rural villages (Green 1998). In the Victorian era, accounts such as that of the establishment of the Congo Institute in north Wales and the presence of African students in Scottish universities indicate that, with some notable exceptions, prior to the post-war mass migration ethnic minority settlement was a much more sporadic affair (see Fryer 1984; Visram 1986; Dabydeen *et al.* 2007). Gypsy/Travellers, Chinese entrepreneurs and itinerants such as travelling musicians or the Indian pedlars of the Scottish islands meant that the countryside was always subject to what Sibley has now classically termed the 'discrepant others' (1998: 93) – people who are somehow there but always out of place. The curiosity value of these individuals and their quiet assimilation into village life is a matter of historical and literary record but of much import to contemporary understanding of rural life in as much as it indicates that the countryside was never quite as homogeneous as it is imagined or represented (see, for example, Day 1998 on Welsh rural life; Cloke *et al.* 1998). This leads us to question why certain conceptions of rural life have been allowed to prevail at the expense of others. A body of theory focuses on such representations of the countryside and ways in which these socially constructed imaginings promote the 'othering' of minority individuals (Agyeman and Spooner 1997; Neal 2002; Cloke 2004; Neal and Agyeman 2006). In these imaginings the rural idyll is contrasted sharply with urban life and perceived as a safe haven: harmonious, unchanging, community-spirited and homogeneous. Such accounts illustrate the ways in which the countryside is constructed as exclusive, 'collapsing . . . rurality into whiteness', such that it becomes, as Neal argues, the haven of 'white safety' (Neal 2002: 443). These dominant perceptions of the rural render invisible the presence of ethnic minority groups, only affording them recognition in more negative or inflammatory reporting; for example, as in the Caie Park disturbances in Wrexham, north Wales in 2003, the government plans to build asylum seeker accommodation centres in rural areas and the deaths of the Chinese cockle pickers in Morecambe Bay (Bright 2004). As rural stakeholders, ethnic minorities are placed in a highly contradictory positioning, being largely invisible to service providers but simultaneously highly conspicuous/visible as rural residents by virtue of their perceived difference (Chakroborti and Garland 2004: 8).

This type of analysis highlights how deeply embedded constructions of the rural idyll are, not only to notions of 'whiteness' but also to notions of British national identity, and more specifically constructions of English, Welsh, Scottish and Irish national identity (Neal and Agyeman 2006). As ethnic minorities are excluded from recognition within images of the rural, it is argued, they are effectively excluded not only from migrating to these areas and forming part of these rural communities but from the dominant constructions of UK national identities (Chakroborti and Garland 2004; Williams 2007).

The assumption of the homogeneity of the countryside as contrasted with the heterogeneity of the city illustrates the ways in which the countryside imagery is rendered 'racially' pure and accordingly *not* multicultural. This has not only fostered a sense among policy makers and practitioners of 'no problem here' but has led to rural race issues being seen as something marginal to or separate from wider debates on British multiculturalism (Williams 2007a). This powerful exclusionary ideology of the countryside is not divorced from issues of public policy, for it informs policy makers' and practitioners' ideas of 'who belongs', who is entitled to the resources of a community, and who is entitled to participate in community life. Issues of rights of entitlement to the resources of an area such as housing, health care, safety and protection are mediated by these deeply embedded ideas. Pugh (2004) has argued that rural agencies need to acknowledge the ways in which predominant ideas about who belongs and who does not, and the ways in which rural identity is constructed, can lead to exclusionary and prejudicial actions.

The rapid diversification of the rural space may ultimately serve to dislodge the powerful exclusionary ideologies of the countryside and the stereotypes of rural dwellers, and revoke Trevor Phillips's segregationalist thesis of the existence of 'a passive apartheid' (2004b). The evidence demonstrates a settled ethnic minority presence in every local authority in Britain (LGA 2007), including those seen as the most rural and remote such as rural north Wales, the Scottish Highlands and Islands, the Antrim coast, and Devon and Cornwall. What is also now becoming more apparent is that transformations to the demography of these areas are rapid and significant. Following EU enlargement in 2004, it was estimated that as many as 720,000 migrant workers from the A8 ('Accession') countries found work in parts of the UK with over 40 per cent of migrants from the new Europe ending up in rural areas (LGA 2007). A8 migrants have so far been predominantly from Poland, generally young and without dependents. They have, however, attracted attention because of the sudden increase in their numbers and their geographical distribution beyond the traditional areas of international in-migration and diversity (2007: 3). The LGA report itemizes in the top 100 local authority areas for migrant worker registrations places such as Cheltenham, Corby, Crewe and Nantwich, Great Yarmouth, Herefordshire, Isles of Scilly, or Stratford upon Avon, all of which had ethnic minority populations of less than 3 per cent in the 2001 Census. In relative terms these 'diverse' populations, while still small, are growing more rapidly than in urban areas (LGA 2007).

In addition there is some evidence that this diversity is the result of ethnic minorities migrating to new contexts such as the suburban areas of British cities and beyond, with people moving for work or seeking a better quality of life (Ratcliffe 2004: 70; Pacione 2005). In Magne's (2003) study of Devon, ethnic minorities' settled residence averaged eight years and respondents gave as reasons for migration factors such as moving to take up work and for a better environment. In a study conducted in north Wales, factors such as moving to join family and moving for work were cited as reasons for migrations (Williams and Hong Baker 2009). The LGA report (2007: 5) uses the concept 'churn' to illustrate the flux and change to such communities and the likely impacts of this on welfare services. Under New Labour policy, asylum seekers were dispersed to more rural areas of the UK and consequent refugee settlement forms part of this pattern (Johnson 2003b). In addition the movement of Gypsy/ Travellers has already changed the profile of many rural communities and is continuing to do so (Heatherington 2006; Bhopal 2006).

Access to the countryside and involvement in environmental issues, as a means to combating disadvantage, have become the focus of policy interventions, with organizations like the Countryside Agency and the Council for National Parks and the Black Environment Network (BEN) attempting to encourage more visitors to the countryside. The appointment of Narendra Bajaria as the first ethnic minority Chair of the Peak District National Park

Authority in 2007 forcefully signalled such an ambition (*Guardian Society* supplement, Wednesday 22 August 2007). However, as Neal argues (Neal and Ageyman 2006: 242), although positive in themselves, these messages continue to reinforce the predominant space notions of the rurality/ethnicity debates as being based on an axis of insider/outsider, exclusion/inclusion. Neal and Agyeman urge a new narrative of the countryside which sees it as an arena of struggle in which individuals act upon and claim their legitimate presence in these social spaces as inhabiters and users. Thus we may discern transformations within as well as across the urban/rural divide, with ethnic minority individuals also appearing as indigenous to such areas as a product of intermarriage and long settlement (Williams 2007a).

Not only the dispersal but the diversity of ethnic groups is a rural reality. The absence of large co-ethnic concentrations or spatially located communities, such as those typically found in more urban areas, is a feature of rural areas. Magne's study (2003) notes individuals attracted to Devon for individual as opposed to communal reasons, giving rise to a very diverse range of ethnic identities in the population, and typically she could not identify co-ethnic clusters of more than ten people in any of the rural wards she studied. In a similar vein, the study by Williams and Hong Baker of north Wales's minorities (2009) found the majority of residents had neither co-ethnic friends nor, indeed, extended family living in the area. Consequently the notion of Black and ethnic minorities as discrete spatial communities is largely rejected in the rural studies, with rurality in itself being seen as inhibiting inter-ethnic networking or association. In as much as the term 'community' has relevance in relation to ethnic minorities in such areas, it is mobilized by service providers as a shorthand for a collective experience of marginalization from mainstream service delivery or, as Garland and Chakraborti (2006:159) have suggested, to denote what they call 'communities of shared risk'.

Mapping the experience

The traditional assumption that 'race' is a non-issue for the countryside has been almost wholly revoked by significant shifts in political and policy attention since 2000 and indeed associated media discourses (Neal 2002). Research studies and policy development on issues of 'race', racism and rurality now have an established place in the lexicon of public policy concerns. It is well over a decade since the Jay Report (1992) launched the issue of rural racism onto the public agenda. Jay's study was pioneering in as much as it established the dictum that problems of racism in areas where ethnic minority populations are small are no less significant than in areas of minority concentration. In addition, it validated the need for research and systematic documentation of this phenomenon and a considerable number of such studies and reports have followed (*inter alia* Derbyshire (1994), Nizhar (1995), Kenny (1997), Dhahlech (1999), Henderson and Kaur (1999), de Lima (2001). More recent examples are Garland and Chakraborti's (2002) study of Suffolk, Magne's study of Devon (2003), Robinson and Garner's study of Powys (2006) and Williams's study in north Wales (2007a).

The messages from the pre-2000 reports were unequivocal and largely summarized by de Lima in her well-named article 'John O'Groats to Land's End: racial equality in rural Britain?' (de Lima 2004). Minorities in rural areas were reportedly isolated, largely invisible to public services, lacking access to appropriate service provision and frequently subject to a plethora of racisms which ranged from the overt to the banal. The cultural and social support networks available to their urban counterparts are notably missing in rural areas, making them vulnerable and adding further layers of disadvantage. Typically minority ethnic citizens and families in rural areas still encounter lack of sensitivity to their needs from service providers, lack basic information on services (including interpreting and translation facilities) and face additional costs in mobilizing appropriate services for themselves (Williams *et al.* 2005).

What de Lima (2004) identifies in her review of the literature are a number of perennial themes that can characteristically be called rural racism, both direct and institutional, most of which have proved resilient to the policy and legislative changes that have ensued since 2000. The evidence she assessed on the startling extent of racism, overt and banal, captured by the participants in these studies, was confirmed by Jay Raynor's analysis of police statistics which graphically indicated that ethnic minorities living in more rural locations were twelve times more likely to be attacked on racial grounds, with a number of 'hot spots' for racial incidents that included areas such as Devon and Cornwall, Somerset, Norfolk, Cumbria and north Yorkshire (Raynor 2005). The picture of neglect, inaction and poor victim support identified in these early studies continues and appears resistant to any change (Garland and Chakroborti 2007).

Perhaps an inadvertent result of the emphasis on racist victimization in the early rural studies was the rather passive and static picture presented of ethnic minorities living within them, too often based on the presumption that they were incomers to an area. There is, however, little doubt that the composition of rural spaces is increasingly challenged by the facts of hybridity and intermixing, long settlement and new forms of identifications by ethnic minority individuals and groups. It has perhaps been little acknowledged that people from minority ethnic backgrounds hold long residence or have been entirely born and brought up in rural areas. The 'discrepant other' (Cloke 2004) of the literature may be not so much of an 'incomer' as an 'insider' in many rural communities, but little attention is given to how these identities are negotiated and become significant to the transformation of how a community is imagined. This calls for an understanding of the way these individuals shape and are reshaping these spaces and for an account of their lived experiences of negotiating rural realities (Williams 2007a).

If these early studies had a tendency to homogenize the experience of ethnic minorities in rural areas, later evidence suggests considerable diversity of experience in the lives of such rural dwellers. For example, the experience of children has slowly become more apparent as in studies by Scourfield *et al.* in Wales (2002), Holder and Lanao (2002) and Bhopal (2006). These studies have highlighted the extent of racist bullying experienced by children both in and outside school. Studies by Magne (2003) in Devon, Robinson and Gardner (2004) in mid-Wales and Williams and Hong Baker (2009) in north Wales have began to open up the more differentiated picture, illustrating differences of class, hybrid ethnicities, faith, sex, age and other social status, length of settlement and heritage that cut across co-ethnic status. There is, for example, some evidence to suggest a differential experience for professional and managerial classes in these areas that departs from the more stereotypical 'black disadvantage' model (Williams *et al.* 2005: 11; Craig and Lachman 2008). By contrast the Commission for Racial Equality (2006) noted gypsies and traveller groups as being among the most socially excluded and vulnerable people in Britain. Other writers have contrasted the experiences of what Sarah Neal has called 'other White' groups such as gypsies and Eastern European migrants with those of 'visible' Black and minority ethnic groups (Garland and Chakroborti 2006).

What is evident therefore is that minorities in these areas defy easy categorization. Service providers can more usually expect encounters with what Vertovec has called 'super diversity' (2007, see also Fanshawe and Sriskandarajah 2010), which runs counter to the traditional service orientation of providing for distinctive and identifiable 'ethnic minority communities'. In these areas it is more accurate to refer to individual families, households or small groupings of multi-ethnic backgrounds rather than co-ethnic communities. If, as the studies indicate, it is impossible to conceive of ethnic minorities in rural areas in any collective sense then Garland and Chakroborti's notion of 'communities of shared risk' (2006: 159) may provide a more fruitful focus for service intervention. Such approaches cut across geographical boundaries, as did the Welsh Assembly's anti-poverty strategy Communities First which networked ethnic minorities across Wales as a 'community of interest'.

The knowledge, resources and initiative of ethnic minorities in rural areas have barely been accessed and are yet to be significantly engaged. More recently, rural projects are mobilizing the narratives, contributions and heritage of minority rural dwellers as a strategy of inclusion (see Carnegie RARP 2009). In a study in north Wales the responses of over 90 individuals and three focus groups produced a rich account of minority views of living and working in the area (Williams and Hong Baker 2009). By far the greater number of participants in this study had been resident in the area for over five years and a third for over 20 years. Similarly, Magne's Devon study found a rela-tively settled minority community (2003). In the Welsh study respondents valued many of the traditional features of rural living, including the beauty, peace and quiet, environmental benefits, pleasant homes and good schools. There were reportedly significant numbers among ethnic minorities who spoke some level of Welsh. People reported contributing to a variety of activ-ities in their community motivated by a sense of 'duty' and 'putting back into society'. Key barriers to participation in civic activities include lack of time and carer responsibilities but also language and culture barriers and concern about discrimination and racism. In confirmation of the literature on rural racism it is clear that the noted constellation of factors of isolation, conspicu-ousness, fear of racism and discrimination overlay an individual's ability to participate meaningfully at local level. As in other studies (Magne 2003), people in this study did not expect or necessarily seek co-ethnic association at local level beyond family and religious association, but sustained positive 'ethnic' association nationally and internationally through actual or virtual networks.

The findings of the Williams and Hong Baker study (2009) suggest a pic-ture of individuals with a high investment in their locality and good levels of integration against a broad range of non-political indicators, including neigh-bourliness and associational life. Volunteering and contributing locally were viewed positively but for some were constrained by fears of discrimination, racism and outsiderism. The study demonstrated, however, a low sense of attachment or direct engagement in political affairs at the level of the local state and an apparent weak ability to influence and shape decisions. Representation on local public service bodies was found to be low.

For individuals from minority backgrounds, living in the countryside has its costs and its benefits. The evidence suggests their presence is well estab-lished, that they are not necessarily incomers to an area and that they will have moved to where they are for a variety of factors – social, environmental and work-related. On the downside, they continue to face everyday racisms, including the racist bullying of children, subtle exclusions that communicate unbelonging and feelings of isolation. Alongside this a high degree of resili-ence and resourcefulness is apparent in meeting their own needs, in the face of neglectful and often inept public service delivery. Messages from rurality/ ethnicity research have collectively highlighted many of the key issues facing ethnic minorities in such areas, with tentative assertions of what these issues suggest for the policy and practice of service providers. Few studies, however, get to grips with the mechanics of democratic service delivery based on *representation, participation and consultation*. To what extent are ethnic minorities involved in local decision making as councillors, staff mem-bers in local authorities, sitting on panels, boards and committees? To what extent are they engaged in the design and delivery of services? And how effectively undertaken is the duty to consult with constituent members of the community that includes ethnic minorities? In the absence of true engagement, ethnic minorities continue to be denied social justice in rural communities.

Can't see the wood for the trees: the inadequacy of policy and service responses

In the wake of the Race Relations Amendment Act 2000, and especially in Wales, Scotland and Northern Ireland in the post-devolution era, rural race equality policy has been given a legitimized basis for action and a number of policy levers were made available to rework the landscape of rural race issues. There can be no patch of the UK where public bodies are not now at least aware of their statutory duty to be responsive to race relations and to promote racial equality. Indeed, the Equality Commission for Northern Ireland devotes a significant part of its website and activity to supporting organizations such as NICEM (the Northern Ireland Council for Ethnic Minorities) and local anti-racist groups, as much as community-specific groups supporting Turkish, Polish and other minorities (http://www.equalityni.org/), and the Scottish and Welsh governments have dedicated significant resources and policy initiatives to supporting equality in welfare and access to health care (see Chapter 3). In addition, considerable challenges for public services were identified by the LGA 2007 report as a result of the increased range of ethnic diversity in local communities. Looking at information collected from over 100 councils and other public bodies, the report identified:

- The impact of 'churn' in schools – with pressures including translation services, coping with cultural differences, mid-term arrivals and the numeracy and literacy of young children.
- Child protection – the difficulties of safeguarding children given cross-cultural assessments and the issue of care of unaccompanied children.
- Language barriers – including the need for basic information for migrants.
- Housing – in areas experiencing rapid growth migrants are living in overcrowded and unsuitable properties.
- Community cohesion – seen as a high priority by the respondents in the survey given potential tensions between migrants and host communities.
- Community safety – with many migrants being the victims of crime rather than perpetrators.
- Health – specifically the inappropriate use of A&E services instead

of GPs by migrants and the mental health needs of asylum seekers and refugees who have experienced trauma.

(LGA 2007: 5–6)

De Lima (2004) has argued that the overriding shortcoming of local service providers is the result of a reliance on a numbers-led rather than a needs-led approach to service delivery, and reactive policy making. The inadequacy of policy and service responses has been a recurring theme in rural studies and continues to be so even after the implementation of the Race Relations Amendment Act and despite concerns raised by more recent migrations. Short-termism, reliance on separate special projects rather than mainstreaming, lack of forward planning and failure to consider financial projections to manage rapid change continue to bedevil rural authorities. The likely reasons for the inadequacy of responses are multiple, ranging from lethargy and neglect, lack of political will, ignorance or incompetence at one end of the spectrum to lack of resources, lack of policy learning or lack of sustainability of good practices at the other. Pugh's starting point is that members of Black and ethnic minority groups face many of the same sorts of problems as other individuals living in rural areas, including factors such as transport difficulties, higher living costs, patchy or non-existent services and the stereotypical perceptions of policy makers of rurality (2004: 177). Overlaid on these generic factors are the problems arising from racism and discrimination, including the prejudicial attitudes of service providers. He argues that a pervasive 'urbanist assumption' has characterized the service responses (2004: 182), with agencies both statutory and voluntary slow to make the adjustments and compensations necessary to fit rural circumstances. Pugh argues for effective training strategies on equality issues, accurate data collection, consultation with a range of minority ethnic groups and collaborative cross-agency working. Other authors have suggested that, in the absence of a 'critical mass' of minority users, rural agencies should collaborate and share facilities such as language support (Johnson *et al.* 1989). What is clear is that lack of policy learning in relation to the settled minority population left many authorities on the back foot when faced with the challenges posed by new migrations to the countryside.

Mountains to climb – policy responses

The challenges to rural service providers in this respect should not be underestimated. De Lima (2004) has called for accurate data collection and monitoring and creative solutions to meeting need, with an emphasis on the contributions and potentials that ethnic minority groups and households make to rural communities. The issue of data collection alone, however, is a challenging one. Detailed data at ward level on ethnicity is difficult to capture and its uses are made problematic through the limits of statistical comparability and issues of confidentiality. Take, for example, published data on the levels of child maltreatment, take-up of free school meals, domestic violence, poverty or even racist crime in a small population where two or three ethnic minority families are highly conspicuous. In addition service providers are challenged by the mechanics of reaching out to minority families without stigmatizing and labelling them or indeed overburdening them with frequent consultations. Further, in their efforts to find creative solutions through cross-service collaborations, they are too often confounded by bureaucratic boundaries, funding cycles and the failings of inter-professional working. These are very real constraints in practice. Neal and Agyeman (2006) provide a more specified framework for policy makers, planners, service providers and countryside agencies, calling on them to work from the four 'R' premise: *Recognition, Relevance, Resources, Review* (2006: 246). This is an approach that recognizes the heterogeneity of rural communities, that designs policies relevant to their diverse needs that are adequately resourced, and that keeps under constant review the effectiveness of policy interventions.

Whilst there is an emerging grey literature on Good Practice Guidance for effective engagement with ethnic minorities and other so-called 'hard to reach groups', there are few worked examples of how these techniques might be deployed in rural areas (Brackertz 2007). An action research project conducted in north Wales aimed to explore the nature of the engagement between ethnic minority groups and public service bodies and to seek to enhance consultation strategies between public bodies, which were reportedly poor (Williams and Hong Baker 2009). The public bodies targeted in this research reported a number of the familiar barriers to engagement with ethnic minorities in rural areas (Scottish Executive 2002; Magne 2003; Caust *et al.* 2006). Engaging effectively with ethnic minorities was seen as daunting, challenging and frustrating given the small and scattered nature of the population in the area, and participants needed considerable support to develop strategies. A widespread feeling of frustration was voiced by one of the respondents in the study regarding the statutory duty to consult, which she suggested is simply 'parachuted down from on high without additional funding or support' to facilitate the process (Williams and Hong Baker 2009: 19). Ignorance about how to access participants and lack of know-how were evidenced in the study. Participants had failed to learn from available resources, or from tacit knowledge within the organization or available in the area, and therefore continued to replicate weak practices. The triple jeopardy of overcoming the barriers of time, budget and capacity was frequently expressed. While the study found participants well motivated towards engagement and willing to learn, they lacked experiential know-how and were overwhelmed by a number of political and institutional barriers. Consultation with the minority ethnic community was, in places, seen as the sole responsibility of one person or department rather than as a strategic issue or one that was embedded across the organization as a whole. Concerns were also raised about being seen as singling out particular groups, and some felt that they needed to justify, to both internal and external challenges, expending time and funds on consulting with what is still statistically a very small percentage of the population. All too frequently, the sole representative of the minority voice in such situations is a token 'non-executive' with an interest in diversity or equality matters, appointed by a central civil service or similar appointing body, rather than an authentic representative of a local minority voice. A number of the respondents talked about the reluctance of institutions to change, of resistance to letting go of models of consultation which don't work and of 'some people who have remained in post for years . . . who don't want to move away from . . . the same thinking, same way of working and with the same people' (2009: 19).

The findings of this study are instructive. Issues of lack of leadership from the top in terms of commitment to initiatives, the allocation of appropriate resources and capitalizing on gains made by front-line workers were identified. The study found organizations not being creative or utilizing sufficiently innovative techniques to meet the evident challenges and the insufficient use of mixed methodologies. Organizational cycles that produce their own constraints to the development of cross-authority partnerships and the sharing of good practices, with organizations frequently reinventing the wheel, were noted in the study alongside staff turnover that resulted in a loss of expertise, capital and established networks conducive to sustained and good practice. Overall the institutional memory was identified as poor, with pockets of good practice falling into attrition. Third sector organizations in the area, vital to supporting effective consultation and engagement, lacked the funding and resources to respond and, while a high value was placed on their expertise, public sector organizations were little prepared to provide sustained funding. This is, of course, a familiar refrain for Black and minority ethnic third sector groups, especially where their members form a politically insignificant quorum.

There can be no quick fix in solving these issues of engagement with ethnic minorities in such areas. It requires building of trust, the commitment of time and resources and sustained capacity building. Models of service delivery borrowed and adopted from areas of minority concentration will inevitably have limited application in rural areas and creative solutions have to be devised, trialled, evaluated and then mainstreamed. The challenges of engaging with less powerful 'weaker' partners in the new arenas of governance have been discussed elsewhere in this text (see Chapter 4) but third sector organizations are central to policy development and good practice with rural ethnic populations. The absence of a critical mass of people from minority ethnic backgrounds will remain a challenge to rural policy making while parochial approaches are taken to policy development. Where ethnic

associational ties are weak these populations will remain a relatively depoliti-
cized constituency, subject to tokenistic co-option or consigned to official
marginality. The lack of experiential prompts (sometimes referred to as 'the
elephant in the room') means that issues of 'race' and ethnicity inevitably
carry low salience in such areas and are subject to minimalist technocratic
responses stripped bare of moral and affective content. It is difficult to progress
social justice ambitions for inclusive rural citizenship under these conditions
and progress too often relies on a small number of committed individuals.
What is needed is a strategic, committed and corporate approach to tackling
race equality and social inclusion in rural areas.

Between the mountains and the sea: gaps in the agenda

All too often rural 'race' projects are short-lived, poorly funded and lack sustainability. Craig and Manthorpe (2000) suggest that the nature of much rural
research has been self-limiting, with findings often confined to the publication
of a local research report and lessons lost through not being disseminated
beyond the immediate context. There has been a lack of strategic funding
streams to support work of this kind. Over the years several major government
policy initiatives such as the Community Cohesion strategy, Social Inclusion
policy and even rural policy itself have been neglectful of issues of racial
and ethnic diversity in rural areas (de Lima 2004). In 2007 the Commission
for Racial Equality was replaced by the new Equality and Human Rights
Commission (EHRC) but to date the EHRC has no specifically rural-related
agenda. In 2009 the Carnegie UK Trust, a major funder of rural research, commissioned a rural action research project (Carnegie RARP 2009). This multi-
stranded programme provided support for a range of community-initiated
projects across the UK, in Wales, Scotland, Northern Ireland and England. It
included a project undertaken by Citizens Advice to enhance information and
advice giving to minority groups; a digital diary project aimed at capturing the
narratives of Gypsy/Traveller families; a theatre project working with young
people's attitudes to newcomers; a project aimed at fostering understanding
and good community cohesion between religious minorities and a project
aimed at enhancing public sector services' engagement with rural ethnic
minorities. Participants in the project concluded: 'It's like throwing a small
stone in a big pond: it has a ripple effect', attesting to the potential to influence
change (Carnegie RARP 2009: 5).
    A number of overarching messages emerged from these projects that
indicate directions for policy development.

- Leadership: the need for greater and explicit public sector leadership in addressing race equality and discrimination, including

the development of infrastructure, skills and the commitment of resources.

- Rights to services and resourcing: the need for appropriate and adequate resourcing to ensure 'equivalence' in access to rights.
- Building infrastructure and capacity: the need for partnerships between the range of providers, statutory and voluntary sector and the engagement of a wide range of policy actors.
- Inclusiveness: recognition of the fact that integration is a two-way process and the need to support and develop fora that allow for exchange and dialogue.

(Carnegie RARP 2009)

There is still a long way to go for the rural race agenda. There has not been enough detailed work on the take-up or non take-up of services or on the ways in which ethnic minorities in rural areas mobilize services beyond their localities in meeting their needs, for example services such as breast or prostate screening. What do we know, for example, about the care of older people from minority ethnic backgrounds in rural areas? What are their pathways of care and how do they manage them? How do people from minority backgrounds achieve appropriate hospice care or funeral arrangements in areas of sparse service provision? What is the level of child poverty or what are the specific mental health needs? The literature on rural race issues to date has had the effect of reducing experiences to the issue of rural racisms and it is timely now to pursue more fine-tuned monitoring of the health and social care needs of these households.

Conclusion: towards rural citizenship

While the population of ethnic minority communities in rural and remote areas is relatively small compared to their presence in the UK population as a whole, there is no local authority area without a minority presence, including those considered the most remote. These communities have been subject to considerable transformation in recent years with both the settled minority ethnic population of rural areas growing and the substantial movement of migrant worker populations and other minority peoples to rural areas. Diversity is now the norm. Recognition of this presence has operated to challenge the assumptions of much multiculturalist policy making, that is, its focus on areas of ethnic minority concentration. The debate on race relations is gradually shifting to accommodate a view from the countryside from small communities, and the town as well as the metropolitan city.

It is nevertheless the case that minority ethnic individuals and groups within rural areas have struggled to be visible in terms of public policy and service delivery. Their citizenship rights have been severely compromised. Their lack of concentration and the fragmented and diverse nature of this population means they lack political clout, effective representation and a collective voice, such that they continue to be overlooked and marginalized. It is well established that the impact of racism and discrimination in these communities is no less substantive than in areas where they are more populous; indeed, these issues form a complex interplay with service delivery that continues to ensure the denial of access to key services for many. The low numbers of minorities living in rural areas typically means that networks, minority organizations and other forms of social support that may be available in areas of more dense populations have not developed in the locality. Accordingly many of the assumptions of partnership working, community engagement and community consultation at the heart of contemporary policy have to be rethought.

The concern to build strong and responsive communities that have a voice in the design and delivery of public services is a core policy mandate. This extends to building the capacity of the most marginal voices in order that they can be heard in the policy process. Local authorities and other public bodies are increasingly acknowledging the issues involved in effective engagement with minority individuals and households in their area but will insist on using the rhetoric of the 'hard to reach', rather than, as some grassroots bodies suggest, describing them as 'easy to ignore' (Afiya Trust in Johnson and NBCCWN 2008). At the same time public sector organizations in rural areas often lack the infrastructure, skills, commitment, leadership and resources required to respond appropriately to diverse communities. Goodwill and commitment on the part of front-line workers falls into dismayed helplessness in the face of inadequate support from the top. Organizational constraints such as lack of appropriate funding, time and resources deployed to consultation activities and failure to give scope for innovation and creativity at the front line hamper progress. The effect of competing priorities (or a fear of challenging existing established expectations and power bases) easily shifts attention away from the equalities agenda and accordingly inhibits the accumulation of expertise and sustainable practices. This lack of leadership and support needs to be addressed. What is clearly needed is leadership and support to build capacity and to promote sensitive experimentation and innovation.

Third sector partners are crucial to the building of capacity both among public service staff and among minority ethnic individuals, groups and households in the community to promote meaningful and effective engagement. The voluntary sector is not only filling gaps in service provision but actively involved in this work of building capacity in communities and skill development in agencies. Investment in this sector by local authorities, devolved government and other public sector agencies is vital if governments are to achieve their ambition of building inclusive rural communities beyond tokenism.

Clearly greater steps need to be taken to capture the involvement of minority ethnic individuals in the local state, including their representation in decision-making roles and on decision-making bodies. Minority ethnic and migrant households are making a vital contribution (economic, social and civic) to rural communities. Their contribution needs to be recognized, valued and appropriately engaged in the policy process.

PART 3
Responding to Diversity: Future Agendas

8 Black and minority ethnic workers in health and welfare services

Introduction

The issue of fair treatment in the workplace, and in particular interventions affecting recruitment into the ranks of welfare professionals, promotion within them and general well-being at work, are all important to our understanding of welfare society. This chapter therefore considers the significance of the contribution made by the labour of Black and minority ethnic workers in health and care, whether by muscle or mind. It is concerned with issues of equal opportunities, workers' rights, freedom from harassment and discrimination as well as well-being at work, but also highlights the intellectual and symbolic importance of having a diverse workforce.

The representation of Black and minority ethnic individuals within the welfare sector workforce has at various times in history received sponsorship for a number of reasons: to address labour shortages, for symbolic and tokenistic imaging, or for its transformatory potential. One line of argument suggests that greater representation of Black and minority ethnic individuals in the health and welfare workforce could create services more responsive to the needs of ethnic minority communities. The core of this idea emerged in local government during the 1980s under a variant of what Paul Gilroy (1987: 136) has called 'municipal anti-racism'. This particular brand of anti-racism engaged local authorities as an instrument of change in terms of actively campaigning against racism, targeting funding and initiatives towards marginalized groups and recruiting from the ranks of under-represented groups. The Race Relations legislation of the late 1990s gave momentum to these strategies in the ambition to tackle institutional racism, and in an early response the then Home Secretary set targets for recruitment of Black and ethnic minority police into senior management. Bhavnani *et al.* (2005: 79) suggest this 'top-down' model of organizational change came gradually to replace employee-led initiatives on anti-racism. The direction of travel of these ideas, then, is clearly significant, as is the focus, whether on employment, service delivery or for ideological aspirations.

The 'ethnic penalty'

As in other aspects of life, whether regarding housing, education, health care or industry, there is long-standing and substantial evidence of disadvantage affecting the employment of Black and minority ethnic people in the health and social care professions. Across all the post-war research and campaigning literature related to migrants and minority ethnic people in Britain (i.e. since 1948), poverty, discrimination and exclusions from the labour market are central concerns. The 'ethnic penalty' is well researched (Heath 2001), and was described initially in relation to housing, where it appeared that Black and Asian people had to pay the equivalent of an 'ethnicity tax' to obtain council housing or to achieve accommodation of a comparable quality to that enjoyed by the white British working classes (Flett 1979). The same sorts of processes are apparent in relation to employment – both in terms of under-employment (for example obtaining a poorer return on investment in skills by the need to offer higher qualifications to obtain a post: Esmail *et al.* 1996) or in relation to income for work of a similar or higher level, being paid less and prevented from obtaining promotion (DCLG 2010: para. 1.19; Cabinet Office 2003: 38). In industry, this was sometimes described as being in effect a separate job market for Black (and Asian) workers (see for example Iganski and Payne 1996, 1999) or, at the very least, representing a substantial gradient between the career experiences of white and non-white employees, across industrial sectors. Black and minority ethnic (and migrant) workers universally, it seems, tend to occupy lower status employment roles, not commensurate with their educational qualifications, and frequently experience downward social mobility (see, for example, Johnson 1988). This is not, of course, purely a UK phenomenon – it has been noted in the United States (see, for example, Lieberson 1980) and elsewhere in Europe as well (Wrench 2007).

The existence of an 'ethnic penalty', and discrepancies in status and distribution of Black and minority ethnic workers in a sector, were not always accidental or related to the inferior expertise, qualifications or actions of the minority workers. Leiberson's analysis shows clearly that the latter explanation cannot hold water. Indeed, in many cases the employment of minority and migrant workers was an element in a strategy to transform the workforce or workplace, whether through the introduction of new roles and structures or as a means to overcome the preferences or practices of the majority 'indigenous' workforce (Duffield 1988). Indeed, even in the UK in 2009, it has been reported that, despite the current economic recession, many employers are still intending to recruit significant numbers of migrant staff in the near future, because of problems in recruiting 'British' labour (this now includes significant numbers of UK-born Black and Asian British people) to fill significant roles, including care service positions. An article in the *Guardian* (Osborne *et al.* 2009) stated that 'despite predictions that the recession would lead to an exodus of non-UK nationals, one in 12 employers in the UK plans to recruit migrant workers in the next few months'. It quoted Gerwyn Davies, public policy adviser, Chartered Institute of Personnel and Development, as saying: 'The idea that migrant workers comprise a marginal segment of the UK workforce that is dispensed with when times are tough is clearly wide of the mark. Most are recruited and retained by employers because they provide skills or attitudes to work in short supply among the home-grown workforce' (Osborne *et al.* 2009).

The same approach to the employment of migrant labour – what Marx once described as a 'reserve army' – whose true costs of reproduction and rights are not fully borne by the employer or the state, is true across Europe (Palese *et al.* 2004, 2006; Wrench 2007). Perhaps it comes as more of a shock when it is reflected in differentials in the personal health and well-being of migrants and migrant-descended people working in the health and welfare sector. However, the evidence tends to suggest that migrant and minority workers – especially when their citizenship status is unclear or can have doubt cast upon it – not only have lower wages and less prospect of secure careers but also poorer health and, even so, may be denied access to the 'social wage' of benefits and support including possibly even the services that they have been hired to deliver (see Chapter 6). That said, it is also hard to obtain unequivocal data on this matter, since (almost by definition), being marginal workers, additional savings are made by failing to monitor – or include in workforce monitoring – the position of such staff. Criticisms of this failing are legion, from the CRE (2007), the European Confederation of Trades Unions (Carr 1996) and the Cabinet Office (2003), yet the 'national minimum dataset' on the social care workforce (Hussein 2009) still reports that social care employers failed to provide ethnicity data on more than a quarter of employees, and there is still no formal coding to identify migrant workers.

Recruitment: getting there

The creation of the modern British welfare state would not have been possible without the contribution of huge numbers of migrant and minority ethnic staff, including Asian doctors, Caribbean and Mauritian nurses, social workers, housing professionals and teachers. Members of the Caribbean and Asian diasporas in particular have contributed in many and various ways to the development of the British welfare state and its ability to deliver health and caring services to all in Britain (Kyriakides and Virdee 2003). This contribution has primarily been seen as their disproportionate representation in the 'foot-soldiery' of the hospital labour force, as documented by Lee-Cunin (1989), for example. Attention, however, should also be given to their role in leadership and intellectual capital, such as that demonstrated by Dr Chuni Lal Katial (1898–1978), Britain's first Asian mayor and the founder of the pioneering Finsbury Medical Centre in 1938 (Esmail 2007), or Lord David Pitt GP and parliamentarian, as well as many other unsung heroes (this word is, in the original Greek, genderless). The Caribbean was also, in the mid-nineteenth century, the birthplace of a relatively unsung heroine of British medical history, Mary Grant Seacole, who described herself as a 'doctress' and was credited with saving many lives in the Crimean War (Dabydeen *et al.* 2007). Perhaps the earliest 'nurse-practitioner', she laid the trail for many subsequent migrants who formed the backbone of the British National Health Service during its formative years after 1948.

Strangely, the fact is that one of the major differences in the health status between the Black and minority ethnic and white majority populations is the gap between white and Black older women (Nazroo 1997: 59). The particular irony of this finding lies in the fact that a very significant proportion of the older generation of Caribbean-born women in Britain came here specifically to work in the National Health Service and one might have expected this group above all others to have known how to maintain their health and to use the NHS effectively. These latter-day 'daughters of Seacole' (Lee-Cunin 1989) were, in many cases, recruited directly through offices set up in the aftermath of the Second World War to relieve the population shortages foreseen by the Royal Commission and Beveridge, the architect of the NHS and the welfare state. No precise figures are available to say how many nurses were recruited from the Caribbean, but it is well established that in addition to the large numbers of male workers recruited to British industry from the states of the former empire (and Commonwealth), a significant female labour migration took place from the West Indies to Britain. In 1971, overseas nurses formed 9 per cent of the total hospital workforce, and half of these came from the Caribbean (Thomas and Morton-Williams 1972). This reliance on internationally recruited nurses did not decline in subsequent decades, even if the focus of origin was to change over time.

The concerns of 1980s race politics inevitably resulted in an increased recruitment of Black and minority ethnic people into the professions, and especially in occupations such as social work, teaching, nursing, housing and the police, but also in more high-profile locations. The most recent government *Statement on Race* (DCLG 2010), as we bring this text to press, notes with approval that since the Prime Minister's challenge in 1997:

... we have and have had ethnic minorities as Chief Constables, Permanent Secretaries, High Court judges, an Admiral and currently we have five ethnic minority MPs who are Government Ministers.

(Malik, foreword to DCLG 2010: 4)

While some of this recruitment could be attributed to demographic and labour market changes, there is little doubt that much of the impetus came from political and moral concerns that service providers in areas of ethnic minority concentration should somehow be more representative of their local constituents. Positive action strategies, although variably adopted, ensured sponsorship of students into nursing and social work education (de Souza 1991). Gail Lewis (2000a) tracks the particular story of the recruitment of Black women into social services departments of the 1980s, as a 'new cadre of social workers' (2000: 8) recruited specifically as a response to the identified shortfall in meeting the needs of racialized populations of colour. She is scathingly critical of what she calls 'the black staff model' (2000a: 129), which she argues pivots on the assumption of essentialized cultural knowledges which social services departments need to access, and these are seen as residing in the racialized bodies of particular types of people.

> Thus black staff were thought to ensure equality of service provision, free from racist and cultural misunderstandings, because they would be like, indeed replicate, their clients regardless of divisions of class, gender, age, locality or indeed even the professional/client relation. No learning process would be required because in the social worker/ client encounter like will meet like.
>
> (Lewis 2000a: 129)

This misconception of the position of Black and minority ethnic staff within public service organizations epitomizes the often untenable position of such staff within largely white organizations. The anomaly is that far from commanding a positive value for their work, these workers are often placed in marginal positions within organizations, find themselves overburdened, subject to conflicting and additional demands by comparison with their white counterparts and experience high levels of workplace discriminations (Goldstein 2002).

Stubbs (1985) very quickly identified the ambivalent nature of this positioning in his examination of the organizational and structural location of this cohort of Black staff in social services departments. At one and the same time they were to challenge the prevailing practices and ideologies of white professionalism yet not rock the boat sufficiently to produce organizational change. Accordingly, he argues, they were manipulated by managers within departmental notions towards the categories 'good Black social worker' and 'bad

Black social worker' (1985: 17). This analysis at the level of organizational behaviour illustrates something of the external stressors placed on Black and minority ethnic workers. Lewis (2000a) provides a further dimension, arguing for attention to the ways in which individuals internalize these ambivalences and ambiguities to the extent that they affect their subjectivities and identities (2000: 130). Additional to these pressures, of course, are those that arise from being expected to represent the minority ethnic community and its needs, and simultaneously be the means whereby those expectations are met as being, naturally, the 'culturally and linguistically competent' resource to provide them with services within the workplace. And, at the same time, the members of that community will also see the 'familiar face' and person who perhaps also speaks their language as being their advocate and insider guide. These together can place impossible demands on minority workers – and may also stereotype them as a minority service provider, rather than as a generically competent member of staff with normal career progression expectations (Johns 2004).

Abuse and exploitation

Nurses accepted from overseas for training in the early days of the Welfare State were very rapidly put into working roles, and frequently they found themselves in psychiatric or other less popular specialist roles, rather than the general nursing and training posts they had anticipated. Few had any help in settling in, and none experienced a formal orientation programme, although a requirement for this was introduced by the Nursing and Midwifery Council, eventually, in 2006 (NMC 2007). Indeed, for many of those earlier recruits, their place in Britain was conditional on their work permit and it is clear that many were forced into lower grade posts than might have been expected on the basis of their previous qualifications. Others were (mis)guided into the less prestigious, lower paid, State Enrolled Nurse grades with little or no prospect of career advancement. Even in other hospital employment, overseas recruits and Black and minority ethnic staff were channelled into the least attractive and most insecure elements of catering, domestic and portering work, and hardly ever accepted into the higher status and better paid ambulance work, whether as drivers or clinical staff (CRE 1983). Indeed, Black and minority ethnic staff are still under-represented in the ambulance services (see for example Lyfar-Cisse 2008). Those who tried to upgrade their status faced a series of barriers and few were successful. In addition, many faced racial abuse from their patients and even from their colleagues (Lee-Cunin 1989; see also Bowler 1993) as well as being largely confined to night shifts, particularly in mental handicap, psychiatric and geriatric care wards, which are recognized as 'dead-ends' for subsequent promotion. Not surprisingly, one result has often been a determination that their children should not repeat their own experience, even at the expense of having to work longer and harder them-selves. As two of Lee-Cunin's respondents commented:

> George: I will stay in nursing, to keep my children away from it. I want them to be a doctor or lawyer. I have made my bed, so I have to lie in it.
>
> (Lee-Cunin 1989: 9)

and

> Elaine: I wouldn't get a job now (following the 1988 regrading exer-cise). No-one would take me. I have to stay in nursing. Soon they will have no young black nurses in my hospital. They are not taking them, and anyway my kids are not going to get into that profession.
>
> (Lee-Cunin 1989: 11)

More recent figures show that there have been significant changes in the health services, and there are indeed a few high-profile or highly graded staff of minority ethnic origin. Monitoring of entrants to nursing, while showing that 6 per cent come from a 'minority' background, also shows that they are much more likely to describe themselves as being of Black African origin, and less often of Black British or Caribbean descent (Gerrish *et al.* 1996). How-ever, at least 100 NHS employers (health authorities, colleges or NHS Trust hospitals, ambulance services and community health trusts) in 1997 were shown to be employing no Black staff of Caribbean origin. Places such as Brent, Ealing and Lambeth, which have significant Black populations, had proportions of Black employees which were noticeably below the levels that might have reasonably been expected (Navidi 1997). Only a very few (such as Croydon Mayday NHS Trust) employed more Black staff than might have been predicted on the basis of their catchment areas. There has been a dramatic fall in recruitment from UK minority ethnic groups, so that while in 1995 8.7 per cent of nursing grade staff aged 55–64 were Black (African–Caribbean origin), less than one in a hundred staff aged under 25 were so in those organizations for which the data were available. This cannot be attrib-uted to the lack of educational qualifications or labour market engagement of this group: a high proportion are either in further educational study or unemployed and seeking work (Owen 1994). The 1991 and 2001 censuses show a distinct move into clerical and secretarial work, and self-employment. Anecdotal and incidental evidence from other sources suggests that some at least of the latter arises from the development of nursing homes, following a 'West Indian' tendency to develop 'skill-based' entrepreneurial activity (see Johnson 1988), although we have been unable to locate sound research on this phenomenon.

Among the women in the 1996 Policy Studies Institute (PSI) survey, those of Caribbean origin were twice as likely (around six per cent), compared to whites, to be nurses, and in general this was the most highly qualified of all migrant groups. Of older women, more than one in eight of all Caribbean female migrants were (or had been) nurses, but below the age of 44, the figure fell to less than one in twenty. The same survey also noted that 25 of the 32 Caribbean female employees in the hospital sector (out of 175 working Caribbean women in the survey) denied that there were 'equal opportunities' where they worked. These two facts, as was also suggested by the Beishon *et al.* study of the nursing profession (1995), may be linked. Indeed, even in 2003, a study of nurses found that 40 per cent of ethnic minority nurses reported experiencing racial harassment from their colleagues and, perhaps more surprisingly, 64 per cent said that they had been racially abused by patients (Shields and Price 2003).

While we have some research evidence and monitoring data relating to NHS professionals and health care staff, there is a serious evidence gap in relation to care workers, especially those working for local authorities or in the private sector. Social work professionals have been heard to complain about racial discrimination and harassment at conferences and on internet blogs (e.g. communitycare.co.uk/blogs), but there seems to be almost no published research to substantiate or measure this (though see Channer and Doel 2009). It has, however, been reported that at least 16 per cent of the care sector workforce was born overseas (some estimates place this higher: in 2006 this was at least 105,000 people, and in London they represented 68 per cent of care workers: Rawles 2008, http://www.guardian.co.uk/society/2008/mar/26/long termcare.socialcare), and that their conditions of work were significantly worse than UK-born workers. Clearly, there are also aspects of racialized discrimination and harassment alongside the exploitation of European-born staff, particularly those from the recent accession states of the EU, with overseas-born staff being better qualified and employed in lower status roles. The recording of data is still poor, however, even in statutory datasets such as the NMDS-SC (Hussein 2009), and much reliance has to be placed on anecdotal, journalistic evidence or reports at conferences, such as those of professional associations and trades unions.

That said, it is also important to note that many trades unions have come late to the defence of minority ethnic and migrant workers (Carr 1996), having in the earlier period of migration and settlement been content to protect the jobs and conditions of white workers (until, perhaps, the events such as the Grunwick and Imperial Typewriter Works strikes, which highlighted the role of Asian and Black people in the union movement: Wrench 2004; Jefferys 2007). Conversion to fighting the corner of Black and minority ethnic and migrant workers may also have been a reflection of the change in membership of the professions and a need to keep membership of the unions and subscriptions up. Now, however, it is important to recognize that both trades unions and professional associations play a very important role in fighting racism and supporting migrant and minority ethnic staff (TUC 2009). Indeed, the RCN (which performs both roles) played a very significant part in the struggle, supporting a major research report into the experiences of 'internationally recruited nurses' (IRNs) (Allen and Larsen 2003), which highlighted also the racialized experiences of many of those who came to work in the UK around the turn of the twentieth century:

> (Many) reported having been manipulated and cheated, especially in the private sector, but all reported frequent experiences of racism and even white IRNs felt discriminated against because they were foreign . . .
>
> (Allan and Larsen 2003: 4)

Their report makes it very clear that there had been failings in the support given by the RCN and other union bodies, but that such professional bodies are essential elements in a strategy to improve matters. We should also note that while there has been a fair amount of criticism of the role of unions in the past, Virdee (2000) has challenged this view, and reminds us that unions also had to accommodate a variety of other agendas, and that they have at least now 'changed their spots' and have an important part to play in the future.

The future of a diverse workforce

The irony remains that many who came to care have now none to care for them, for various reasons. Further, those who have chosen to live alone rather than marry have ended up caring for each other in the absence of support from the Welfare State they helped to found. There is no doubt that migration can present challenges to health and health services, by bringing medical services in contact with people of different cultures and health needs, some of which may be inherited and genetically linked to the countries of origin. However, it also brings solutions to those problems, by supplying labour and indeed also forms of experience and expertise which are of value to the wider community, provided that the existence of controls on migration does not prevent family completion and thus the existence of future generations of carers. As has been shown in many studies, linguistic and cultural differences between nurses and patients have hindered efforts to improve the quality of care provided to these communities, both in primary and acute settings (Johnson 1999). Negative stereotyping and insensitive treatment of patients of South Asian background by nursing staff also remains a problem, examples of which abound in the fields of mental health (Bhui and Sashidaran 2003), maternity care (Baxter 1997), diabetes (Fleming and Gillibrand 2003), cardiac care (Nazroo 1997) and haemoglobinopathies (Anionwu and Atkin 2001). It has therefore been suggested, in many places, that the employment of more minority ethnic nurses would help the NHS to meet the health care needs of multicultural Britain more effectively (Johnson 1998). Similarly, it has been suggested that an NHS serving diverse users needs more diverse doctors (Bowler 2004). This understanding has been given added force more specifically by the Race Relations Amendment Act 2000, which stated that all NHS trusts and bodies must have a Race Equality Scheme detailing their plans to work with Black and minority ethnic communities in their areas (Johns 2004).

As far back as the early 1980s, however, there was a growing recognition that the shortage of nurses of South Asian background in the NHS was hindering the provision of culturally sensitive care (see CRE 1987; Culley and Dyson 2001: 231–49). We now understand how the nursing profession could gain valuable understanding and practical experience by drawing on the insight and experience of health care professionals from different communities (Darr and Bharj 1999). Further, a culturally diverse workforce would be better equipped to challenge racism in service delivery and confront racist constructions of people's health needs (Ahmad 2000). The same, of course, would be true in other professions delivering caring services.

However, despite this consensus of opinion, and legislation that obliges all public sector bodies to offer equality of access in recruitment to people of minority ethnic backgrounds, there has over recent years not only been a decline in the proportion of workers from African–Caribbean origins, but also little change in the proportion of South Asian nurses employed in the NHS workforce (Gerrish et al. 1996; Navidi 1997; Iganski et al. 2001). Recent data suggest that less than 2 per cent of nursing, midwifery and health visiting staff are of South Asian background; a figure that would need to double to match the proportion of people of South Asian origin in the general population (Darr et al. 2007). The under-representation of people of South Asian origin within the student nursing population has been especially apparent in areas with large South Asian communities. In 1997, for instance, less than 3 per cent of Bradford's nursing students were of South Asian background, while the South Asian population of the city totalled 15 per cent (Darr 2001).

Improving the number of students of South Asian background on nurse education courses is a major challenge facing NHS Trusts and the higher education institutions (HEIs) who train the now increasingly all-graduate entry professions and thus, in effect, determine the profile of clinical and care staff working in the NHS (Alexander 1999; Chevannes 2001). Much of the literature which seeks to explain the under-representation of students of South Asian background on nursing courses is based upon anecdotal evidence which is largely unsubstantiated (Gerrish et al. 1996; Culley and Dyson 2001). Among education managers within schools of nursing, for example, there is a widely held view that problems in relation to the recruitment of students of South Asian origin may have cultural causes (Darr *et al.* 2007). The 'hands on' and intimate nature of many nursing tasks is thought by some to be a major deterrent for many females and it has been assumed that within the South Asian population nursing is an inappropriate career choice for young people with five or more GCSEs (Karseras and Hopkins 1987). This stereotype, however, does not necessarily accord with the choices made today by young people and their families.

In contrast, other health care professions such as medicine, pharmacy and dentistry have continued to attract large numbers of applicants from students of South Asian background (Vellins 1982; Taylor 1993; Esmail 2001) Recent statistics show that British-born Indian, Pakistani and Bangladeshi people account for 19 per cent of places on medical and dentistry degrees in England (UCAS 2005) and it is predicted that the over-representation of these groups in medical and dental schools will continue (Goldacre *et al.* 2004). Recent success stories include medicine where in the NHS in 2007 25 per cent of doctors at consultant level and 47 per cent of registrars were from Black or minority ethnic backgrounds (Fanshawe and Sriskandarajah 2010). Nevertheless, given the high percentage of people from Black and minority ethnic backgrounds in the public services as a whole, it is more the case that they are strongly represented in the lower grades and not in middle or high levels of management.

An overemphasis upon cultural barriers fails to consider other reasons why individuals might be deterred from pursuing nurse education or other routes into caring professions. Lee-Cunin (1989) found that twice as many South Asian women suggested that 'racism' and discrimination were disincentives to a career in nursing and midwifery as those who suggested that their families would not approve such a career choice. Similarly, Darr (2001) identified a lack of work experience opportunities in local health care settings and limited provision of information about the profession in schools as significant barriers preventing pupils of South Asian background from pursuing their interest in nursing. More recently still, reports on the experiences of migrant care workers and, indeed, higher status professions such as doctors, have continued to show that they face unacceptable levels of discrimination, abuse and poor career mobility, even though the Improving Working Lives Standard (IWL) introduced in the NHS Plan makes it clear that every member of staff is entitled to work in an organization which can prove that it is investing in improving diversity, tackling discrimination and harassment and developing the skills of all its staff to improve patient services. This aspiration has been given high level support: in February 2004 at the NHS Leaders' Conference both the then Secretary of State John Reid and the NHS Chief Executive Sir Nigel Crisp emphasized that race equality is core business for the NHS and that senior staff must take the lead to ensure that their organization really delivers race equality for both patients and staff. However, research and anecdotal evidence continue to show that there is a gap between this aim and the reality experienced by Black and minority ethnic staff.

There is, we accept, very little solid evidence of discrimination and abuse that would meet the test of scientific enquiry: partly because of the institutional barriers to collecting and analysing data which could demonstrate this (Lemos and Crane 2000; Coker 2001). However, if professional and social networks of Black and minority staff continue to hear and transmit stories of individual experiences, and to believe that they represent groups subjected to such treatment, then this understanding will in turn transmit to the wider communities, and affect recruitment and attitudes. Indeed, there is also some evidence, collected by groups seeking to make a difference, which gives support to this assertion. A recent review by the BME Network of staff working for the 27 NHS bodies in the South East Coast Strategic Health Authority region (SECSHA BMEN) (Lyfar-Cisse 2008), which itself caused considerable controversy and adverse reaction by some managers, was able to demonstrate that differentials existed. It also showed that there was consistent and systematic under-recording of 'ethnicity' data that might have been able to advance understanding of the processes at work, only 93 per cent of staff having their ethnic origin coded in the personnel files. None of the NHS organizations surveyed at that time had completed the statutorily required Race Equality Impact Assessment, and thus all were in breach of the Healthcare Commission's Core Standard c7e.

In particular, the analysis of officially collected administrative data carried out by the SECSHA BMEN group showed that a disproportionately high number of Black and minority ethnic staff were involved in bullying and harassment, grievance and disciplinary procedures. In addition, there was a significant under-representation of Black and minority ethnic staff at higher executive levels – especially as executives and non-executive directors of trusts (less than 3 per cent of all trust board directors were of Black and minority ethnic origin), and while all trusts in the county had a disproportionately high amount of Black and minority ethnic staff in pay band 5 (just below middle management level) there were very few in posts graded above that, and there was a very much higher attrition rate in the recruitment process, with significantly lower success rates for Black and minority ethnic applicants. At West Kent PCT, Black and minority ethnic staff were involved in 43 per cent of bullying and harassment procedures, but only accounted for 7 per cent of the overall workforce. At Kent and Medway NHS & Social Care Partnership Trust, delivering mental health services, Black and minority ethnic people made up 58 per cent of job applicants, but out of the 49 per cent shortlisted only 7 per cent were appointed. Over the region, although Black and minority ethnic people comprised 15 per cent of the workforce, twice the national and regional representation in the population, they were involved in more than half the bullying and harassment cases in the region's mental health trusts (that is, were represented at a risk ratio of 1.72, compared to white staff), were involved in 25 per cent of disciplinary cases and nearly twice as likely to have submitted a claim to an industrial tribunal than white staff (Lyfar-Cisse 2008; see also Santry 2008). These weaknesses also appeared to spill over to the treatment – or at least, the administration of racial justice – for patients, in that nearly two thirds of the trusts were failing to comply with the Health-care Commission's requirement to collect ethnicity data on patients (Core Standard C18).

The 'action plan' which came out of the deliberations of that group iden-tified a series of actions to address these inequalities. These, unsurprisingly, included consistent recording and production of ethnicity monitoring data across all trusts, better consultation and engagement with both Black and minority ethnic communities and staff, targeted recruitment of Black and minority ethnic directors (especially non-executive directors), and regular audits of disciplinary, grievance and capability reviews as well as training for relevant staff in cultural competence and anti-discrimination practice (SECSHA BMEN 2008).

Well-being at work

Outside the statutory sector, there is evidence that care workers of migrant origin are equally or worse treated, and may have even worse health con-sequences (Darr *et al.* 2007; see also Cangiano *et al.* 2009). A report conducted by Oxfam in collaboration with a migrant worker support group (Oxfam 2009) describes widespread exploitation of migrant care workers, revealing that they are routinely forced to work excessive hours, often with no holiday or sick pay, and may also be required to be on call for no extra pay. It was apparent that employers and agencies were willing to exploit the vulnerability of such workers in order to keep costs down and compete with other social care pro-viders. In this, they drew parallels with the exploitation of agricultural workers (which is now regulated by the Gangmasters Licensing Authority (GLA), set up in 2006 in response to the Morecambe Bay tragedy two years earlier, when 23 Chinese cockle pickers drowned). The author of Oxfam's report, Krisnah Poinasamy, argued that there was little to distinguish gangmasters recruiting agricultural labourers from abroad from the employment agencies that supply migrant care workers to care homes, both demonstrating a tendency to under-payment of wages, debt bondage, excessive hours, spurious deductions, dan-gerous and unsafe working conditions. The report noted (as previously observed here) that care work in Britain is perceived as low status and badly paid, making it difficult to attract UK workers. There is high turnover and agencies are increasingly relied upon to supply staff to make up the shortfall. According to the report, about a fifth of the estimated 1.5 million workers in the care sector are migrants, and particularly those employed through agencies 'experience significant abuse and exploitation at work'. Evidence that this experience is not confined to the UK comes from a recent paper about migrant care workers in Denmark, who – while taking an average of five fewer days sick leave than their local counterparts – reported consistently poorer health than Danish-born care staff (Carneiro *et al.* 2009).

The Oxfam study presented a case study of Magda, a care worker from Poland, who told the report's authors that she was recruited in Poland by a representative of a well-known British care company. She was made to sign a binding contract for a year, which she was not able to break unless she repaid £1000 in travel and accommodation, which she was unable to do.

> I had to do a minimum of 60 hours a week for almost two years. I was doing the night shift five to six days per week, from 8pm to 8am, she said. She added that she was too afraid to complain about her excessive workload for fear that she might lose her job, and said she felt employers took advantage of migrants who were 'desperate'.
>
> (Oxfam 2009)

There are an estimated 1.5 million workers in the adult social care workforce in the UK. Labour Force Survey estimates suggest that one in five care workers is paid below the national minimum wage, with one in ten paid below £4.95: if the Oxfam report is to be believed, the situation is probably even more problematic for migrant and minority ethnic workers. Further, there are signs in present policy that this could be worsened by new developments such as the 'personalization of care'. This approach to service delivery is also encouraging the use of more self-employed care workers to deliver care in a client's own home, and may increase the vulnerability of care workers (see Chapters 5 and 6). Few people arranging their own care will have much knowledge or capacity to employ staff directly, and it is highly probable that most will seek out, or be targeted by, agencies who will offer low-cost services relying on the same sorts of 'imported' labour as the care homes already use.

The policy of 'personalization' aims to transform care users from passive recipients of care into agents with choice and control over the care they receive, through transfers of Direct Payments and individual budgets from local authorities to older people, to enable them to purchase the care they feel is most appropriate to their needs. However, it does not provide much support or guidance to users in how to do this. It is true that individuals who have a personal budget can continue to purchase traditional domiciliary care through an accredited care agency, but many may prefer to have one or two personal assistants who are self-employed, as this can provide continuity and flexibility of support, and avoid the perception that 'local authority' staff are impersonal and less reliable or flexible in their attendance. However, it raises risks that such workers will have even less opportunity for redress or enjoyment of fair employment rights, especially if (as is likely) they are migrant workers. Indeed, the Oxfam study suggests that the perception that there are links between government-funded employment rights enforcement agencies and the immigration authorities is likely to deter workers from reporting abuses, even when they have every legal right to work in the UK. The risk of deportation is one which most migrant workers are unwilling to take.

In the circumstances, it is perhaps not surprising that there is little data on ill-health in this sector, but it is unlikely that there are no adverse aspects to the occupational health status of migrant workers in the care sector, although the Oxfam and COMPAS reports were not able to collect data on this specific outcome. It would, however, be depressing if this were to be final word on the story of the contribution of migrant and minority ethnic workers to the provision and enjoyment of welfare in Britain.

Conclusion

Despite a very patchy and unbalanced evidence base, and near silence in the literature on the conditions of certain welfare sector workers, it is clear that health and social care in Britain is dependent on migrant and minority ethnic workers. Such workers will face double pressures – first from their employers and the service-providing agencies to be transformatory and to be bridges to, and resources for, minority service users (not least in language support). But they will also be seen by those communities as their spokespeople and role models, challenged to make a difference for their communities of origin. These bridge-builders (Abrahamsson *et al.* 2009) are not drawn only from the more traditional Black and minority ethnic and overseas-qualified worker backgrounds, but also include significant numbers of more recent European origin workers, who are also experiencing similar racialized discrimination – while recruitment continues almost unabated from southern and central-eastern Africa, west Africa, the Pacific rim, Philippines and Asia. It is also clear that inequalities persist and that Black and minority ethnic staff are still not fully represented at all levels of the professions, and that they are subject, even in places where they form very large proportions of the workforce, to 'unexplained differences' in their treatment in disciplinary cases (Esmail 2007). Indirect measures such as 'life satisfaction' (Van Stolk *et al.* 2009) continue to show that there are matters which need to be addressed, while reports repeatedly call for better monitoring and subsequent action (Boorman 2009).

Most of the solutions proposed are familiar: better record keeping and monitoring, reporting and review of targets, more support and mentoring for Black and minority ethnic professionals, and an end to denial of what is effectively institutional racism across all sectors of the welfare system. Central to this will be the role of networks and alliances, both 'ethnic' and professional. There have been some changes: Race for the Professional, an association set up by the CRE to provide mentoring and mutual support (CRE 2007: 21), has now been funded by the government's TRIF (Tackling Race Inequality Fund) initiative as the 'Network for Black Professionals' (www.nbp.org.uk) to provide some support for the taller minority poppies. There have also been, as we have seen, a few more high-profile Black and minority ethnic faces in leadership roles. But to bring about lasting change, there must be a positive element of leadership as well as continuing effort by Black and minority ethnic workers themselves (Carr 1996; Bhavnani *et al.* 2005). This will require reserves of resilience and continued struggle or resistance, as well as strategic alliances, as suggested by Allan and Larsen's report for the RCN (2003). It will not be enough to rely on the 'inevitability of gradualness' (a phrase attributed to Sidney Webb, the Fabian socialist, in 1923). There have been successive waves of small gains, but also times in the wilderness and reverses, such as the fleeting enthusiasm for positive action in the 1990s, which have only slightly ratcheted up the position of Black and minority ethnic staff, while perhaps leaving newer arrivals further behind. More transformatory change could in fact ensure not only better services for Black and minority ethnic and other disadvantaged populations, but also, as shown by the intellectual and energetic contributions of earlier generations, more effective and efficient services for all, as demanded indeed by the so-called 'QIPP' agenda of the new NHS. Change cannot be either 'top-down' or 'bottom-up', but needs to be 'both/and'. This is an essential part of the creation of a welfare society, with mutual respect and support between all groups.

9 Professionalism and cultural competence

Introduction

The importance of acknowledging and actively addressing ethnic and cultural diversity is recognized in a range of government policies, with policy initiatives often being augmented by specific guidance for front-line practitioners. It is increasingly the case that health and social care providers at all levels of service delivery are being expected to conform to and design services around culturally and linguistically appropriate service standards. Social work, social care, medicine, nursing and a range of clinical professions have developed benchmark standards to guide professional practice and redesigned curriculum requirements to guide training that addresses ethnic, cultural and linguistic diversity. These commitments are now seen as fundamental to professionalism and are being embraced as core principles and part of the value basis of the professions. Concepts such as anti-discriminatory, culturally competent or culturally sensitive practice have become commonplace in the language of welfare professionals. Against this policy push a not insubstantial body of literature points to the shortcomings of practitioners in this respect and calls for appropriate and adequate training and continuing professional development to enhance skills and sensibilities in responding to ethnic diversity. The Parekh Report (Parekh Commission 2000: 306), for example, as one of its many recommendations, suggested that 'all those employed in the health and social welfare services should be trained in cultural awareness and sensitivity' and, in its testing list of questions to prompt organizational change, asked of institutions (2000: 283) 'Is there a satisfactory system of developing staff skills in relation to equality and diversity issues?' Despite the requirements of the Race Relations Amendment Act, professional interventions have continued to lack competency and confidence with results that at best undermine public service values or at worst lead to tragedies on a grand scale. The cases of Jasmine Beckford (1985), Tyra Henry (1987), Liam Johnson (1989), Sukina Hammond (1991) and Victoria Climbié (2003) are only some of such cases that reflect the shortfall.

The transformational potential of frontline workers, the 'street-level bureaucrats' (Lipsky 1980), in crafting more appropriate responses to ethnic minority communities is immense. They are key arbiters of access to welfare and key determiners of equality of outcome. They are also pivotal to changing the cultures of organizations and the image and messages organizations communicate to their users. Accordingly they can contribute significantly to the 'public value' their organizations can bring to society in responding to a divided society (Moore 1995). Through improving the relational processes of everyday encounters they can critically shape and change welfare experiences in creating what we have broadly called a welfare society. Yet for a number of reasons this potential has been under-exploited, and has had a limited impact on the wider social relations of welfare but not led to any significant shift in the experiential narratives of ethnic minorities. Such accounts still too frequently attest to the stigmatizing, discriminatory and inept actions of service providers and contribute to the sense that a service is 'not for people like us'. This chapter seeks to explore the transformatory potential of professional workers to contribute to more flexible, appropriate and sensitive service delivery.

Setting the standard

While the definition of professionalism is somewhat contested (Svensson 2006), it is generally accepted that in return for commitment to higher education and continued learning of arcane or advanced knowledge, and the principle of altruistic behaviour, members of a profession receive respect and a level of freedom to practise self-regulation and monopoly. Traditionally professionalism was a characteristic associated with knowledge-based activities requiring long periods of education and training, and entailing service for the common good. The model was probably that of medicine, in particular the services of the healer, whose roots can be traced to Hellenic Greece and the Hippocratic Oath. The role of the healer may have remained fairly constant even if the technology has advanced considerably, but the concept of professionalism has also changed in response to societal and professional needs. In particular, medicine's status and autonomy were challenged and its performance questioned by a succession of changes – social, political and economic. In order to retain the autonomy and respect associated with professional status, the professional may now be subject to some regulation, and be required to maintain higher standards than are required of 'the general public'.

As Cruess and colleagues have noted,

> There is a social contract between society and medicine that hinges on professionalism. This contract has been and remains largely

unwritten, leading physicians to treat it as an implicit rather than an explicit concept. As societal expectations have changed and new demands (are) made upon the medical profession, the social contract has changed and the profession must adapt.

(Cruess *et al.* 2000: 157)

In particular, it behoves professionals to carry out their duties in a rigorous, effective and transparent fashion, in order to retain their right to monopoly and self-regulation. Consequently, bodies such as the General Medical Council, Nursing and Midwifery Council or General Social Care Council have come into being, maintaining registers of permitted practitioners and setting standards for their practice. More recently, the Council for Healthcare Regulatory Excellence (CHRE) (www.chre.org.uk) has been formed to oversee and coordinate the actions of the nine major professional bodies, including the Health Professions Council, which exists to add and regulate 'new' professions allied to health care. At present, however, CHRE has only published policies for employment under its Equal Opportunities and Race Equality Scheme, although it does state that its employees are expected to respect people's ethnicity and cultural background, and it is clear that it will expect this to be a policy observed and enforced by its member councils. We anticipate that in due course more explicit statements of competencies and behaviour may be added to these guidelines.

As the president of the GMC has noted,

Patients may not want to talk openly and honestly with their doctor if they feel they are being judged on the basis of their religion, culture, values or political beliefs. Our core guidance, Good Medical Practice (General Medical Council 2006) makes it clear that doctors must treat their colleagues and patients with respect regardless of their personal circumstances or background, life choices or beliefs.

(Catto 2008: 235)

To achieve this end, professional training will need to incorporate some element of familiarization with such values and beliefs.

A key element of professional regulation has been oversight of the curricula used in institutions of higher education in the formation (or training) of professional workers, and the gradual creation and refinement of sets of 'core competences' against which would-be members of the professions are judged. Competence is a complex concept, and includes elements of knowledge, attitudes and skills or behaviour and, according to the specific profession, may require more or less knowledge, or technical skill, and achievement of these at different levels or standards. As Cruess *et al.* (2000: 158) note, 'compliance with (these standards) are not options but obligations'. Entry on to the registers

in any of the main professions depends on fulfilment of a programme of training, which is now very much defined in terms of 'occupational standards'
and 'competences'. Thus, in social work, graduates are expected to understand
the processes that lead to need and inequality including attention to issues
of 'race' or ethnicity, alongside other social factors of diversity. The National
Occupational Standards for Social Workers contain repeated statements referring to the competences required to perform the role – these include attitudes
and behaviours, such as being able to: 'Talk to those requiring and using
services, and their carers, with due respect for their age, ethnicity, culture,
understanding and needs' (TOPSS UK Partnership 2002: Section 1). Similarly,
social workers are expected to have enough insight and knowledge about the
diversity of their clients be able, in all 'key roles', to 'Identify the nature of the
relationship and the processes required to develop purposeful relationships,
taking account of ethnicity, gender, age, disability, sectarianism and sexuality
issues' (TOPSS UK Partnership 2002: Section 5).

In the NHS, where all professions and occupations are now expected
to define their roles and competencies in terms of a 'Knowledge and Skills
Framework' (KSF) as a part of the 'Agenda for Change' reforms initiated in
2003/04 (DH 2004), a common framework has been established to describe
what is needed to be learned. A number of those skills include explicit reference to competence in communication with, and support of, people of minority ethnic or cultural backgrounds, and the final 'core' dimension is listed as
being the skills and knowledge required to advance and support equality and
diversity as an objective of health service delivery. It notes that this will require
appropriate competences within the other 'core' dimensions, of communication, personal and people development, health, safety and security, service
improvement and quality as well as the generic competences such as learning
and development, and complaints and issue resolution (including harassment
and bullying).

Some of these are yet to be fully defined: and in nursing there remains a
great deal of debate about the meaning of cultural competence and what
should be included (Johnson *et al.* 2008; Kelly and Papadopoulos 2009).
Similarly in social work and social care the focus, nature and impact of developing competency in anti-discriminatory and cultural sensitivity is hotly
debated (O'Hagan 2001; Sakamoto and Pitner 2005; Graham 2007; Laird 2008;
K. McLaughlin 2005) and is the subject of some considerable professional
anxiety (Burman *et al.* 2004). A key aspect of this debate relates to how such
competency can be measured, although in Australia and New Zealand (Papps
and Ramsden 1996; Walker *et al.* 2008) and the United States of America (Like
2008) there has been considerable advance in definition of 'cultural safety' and
requirements for culturally competent practice.

The guidelines of the new British NHS KSF make it very clear that while
different levels may exist (ranked from 'basic' to those required of more senior

staff, who will be expected to 'develop a culture that promotes equality and diversity'), 'all core dimensions including Core Dimension 6 (equality and diversity) have to be in every KSF post outline, at least at level 1' (DH 2004: 80). That is, the NHS has made it quite explicit that it is the responsibility of every employee to act in ways that support equality and diversity and to recognize that equality and diversity are related to the actions and responsibilities of everyone, including not only attention to ethnicity and 'race' issues but also age, gender, social and economic status and sexual orientation. Even at the most basic level, staff in the NHS will therefore be expected to be aware of, and act in ways that are in accordance with, legislation related to racial and ethnic discrimination, recognizing that people are different and making sure they do not discriminate against other people, while recognizing and reporting behaviour that undermines equality. More senior staff would be expected to 'develop a culture that promotes equality and values diversity', for example by actively challenging individual and organizational discrimination, and perhaps acting as a mentor to people from diverse groups or as a role model, and using their strategic position to focus resources to deliver equitable outcomes (DH 2004: 85). Clearly some of these will require standard generic skills appropriate to the level of the staff member, but the requirement is stated in terms that indicate that these actions and skills should be reviewed and evidenced during annual appraisals, and where necessary addressed through a personal development plan and additional training.

Nowhere in the documentation of either body, or indeed in documents such as the General Medical Council's 'Duties of a Doctor' series, is there a statement of specific knowledge required about, or competence in, any aspects of particular minority ethnic group cultures. It must be taken from these broad statements that qualified and competent social workers or clinicians should be able to keep themselves abreast of changes in these, and the diversity of cultures that they might encounter. It is also worth noting that workplace assessors and appraisers are charged with ensuring an ability to understand and confront racism among the placement students and staff that they supervise, although again this is not spelled out in detail anywhere.

Indeed, we may still query the degree to which such professional competencies relating to ethnic diversity do appear in the curriculum. In medicine and nursing, where a clear clinical link between patient safety and knowledge about ethnicity can be demonstrated (Johnson *et al.* 2008), it has taken many years to ensure that at least some token inclusion of these topics is required in the curriculum (Poulton *et al.* 1987; Dogra 2005) and there still remains some resistance to this (Dein 2005). In social work few studies have been conducted but where there is evidence it appears these elements remain marginal rather than mainstreamed into the curriculum (Williams 2010). The problem is that service users and service providers cannot agree on what knowledge is essential, and how much can be expected to be absorbed in an already crowded training programme. Consequently, much 'diversity' training has been criticized as being the provision of 'toolkits' and 'factfiles' or lists of key facts, running the risk of reducing the rich diversity of minority ethnic cultures to a set of tick-box stereotypes (Culley 2000) and essentializing 'ethnicity' to an invariant category associated with determinist ways of living and thinking.

What is clear, however, is that knowledge alone is insufficient, and that the new approach, which includes attention to attitudes, skills and behaviour, is more appropriate, and allows or assists professionals to use their own 'skill and judgement' to work with a whole person, against a background of probabilities and norms from which they can select, or against which they can react and develop as individuals. This will also assist in challenging the stereotypes and prejudicial behaviours of others who seek to discriminate on the basis of just such stereotypes – or what we have elsewhere referred to in this volume as 'racialized' categories. In the new model of the reflective and autonomous practitioner drawing on a reservoir of information, and using or acquiring skills that relate to diverse needs, the expectation is that 'lifelong learning' and continual professional development will parallel and complement the changing nature of cultures and the needs and aspirations of people of diverse backgrounds as they too 'integrate' or develop within a society that does not merely tolerate, but actively encourages and celebrates diversity as a resource to meet and overcome new challenges.

Organizational competence

However, while we have here placed some emphasis on the way forward being self-directed learning and the cultural change of professions, it also has to be recognized that, however competent and committed workers may be, they will not be able to deliver appropriate services or meet the expectations and needs of their diverse clients if the organizations in which they work, and the structural constraints that are posed by the system of service delivery itself, are not also addressed (Bhavnani *et al.* 2005). Cultural capacity cannot be simply addressed by one or even a series of training events for junior and front-line staff. There is a sense in which the higher level competences of the NHS KSF suggest that senior managers may have some responsibilities and capacity to address this issue, but there are also political or other social pressures that have to be negotiated to enable or assure such changes, including the release of adequate resources to supply the necessary facilities and support required by professionals. Organizational cultural competence, however, is an under-theorized and under-documented issue (Bhui *et al.* 2007).

One study which did attempt to address this (Johnson *et al.* 2000) asked a selection of focus groups drawn from minority ethnic community organizations what they would wish or expect to find in a 'culturally competent' health care body. The overwhelming response was a degree of respect for cultural traditions and diversity, along with a preparedness to work alongside community-based groups, and to learn about cultures, languages, religions and dietary restrictions, while having access to 'expert' knowledge from within the community (such as chaplaincy and interpreter support) and lists of contacts within those communities, along with an awareness of their cultural calendars, so that festivals and days of religious obligation could be recognized and, when appropriate, celebrated together. They also expected the hospitals and primary care teams to monitor their own activity and to be aware when specific minority groups were disadvantaged or failing to receive particular services, so that action could be taken to remedy inequalities that were detected.

More recently, Bashford and colleagues (2008a, b) at the University of Central Lancashire have written proposals for a 'basic framework for cultural competency'. They note, in particular, that the diverse meanings of 'cultural competence' may be highly dependent on local contexts and, of course, as the cultural landscape and make-up of local communities varies, it would be inappropriate to enforce a single model across the UK: not all communities of Pakistani origin (for example) will want the same thing, and even within a specific faith group, there will be differences of emphasis, and between congregations in the way they observe and celebrate their beliefs. A comprehensive review of the topic more recently noted that:

> There are no nationally recognized standards by which cultural competence can be measured, let alone defined. However, a basic framework for assessing cultural competence can still be developed ... Organizational competence is demonstrated through a clear commitment to recognizing diversity and the development of pro-active policies which embed equality and skills in working with diverse communities throughout the organization, including:
>
> - A clear commitment to equality, valuing diversity and human rights, articulated in the aims and objectives of the organization.
> - Provision of staff training programmes to a range of personnel, continuing from basic induction through to higher level learning.
> - A system for engaging and consulting with local communities and ensuring that services take account of local diversity.
> - Leadership and management of equality and diversity through performance and monitoring systems.
>
> (Adapted from Bashford 2008b)

It is also interesting to note that the notion of auditing the cultural and anti-racist, pro-equalities competence of organizations is gaining ground. The

Audit Commission and Care Quality Commission have begun to ask those agencies that they scrutinize to provide evidence of their procedures and processes, to ensure that their services are culturally competent and have systems built in to reduce or tackle issues of discrimination (intended or unintended) and inequalities of outcome. A recent publication from the National Cancer Action Team listed the following questions (see box) from its 'BME Baseline Audit' of the 'patient experience', which had been posed to all NHS trusts and cancer networks and which is being analysed as part of its regular quality assurance and accreditation process. This self-assessment audit of both trusts and networks was undertaken between January 2009 and July 2009 to gain an understanding into the range of services offered at a trust level that were culturally sensitive and to ascertain the arrangements networks had in place to support service-level agreements to assess the quality of services provided.

Questions for Trusts and Networks on Cultural Sensitivity (Organizational Audit)

1 Within the Trust/Organization, do BME cancer patients have access to culturally specific advocacy and support services, either provided directly by an NHS provider or commissioned via an SLA from the voluntary sector?

2 Within the Trust/Organization, do BME cancer patients have access to culturally appropriate prostheses which are available at the point of need, in an appropriate shade to suit the patient's skin tone?

3 Across the Trust/Organization do BME cancer patients have access to culturally appropriate wigs and cosmetic advice at the point of need?

4 Across the Trust/Organization, do BME cancer patients have access at the point of need and by referral to culturally and age appropriate counselling?

5 Across the Trust/Organization do BME cancer patients have access to culturally specific diet and nutrition advice from a trained culturally competent nutritionist?

6 Across the Trust/Organization do BME cancer patients whose first language is not English have access to audio/visual and other translated material in tumour areas relevant to their need?

7 Is the Trust/Organization able to demonstrate that staff are trained to deliver culturally competent services and is a workforce plan in place with an up-to-date register system in place to monitor attendance?

8 Can the Trust/Organization demonstrate that staff are trained to work with interpreters around breaking news to cancer patients whose first language is not English?

9 Are Service Providers able to evidence that interpreters used within cancer services have received training specifically around medical terminology

---

associated with cancer and understand how to translate probing questions and/or break bad news in a culturally acceptable manner?

10 Can the Trust/Organization demonstrate that ethnic coding is collected routinely and they have a process in place to access the percentage of data collected and its accuracy?

11 Do Service Providers have a system/framework in place which captures patient satisfaction of cancer services, results of which can be broken down by ethnicity?

(National Cancer Action Team 2009)

What is normally expected in any culturally competent organization, as noted in item 7 of the above self-assessment audit and also in Bashford's (2008b) review and summary, is attention to the continuing professional development and training needs of staff, many of whom will have had little or no initial training in aspects of cultural competence, despite the specific curricular guidelines mentioned above. For some, it may also be still possible that they have not had the experience of living in a multicultural, diverse community (although, as we saw in Chapter 7, this is increasingly unlikely). In such cases, however, and possibly for all professionals, it is necessary to begin with what has been termed 'cultural awareness' (Koskinen *et al.* 2008) – which will include a recognition that they themselves come from, and are formed by, a specific culture which will affect their own decision-making processes, values and expectations. This will enable them to obtain insights into different cultures, changing their thinking about new cultures, helping them to identify with another culture, and confirming their self-awareness, or simply providing them with new personal insights into who and what they are themselves. From this, it is hoped that 'cultural hunger' or 'cultural desire' (Campinha Bacote 2003) – a wish to learn more about other cultures – will develop, and become a self-fulfilling and virtuous circle of personal learning and development, rather than a rote-based learning of 'key facts' and stereotypes. Indeed, Campinha Bacote suggests that if the desire or motivation is strong enough and properly developed, this will encourage the professional to develop a passion for and commitment to the process of cultural competence and become inspired to examine uncomfortable subjects, such as racism.

On the evidence of training to date, this would appear to be desirable, since earlier attempts at 'race awareness' training, often modelled on the systems developed by Katz and based on the experiences of the American army in the 1960s and 1970s (Katz and Ivey 1977; Katz 1978), sometimes led to considerable disruption, resistance and even backlashes and worse outcomes for Black and minority ethnic users of social work services (see Sivanandan 1985). The main criticism of that approach was that it appeared to be based on developing guilt feelings, rather than a positive desire to engage in learning and action to combat racialized injustice, and also that it might 'alert' people to unacceptable beliefs and assist them to conceal, rather than reform, these. More recently, in addition to basic training in 'cultural awareness' and cultural knowledge, a number of other approaches in anti-discrimination and diversity management have been attempted. These have been variously characterized by Luthra and Oakley 1991, Wrench and Taylor 1994 and Tamkin *et al.* 2002, but can be summarized as follows:

> *Information training*, the giving of basic facts on population demography, legal obligations and prejudice, which should affect behaviour. This may also be presented as equalities training (or equity training), which provides participants with descriptions of legally appropriate behaviour, assuming this will bring about the desired behavioural changes: this approach has been found effective in 'directed' hierarchical organizations such as police forces (Holdaway 1997; Tamkin *et al.* 2003).
>
> *Cultural awareness training*, which engages trainees in order to change their attitudes, and assumes that by raising awareness, discrimination will reduce. There is less evidence for the successful implementation of this approach, but the process of giving information about specific cultural practices and needs, which is normally incorporated into this approach, should be effective if combined with and associated with the description of normative skills and knowledge for the relevant profession (e.g. nursing). However, there have been few successful evaluations of the degree to which such knowledge is retained, let alone whether it is used in practice subsequently (Johnson *et al.* 2008).
>
> *Racism awareness training* (and increasingly this approach has also been applied to other 'specific' awareness training), which focuses on racism (or sexism etc.) uses self-awareness and confrontational techniques to bring about changes in behaviour. The evidence for its effectiveness in the UK context is disputed, and in the 1970s and 1980s a number of controversies erupted over its incorporation in social work training. This led to adverse outcomes and press coverage in some cases, and its abandonment. Unfortunately, this sometimes also precipitated a move away from explicit treatment of the issue (Richards JK et al 1985; Johnson 1986).
>
> *Anti-racism training (ART)*, which assumes that racism and discrimination exist in an organization and is therefore aimed at changing organizational practices to combat racism, was developed partly as a response to the reaction to the earlier Race Awareness Training (RAT). This form of training may be more widely described as anti-discrimination training, which tends to focus on specific practices

such as recruitment, and is increasingly required of staff involved in promotion, appraisal and selection panels.

Diversity training has become more popular, targeted towards managers and other power holders and covering a variety of equality strands in order to develop a heterogeneous culture within an organization and address requirements under human rights-related legislation: sometimes this is also known nowadays as 'human rights training', but its focus still remains largely on human resources management, to ensure that staff are treated appropriately.

It is worth noting that nearly all of these studies and activities appear to have been based on 'post-entry' training, rather than foundation training at the initial stages of professional formation. It is true that studies of training given to police cadets on anti-racist practice did suggest that the 'canteen culture' experienced after learners started their practice placements with experienced (and possibly more cynical or prejudiced) station staff rapidly led to a loss of acquired skills, beliefs and behaviours – although, again, we would accept that these were studies undertaken before the modernization of the police training syllabus and a much increased intake of graduate-level officers (Holdaway 1997). However, Tamkin *et al.* (2002, 2003) are very clear that post-entry training is far from the ideal, bringing with it problems of resistance, absence, reluctance or resentment, inaccuracy of information delivered, and also problems of finding trainers who are enthusiastic and not dogmatic or given to reinforcing stereotypes and capable of relating to the institution/ profession's own culture! It is evident that the most appropriate way to deliver such formational experiences is through being incorporated into initial professional education and training, or embedded in induction training delivered to new staff entering an organization and thus linked to the organization's own culture and grounded in its philosophy for all new entrants. However, it may also be necessary to provide 'refresher' training and to ensure that the idealistic values transmitted are not lost during practice placements while working alongside experienced colleagues who have been less well prepared for working with diversity (Johnson *et al.* 2008).

Luthra and Oakley (1991) concluded that in the longer run, the most effective way to bring about change is the so-called 'education approach'. The education approach takes a more long-term view and assumes that change can only come about through the self-driven personal development of individuals. Luthra and Oakley argued that when individuals themselves identify a need for change and find ways to do so, change will happen. This can be stimulated by a number of triggers, including the 'cultural hunger' identified by Campinha Bacote, but also by a recognition that diversity and equality are key components in a professional culture and required for accreditation and professional progression.

An alternative formulation which allies well with our concern for a more structured and structural change in the systems and agencies of the welfare society is the 'racial justice approach', viewing 'race' within an institutional and cultural context, which aims to transform organizational and societal power relations through understanding power and how racism is perpetuated by organizations. More specifically, it is about understanding privilege, developing accountability for racism, and identification of racism and oppression. As Tamkin (2000) suggests, citing an American researcher,

> Rogers notes: 'Diversity training can ask white people to change their consciousness while leaving their dominance intact: a racial justice approach requires an organizational transformation of power relations.'
>
> (Tamkin 2000: 15)

If this is accepted, then it has to be accepted that an anti-racist, structurally informed approach will have to be more extensive and challenging, requiring longer and greater training input, which might need to take a much more political and activist stance, to look at the history of racism, at personal prejudice and institutional racism, and ultimately to suggest the possibility of restructured power relations in society. This has also been summarized as recognizing that both personal attitudes and institutional structures need to change, understanding that the personal *is* political. Certainly, there is no evidence that shorter, 'quick and dirty' approaches have been successful (Brown and Lawton 1991).

This approach rose to ascendency in social work, for example, in the 1980s and was quickly embraced by a profession anxious to reprofile its identity, away from its largely Christian and psychodynamic origins to one more attuned to the dynamic of multicultural Britain (see for example Dominelli 1988). By the 1980s the momentum for a prescriptive curriculum on race equality issues in social work had grown, considerably pushed forward by social work activists, radical professionals, academics and grassroots groups. With the introduction of the Diploma in Social Work in 1990 came a forthright statement in the requirements for qualifying training (Paper 30) that suggested racism was 'endemic' in British society and charged social work with a mandate for change. This statement signalled a particular positioning of race equality and cultural diversity training in the social work curriculum that placed the profession apparently way ahead of other service professionals in terms of tackling the issues of racial discrimination on an individual and institutional level. By contrast professions such as nursing and the police took very different trajectories in terms of their awareness, recognition and training requirements for practice in a multicultural, multi-faith society. By the 1980s and early 1990s a plethora of texts appeared to guide practice, including a series of books commissioned by the professional body, the then Central Council for Education and Training in Social Work (CCETSW). Notable among these was *One Small Step towards Racial Justice* (CCETSW 1991) and CCETSW's *Curriculum Development Series* of the 1990s. It was, however, a trajectory that quickly became destabilized and pilloried for its radical intent and most particularly for its failure to demonstrate tangible evidence of improved practice and responsiveness to the needs of Black and minority ethnic groups. The way in which these issues emerged within the social work agenda and became politicized made them vulnerable to the critique of misguided professional meddling, ideological dogma and to accusations that the movement had become detached from the practical concerns of those it sought to serve (K. McLaughlin 2005). Critics have argued that this trajectory in social work easily became absorbed and tempered within bureaucratic practices and thereby lost its transformational momentum (Gilroy 1987). The competency approach to training, coupled with the neo-liberal incremental and procedural approach to race equality within public service agencies has, it is argued, effectively defused the potential for more radical and widespread changes. There has been an evident shift away from emphasizing the more political aspects of professional practice and its potential to challenge structural racism towards a greater focus on culturally responsive practice related to professional standards. Nevertheless, although painful lessons have been learned about the limits of political action within the parameters of public service delivery, there is a professional openness within social work and social care to developing critical interventions and theories and methodologies of race equality and cultural sensitivity that will be workable in practice.

A development of the more structural approaches to change comes from the new and emerging visibility of 'whiteness' or 'white norms'. It is argued that far too much focus has been placed on considering Black and ethnic minority identities, cultures and lifestyles at the expense of a thoroughgoing examination of how whiteness functions within organizations to protect privilege (Bonnet 2002), through making decisions not to change (cf Bachrach and Baratz 1962). This trajectory prompts an exploration of which norms are privileged over others and how power is assumed and held in organizations. Atkin and Chattoo, for example (2007: 377), suggest that a more rigorous and sophisticated recognition of difference and diversity can operate to illustrate that the 'white norm' of public institutions is no longer securely invisible and non-neutral and through exposure of the assumptive world of public institutions offer challenges to the professional self and the professional ethos. They develop this idea through the notion of the 'reflexive practitioner' who has to negotiate and manage many of the contradictions of welfare delivery on the front line in interaction with the individual or family. Atkin and Chattoo's analysis suggests the need to move beyond formulas, stereotypes and prescriptions for practice, to an understanding of context and organizational practices and processes by which institutions enable or inhibit responsiveness to ethnic minority need. To this end these writers draw attention to 'the process whereby practitioners – and the public agencies within which they work – frame, engage and legitimate the experiences of minority ethnic populations' (2007: 389). Atkin and Chattoo, in seeking ways to enable practitioners to incorporate good practices within the contexts of their existing professional worlds, argue that practitioners do not simply interpret guidance but crucially mediate and act upon it by reference to their professional role and ideology, their own values and assumptive worlds, office cultures and the external political, social and economic environment. What they are seeking to demonstrate is the complexities of the dynamics of service delivery which need to be subject to greater exploration and challenge.

Conclusions: new demands, new challenges

The traditional idea of professionalism with its notion of expert power, expert knowledge and self-regulating autonomy is one little suited to the contemporary complex of welfare delivery. The challenges posed by new governance, greater and more differentiated forms of user involvement and the ascendency of lay knowledges all serve to confront this model of the professional and reshape professional practices. The narrow politics of the public sphere and public service values have been confronted by the claims for recognition, voice and justice posed by a range of service users, user groups and wider social movements. Multiculturalism itself has challenged mainstream professional practice in a myriad of ways: demanding attention to the protection of rights, non-discrimination, recognition of an ever-increasing diversity of lifestyles, cultures and identities and to the values and ideologies of professional groupings. The responses have been largely to adopt assimilation models and to homogenize and stereotype the variety of cultural groups for the purpose of intervention. These types of responses have proved unsustainable in the light of complex, differentiated and dynamic multiculturalism but also collapse in the light of new lines of accountability, new forms of engagement and alliances beyond the public sphere.

Professionals cannot expect sameness in their practice: one of the benefits and challenges of the autonomy afforded to professionals is the expectation that they will be able to respond appropriately to situations for which their initial training may not have prepared them, and that – even without the threat of 'revalidation' hanging over them – they will take steps to engage in 'continuous professional development' and a process of 'lifelong learning'. Thus, whether in medicine, nursing, social work, social care or counselling – or any of the myriad new professions and techniques that continue to develop and seek accreditation under the aegis of the Health Professions Council, the

General Social Care Council and the Care Quality Commission (the new single, integrated regulator for health and adult social care) – the practitioner must be prepared for diverse encounters, expect a complexity of encounters with difference and be ready to work with uncertainty. This means a refreshed form of cultural or anti-racist diversity competence based on a broad range of skills, as facilitator, negotiator, political actor and mediator in more deliberative and open forms of welfare decision making. It means engaging with more reflexive forms of practice and the acceptance of greater levels of power sharing in struggles over welfare and the ability to go beyond the rational pragmatic incrementalism of the neo-liberal modernization project to the notion of public service professionals contributing to increase the value their organizations bring to the broader notion of welfare society.

10 Towards a multicultural welfare

The politics of welfare have been significantly transformed in the modern era as arrangements for the delivery of welfare have become more open, fluid and subject to negotiation by a range of stakeholders. This has led to a significant rebalancing within the mixed economy of welfare toward welfare delivery as a shared responsibility between the state, the family, the voluntary sector and the market, with the ascendancy of the individual citizen as prime negotiator in the refreshed welfare arrangements. The last ten years or so have witnessed widespread changes to the governance of welfare towards a more disseminated network of delivery that has multiple delivery points, is multi-level and multi-funded. There has been a substantive growth in citizen involvement with increased opportunities for participation, the co-production of welfare goods and the claiming of user power. There have been fundamental changes to the approach to equalities and to the role of regulatory bodies in holding the ring and ensuring equitable outcomes. We have been concerned in this text to outline what some of these transformations have implied for Black and ethnic minorities in a period of what may most appropriately be called the post-post-welfare state. Alongside these developments the idea of 'race' itself has been subjected to challenge by a combination of the virtues and problematic aspects of multiculturalism. Minority communities have themselves been changing internally and *vis-à-vis* each other such that mixedness, hybridity, emergent and cross-cutting identities have fractured the notion of the ethnic minority unitary category both as an experiential reality or as a political constituency.

In the light of these widespread changes we have posited the notion of 'a welfare society' as a concept for capturing this broad set of changes but also in the ideal typical sense as a vision of a society that is more inclusive: one where more people are cooperatively engaged in advancing the well-being of all and in protecting the interests of the more socially and materially disadvantaged members who cannot so easily compete on equal terms. This notion appeals not simply to the inclusivity agenda that has come to the fore in policy debates, but also resurrects the redistributionist discourse which we would argue is fundamental to any robust interpretation of inclusion. We must anticipate that further changes to the structures of welfare delivery will come. Under a change of government, organizational and political changes will happen, most likely within the given logic of neo-liberalism. There will also continue to be transformations to the profile of our multicultural society, as migrations old and new reconfigure, as the age structure of settled communities changes and as intermixture becomes the norm. Our concluding task is accordingly a tentative reading of the runes; some speculative assessment of the prospect of the advance towards a multicultural welfare.

Our view of the 'welfare society' is inevitably partial. The focus of this book has, in the main, been on health and social welfare and we acknowledge the many areas of social life beyond the scope of our exploration that impinge on the health and well-being of ethnic minorities and the majority. The criminal justice system, the education system, the immigration system, housing and the workings of the labour market as well as participation (or lack of) in the arts and leisure operate to generate exclusionary forces which undermine or fail to support people's health and welfare. Others, most notably the Parekh Report (Parekh Commission 2000) have attempted to tackle this broad brief (see also Ratcliffe 2004). We have confined our analysis to a visioning of a responsive system of welfare delivery, one that is attuned to the needs of Black and ethnic minorities and sufficiently engaging of them to produce good outcomes that enhance their well-being. Where possible, we have attempted to draw from research or recommendations that have arisen from grassroots organizations supported or led by people from those communities, especially when those reports have been ignored or silenced in wider research and policy debates. At the same time we acknowledge that these good outcomes are almost wholly dependent on wider social changes in the institutions, systems and culture of society. The vision of the Parekh Report outlines a number of major tasks facing British society, including the reimagining of the national story and national identity in more inclusive ways; the balancing of equality and difference, liberty and cohesion; confronting and eliminating racisms; reducing material inequalities and the building of a pluralistic human rights culture (Parekh Commission 2000: 105). The achievement of these far-reaching aspirations demands the attention of a broad range of institutions and fundamental shifts at all levels of society. In a similar vein Ratcliffe (2004: 166) calls for 'a common-sense of nationhood accompanied by respect for, and acceptance of difference and diversity'. He seeks a universal condemnation of racism and racial discrimination, a commitment to the creation of a society that recognizes the need for a greater degree of material equality, and policies that seek out through the provision of appropriate support more heterogeneous and spatially integrated communities (2004: 166). Against broad ambitions such as these we consider what are the potentials and the pitfalls facing the search for a truly multicultural welfare system.

Reading the runes: one step forward, two steps back?

The history of 'race' and welfare makes uncomfortable reading. It reveals a consistent lack of strategy and political will for change on the part of governments underpinned by the negative tones of a wider narrative of the 'threat' of minorities to the resources and solidarities of society. As a consequence this is a tale characterized by an uneven development, by *one step forward, two steps back*, as there has been a failure across time to capture and capitalize on the more progressive movements for change. Neo-liberalist policy towards race equality has shown itself to be Janus-faced, characterized by contradictory imperatives which it cannot square. Given the ascendancy of the neo-liberal paradigm, this tendency is unlikely to change with any change of government, nor is it likely that there will be any radical reduction in the level of public antipathy towards particular minorities in what has been dubbed the era of 'the war on terror'. These wider political and social issues, particularly the attribution of the threat of terrorism, concerns over religious cleavage and ambivalence about increasing globalization, serve to shape public attitudes to ethnic minorities, that in turn will and do shape welfare relationships and welfare arrangements. Concerns about community cohesion and social solidarities populate government policy documents, by inference or directly profiling as problematic co-ethnic community settlement. In the New Labour era the desire to maintain populist approval has largely compromised attempts to institute a coherent and morally defensible position on race equality as in three administrations the government has shown itself unwilling to sustain a forthright stance that might lead rather than be directed by public opinion. This is a tricky context in which to advance the claim for a multicultural welfare.

There is nevertheless an acknowledgement that the 'public' of public service, to use Newman's terminology, has changed, and fundamentally changed forever (Newman 2007). This is a dynamic that will continue to shift, transform and reconfigure like a kaleidoscope and while the desirability or otherwise of multiculturalism remains contentious and its impacts debated, there would be few practitioners and policy makers who can persist in trying to refute this demographic reality or its implications for public service delivery. The ambient cosmopolitanism of Britain's major cities and greater levels of social interaction and encounters with diversity, even in the most rural parts of the UK, are now the norm. In addition the growing intermixture of communities is evidenced by the fact that now one in ten children is born into families of mixed heritage and the overlapping factors of class, religion, belief and culture have produced complex identifications and more fluid associations beyond the co-ethnic group (Fanshawe and Sriskandarajah 2010). Policy makers and practitioners must grapple with – in Vertovec's words (2007) – 'super diversity'.

Migrations will not stop; indeed they will become more complex and more necessary within an increasingly globalized economy. Accordingly, governments need to orientate themselves to how best to respond to a given level of multiculturalism rather than to pursue the birfurcated policy stance of the assimilation/restriction couplet that implies the ultimate levelling out of diversity. The way forward cannot be based on the desire to recreate sameness or maintain a fictitious historic homogeneity, but must be built on a genuine engagement with the reality of diversity. Entitlement to welfare services predicated on a reference to some homogenized notion of nation or national identity is out of step with the contemporary realities. There therefore needs to be a decoupling of restrictive immigration policy and restrictive welfare policy as the overriding formula for managing diversity: the ending of the 'paso doble' between welfare and nation that has existed since the inception of the welfare state. Part of the deconstruction of this axiom comes from a realistic assessment of the contributions of migrants to the economy and to the welfare economy in particular and rejection of arguments that equate in-migration with a drain on welfare resources. It also demands attention to challenging a range of neglectful and discriminatory welfare practices that reinforce the exclusion of ethnic minorities by categorizing them as 'other' or as 'hard to reach' and placing them outside the system of welfare reciprocities.

In addition, sustained efforts will be needed to tackle widespread racial inequalities. We do not believe that the salience of 'race', or racism and racialized relations, is purely of historic interest – William Julius Wilson may have opined in 1978 that the significance of race was declining, but even he in 2009 has recognized the 'structural persistence of the ghetto' (Wilson 2009). The evidence of persistent racial inequalities is indisputable. People from minority ethnic backgrounds were disproportionately affected by two previous recessions and there is little to suggest that the current economic downturn will not have an equally differential impact. We would argue that the government's approach of prioritizing and targeting specific inequalities will inevitably have limited impact given its failure to acknowledge the inter-related nature and complexities of this 'wicked issue' of social policy.

A considerably strengthened legislative and policy mandate on equalities provides the basis for change. This is bolstered by a Europe-wide policy push, in which Britain is no longer a sole player but part of an orchestrated effort to provide a robust system for protecting against discriminations. This has inevitably facilitated, and been part of, the desirable and necessary movement of workers and their families across Europe and served to enhance the transferability of welfare rights between nations and regions. We have witnessed the way in which new and compelling arguments relating to the movement and welfare of eastern European migrants have had the effect of driving policy initiatives on equalities forward at local level across the UK. Whether this push has benefited Black and other ethnic minorities of colour is contestable.

Arguably it has had a filibustering effect as local authorities and health trusts engage with those equalities activities that are more palatable and comfortable to accommodate, their response to the presence of new economic migrants serving to divert attention away from their neglect of the intractable issues and inequalities of the more established minority groups in their areas. At the same time, we recognize, some of those 'new migrants' have become 'racialized' and regarded as once were the Black and Asian migrants (usually unfavourably) compared to the former movements of Jewish, Polish and other central European migrant settlers. The more integrated Europe is thus something of a double-edged sword in terms of race equality. Wider European collaboration provides the basis for more strengthened and transferable rights for all but at the same time presents a countervailing force to more progressive change as it brings in its wake entrenched attitudes to those considered 'outsiders' or non-Europeans. This also may lead to segmentation of those new migrants into 'desirable' and 'undesirable' groups on a basis of perceived 'nearness' of culture (cf Leiberson's 'queuing theory'), and a further splitting of the anti-discriminatory struggle (Sivanandan 2006). The spectre of a 'Fortress Europe' in which pan-European collaborations provide the basis for a concerted effort on exclusions that are anti-Islamic and xenophobic in sentiment and deploy racialized immigration and asylum policy is ever present. Inevitably, welfare professionals will be engaged in either implementing or resisting regressive and repressive regimes that emanate from beyond the context of the nation state. This makes the lobbying and political potential of welfare professionals on a national and wider European political level ever more important to the aspiration of a welfare society.

Acknowledgement of these developments on the wider political stage begs the question of why we so easily lose the ground that was gained on race equality and what can be done to prevent further attrition in future. Some of this can be explained by the complexities of the agenda of multiculturalist policy making itself, an agenda that involves the balancing of issues of equality and diversity, liberty and cohesion in an ever-changing society (Parekh Commission 2000). For example, old and new lines of fracture and poten-tial dissent emerge that indicate the limit of co-ethnic solidarities – such as language and religion or manifest conflicts of interest (Fanshawe and Sriskandarajah 2010). Even more local partisanship, or the influence of cha-rismatic local leaderships, can be used against the greater good, as well as confusing and splitting communities. In addition, particular inequalities are seemingly intractable within certain minority groups because of influences such as culture or religion and attitudes relating to stigma. The mismatch between intention and implementation is a countervailing force against sus-tainable change. While the reverberations of the legislative catalyst are being felt across the public service, public authorities have struggled to translate the statutory requirements into tangible outcomes and sound practices. The process of internalization of the equalities mandate within the bureaucracy has so far largely proceeded along technocratic tram lines with a tick box at each station stop to signal success. This rigid and limited interpretation of the change mandate, coupled with lack of political will, is unlikely to produce good outcomes, hampered as it is by the ever-increasing managerialism of the modern bureaucracy. The conclusion must be that change cannot be left wholly to the organs of the state and its legislative instruments, but there will be a continuing need for struggle and grassroots activism.

Tussles remain about the relative role of the pursuit of ethnically specific services or the value of mainstreaming, and public and indeed professional sympathies waver. Thus a broad sweep of factors compromise progress. But beyond factors such as this, the reasons for most failures to eliminate inequality of well-being must lie at the door of lack of political will and the nature of power distributions in society that consistently remain unequal. Minority groups almost by definition are subject to minoritization – lack of or loss of power. Empowering them and ensuring the systematic representation of Black and minority ethnic communities on public bodies is one point of leverage for the sustainability of the 'race' effort, the capacity building of the 'Black' voluntary sector and opportunities for civic engagement another, while the garnering of sound research evidence to demonstrate inequality and the establishment of a human rights culture as the default are other key steps.

The evidence of the benefits of the government retreat from an explicitly 'race'-based mandate is not compelling, however. In anticipation of the 2010 general election the respective political parties have taken up positions on 'race'. Following on from a consultation on *Tackling Racial Inequalities* and the publication of a government *Statement on Race* (DCLG 2010), the Communities secretary, John Denham, went on record as saying that 'Racism is dead' and argued that roots of the key inequalities in our modern society are to be found in socio-economic disadvantage and class divisions (Sparrow and Owen 2010). Similarly, Conservative think tanks fulminated about community cohesion and national identity, suggesting that faith-based cleavages, and perhaps generational ones, are crucial while the needs of populations can no longer be described along the old, racialized lines (Grieve 2010). Arguably both of the main parties seek a new discourse on 'race' and ways of 'racializing' and reinforcing old traditional cleavages, using new rhetoric or new categories of exclusion and description. The Liberal Democrats, in their contribution to the debate in the Runnymede Trust 'Platform' series (Featherstone 2010), also highlight that 'deprivation is not just about economic deprivation, but also cultural and religious deprivation', but retain the focus on social class and generic struggles, albeit arguing for the need for the Equality Act to recognize the possibility of multiple discriminations. Their policy also, in the end, avoids confronting the evil of racism head on. Accordingly there remains concern that the multifaceted approach of the Equality Act 2010 (as it became, just as we closed the pages of our manuscript to submit it to the printer) will lead to a dilution of the political struggle for race equality that had managed to embed these concerns onto the public agenda or that those concerns will get neglected within a hierarchy of equalities and a competition for priority on the agenda of public bodies.

At the same time, Black and minority-led organizations, headed by campaigning and research groups such as the 1990 Trust, Afiya Trust and Operation Black Vote, have prepared and published a set of demands or issues to pose to would-be candidates and the principal political parties in their Racial Justice Manifesto. The key features of this, as far as it relates to health, welfare and social care issues, are shown in the box below.

What the next government should do:

- An advisory group at the national level to ensure focus on equality and diversity elements from BME perspectives in further development of health and social care which reports directly to the Secretary of State for Health and the Chief Medical Officer.
- Proper investment in raising awareness among communities about health conditions and services, and resources for delivering need-based services for each community.
- Set clear targets in tackling race inequalities in service provision and public health/health inequalities (that is, change the statistics – bring health experiences of minority communities at least on a par with the mainstream population).
- Develop a clear strategy for more effective consultation on policy development and public sector reform with BME organizations, service users and carers.
- Establish a mandatory duty on health and social care services to report on outcomes to service user organizations, BME health forums at local, regional and national levels.
- Invest in developing a skilled workforce and support the leadership and professional development of BME staff working in the voluntary and public sector.
- Establish clear structures for accountability in realizing targets, partnership and leadership building.
- Monitor and regulate high-quality outcome measures, with service users and carers leading the strategy for this.
- Prioritize cross-sectoral working on health inequalities and racial equalities.

(Adapted from Racial Justice Manifesto 2010: Chapter 10 and Afiya Trust 2010)

These are clearly stated and practical pointers for change. The transformations required to the delivery of public services are, however, fundamental and far-reaching if a responsive and effective system of welfare is to be realized. None of the major parties, however, have directly addressed any of these issues explicitly or in relation to ethnicity, diversity or racial justice. A significant shift in public service culture, both in its operation and its fundamental values, is required.

Transforming public services

The decentring of the central state monopoly of the delivery of services towards multiple and multi-level co-production provides significant opportunities for the realization of multicultural welfare and significant opportunities for the empowerment of ethnic minority groups, as well as some dangers or threats. Recognition of difference and diversity in the construction of the 'public' to be addressed by public service now requires a radical deracialization of these categories but without stripping these groupings of the political salience that provides the very basis of their potential power. The collective gains that have accrued to these constituencies should not be dissipated but neither should they be constrained by the rigidities of ethnic categorization. The current government's retreat from the language of 'race' and from policy recognition of 'race'-specific interventions has set a course which is unlikely to change with any alteration of the political party in power. New era equalities strategies are generic, and the new policy language favours terminologies that are generic, with terms such as communities, diversity, social justice, equality of opportunity. At one level this is to be welcomed. If it signals a new and emerging form of progressive universalism that takes us beyond the supplementing of universal services with special and rigidly formulated 'race'-focused initiatives towards a more embedded, equitable and mainstreamed response to diversity, then this must be for the good. The terming of adaptations as 'special provision', and their reliance on 'additional', external funding, makes them vulnerable and emphasizes a short-termism that implies a wish for assimilation and a return to that imagined homogeneous past. A more sophisticated understanding of diversity in the public realm is slowly dawning but it is still the case that practitioners and policy makers too readily retreat to a very particular conceptualization of minorities as distinct ethnic communities, most usually urban-based, as the basis for public policy intervention. Too often this stereotyped depiction drives formulas for action. The 'ghetto' then becomes the (only) locus for action, and freedom of movement and settlement – the ability to 'suburbanize' – becomes a right that has to be foregone in order to achieve cultural satisfaction in services.

The trend toward more open, participatory governance is to be welcomed in terms of its potential to produce greater equality, greater investment in well-being and the benefits of higher levels of civil association. More people than ever before from minority communities are invited into the policy machinery and engaged in determining the shape and nature of services. At the same time the limits of this participatory framework cannot be overlooked. For many the propensity to engage is constrained by factors of class, gender, age, particular ethnic background, religion and other combinations of social status. Those in weak or vulnerable positions are often unable to capitalize on new opportunities for engagement or take advantage of the resources it brings. Most often participatory frameworks empower those most able to take advantage of the opportunities they open up, benefiting those already well positioned in the welfare arena. In addition participatory strategies necessarily rely on artificially constructed groups or categories that individuals may or may not identify with. The constraints of co-ethnic association itself may be a limiting factor as not all members of a group will want the same things. In addition, participatory strategies demand skills and capacities that many do not have and it is usually to be observed that participation in consultation with organizations is undertaken by those *representing* the most disadvantaged, and not by those most affected themselves. This leads many to be sceptical of this policy trend – fearing it is more rhetoric and sham than offering up genuine engagement and inclusive participation. Ethnic minorities remain a weak voice in the new policy arenas and it will take time, commitment and no small measure of risk to build trust and skill on both sides in order to realize the participatory ideal.

All the tinkering in the world with the available structures and with mechanisms of engagement will be to no avail if the social relations of welfare remain largely monocultural. Where welfare interventions are characterized by misrecognition of the issues facing minority communities and where they represent an affront to the values and beliefs of others, they will clearly be limited in their impact. While welfare assimilationism prevails, services will continue to fail the needs of diverse groups. The current focus on consultation and coordination while leaving the mainstream structures untouched will not resolve this ineffectiveness. Variously labelled as 'whiteness', 'eurocentricity', 'monoculturalism' or 'colour blindness', the assumptive world of public service with its liberal values frames the norm and thus ethnic minorities continue to be seen as 'hard to reach' or 'self-segregating' or having 'special needs'. This failure to examine and challenge the so-called neutrality of the 'open access' public service ethos and the nature of its 'generic' underpinning values inevitably produces injustices and exclusions. The future role of public services, following Parekh (Parekh Commission 2000), will be to provide a platform for open dialogue and negotiation, which may include differences of opinion, conflict and contestability about how things are done with respect to welfare outcomes, and hopefully to provide mediation between competing needs or demands, within the parameters of general principles. This is not a prescription for untrammelled relativism but is accommodative of the pluralistic culture in which we live, to reflect a variety of lifestyles, beliefs, passions and personal priorities. The idea of a neutral state arbitrating between competing value systems fails to acknowledge that the state itself is imbued with values that warrant examination in the light of a pluralistic culture.

There is no doubting, however, the limits to this politics of recognition. It could be suggested that over-emphasizing differences in this way has led to a neglect of the fundamental issue of inequality. Diversity is not, nor should it be, an alternative to equality or, at least, equity. Part of the contemporary 'race' trick may be that the increased focus on equal*ities* itself has served to diminish the search for true equality. Indeed, it is possible to argue that all equalities legislation and equalities efforts will achieve is making more equal the status of respective equality strands within a context of considerable and growing inequality between people. The evidence of persistent and widespread disadvantage among black and ethnic minorities stands in stark contrast to the vision of the conviviality of contemporary multicultural society in which different individuals and groups are recognized and respected. Ethnic minority groups experience patterns of inherited disadvantage *vis-à-vis* each other and *vis-à-vis* majority white society. At the heart of this debate is the redistribution/ recognition conundrum of public policy and approaches to equality that suggest greater or lesser emphasis on one or the other. It can be argued that far too much focus has been placed on the discourse of acceptance and recognition of ethnic minority statuses, identities and self-expression at the expense of the redistributionist discourse that stridently calls for greater equality of outcome. Particular vulnerabilities exist among minority ethnic groups including their high representation in areas of deep disadvantage. These will doubtless be exacerbated by the trend towards increased privatization, active consumerism in welfare and by agendas on personal care that relinquish responsibility to the private sphere without the concomitant commitment of resources and audit. Social justice strategies that prioritize the worst off in the context of persistent inequality and seek to establish a robust framework for ensuring a social minimum and the protection of rights are the vital complement to strategies of recognition. Distributional as well as relational elements are necessary for the production of more equal life chances.

The role of public professionals as potential agents of progressive change has long been recognized. Public service professionals, front-line gatekeepers or 'street-level bureaucrats' (Lipsky 1980) are critical to the everyday experiential encounters people from minority ethnic backgrounds have with health and social service institutions and they are also critical definers in the social and cultural representations of these groups. The active recruitment of a more diverse workforce, the potential of sound training in equalities and responsiveness to cultural and other diversity and reclaiming of the possibilities of politicization and collective action in genuine partnerships with user groups is fundamental to the transformation of public services.

There are growing competencies within the professions. Responsiveness to diversity is slowly being embedded within the codes of practice of health and welfare professionals, such as the 'Duties of a Doctor' booklets published by the General Medical Council, and the accreditation processes of the General Social Care Council. Gradually but noticeably practice innovations in cross-cultural working and experimental projects with ethnic minority communities are gaining some ground as recognized processes and procedures, such as new ways of disseminating health promotion information and calls to take up services, but these need more formal evaluation if they are to be valued and sustainably resourced. While communities on the ground may approve of innovations such as meetings held in community centres, and assertive outreach through community-based clinics and events, business managers in the NHS and local authorities may regard these 'new media' as additional and not covered by their regular dissemination budgets. Too often, action taken to address the public health and information needs of 'minority ethnic' groups is seen as an additional add-on to the mainstream workload, and dropped when 'special funding' is withdrawn or comes to an end (as, for example, in the NHS 'pacesetters' programme or the CSIP DRE agenda). Only if such activities are 'validated' through formal evaluation of their cost-effectiveness will they be accepted as appropriate and normal aspects of a response to the public information duty, even when considering the requirements of the Race Relations Amendment Act and Equality Act duties, to address inequality. The extent to which welfare professionals are able to form new and productive alliances with ethnic minority groups and organizations is a delicate balance between their own comfort with new ways of working, the local politics of their area, the degree to which such joint working or co-production is supported and approved by policy makers and professional guidance, and the resource constraints which affect all working in a service where there are continued calls for efficiency savings and tighter budgets. Evidence-based practice requires, regrettably, evidence approved at the appropriate level e.g. by the National Institute for Health and Clinical Excellence (NICE) or the Social Care Institute for Excellence (SCIE) and the Care Quality Commission (CQC) before it is acceptable as a basis for action.

Perhaps less acknowledged is the potential role of research and academic professionals in advancing and advocating for transformations and change in welfare policy and practices. We might, indeed, argue that research is, or at least has the capacity to become, the alternative voice or democracy of the dispossessed – following Friere's pedagogy of the oppressed (1970). Craig (2007b) has argued that research funding for ethnicity research is relatively poor and that high-quality peer reviewed journals with few exceptions have been light on attention to articles on 'race'. Inputs from black and minority researchers in the field of health and welfare are clearly important to this transformational potential. There is an urgent need to expand the knowledge base of ethnicity research, and to explain the evidence base of the new ethnic demography of the UK, as a foundation for well-informed policy making. The CRE in its final report, for example, noted in relation to health inequalities and ethnicity that:

> The main problem is the absence of good qualitative data in the healthcare sector, which makes it impossible to monitor differences by ethnicity in the use of many NHS services. What data is being collected in secondary care is rarely used to change policy. The apparent lack of attention paid by the Department of Health to their responsibilities under the duty to promote race equality is, at least in part, due to the lack of available data on ethnicity in the health sector, and problems with ethnic monitoring in primary care. Systematic collection and analysis of data are vital to providing responsive, appropriate and equitable public services. The NHS has made only slow progress in addressing these concerns.
>
> (CRE 2007: 28)

A number of areas ripe for study are indicated by our review of the literature for this text, and are increasingly being highlighted by lobbying groups, such as the group of grassroots and lobbying organizations which proposed a 'Racial Justice Manifesto' in advance of the 2010 general election (see above). There is an evident need for research on the new legal context that is emerging, the application of equality law and the ways in which this impacts on the nature and standards of local governance and public service delivery. The potential impacts on minority ethnic groups of new directions in welfare delivery such as personalization of care and the privatization of care are areas which are under-researched, despite the statutory requirement for 'equality impact assessments' in all new areas of public policy, as is the role of faith-based and other third sector organizations in the development of the mixed economy of welfare. We need a greater understanding of the implications of ethnicity and racialization for democratic governance across the four nations of the UK and an in-depth understanding of the ability of ethnic minorities to engage with the new structures of welfare delivery. The prevalence and street-level influence on policy implementation of racism in all its manifestations requires deeper exploration, as does its impact on Black and minority ethnic welfare professionals. How do policy makers, advisers and practitioners understand concepts of ethnicity, culture, nation and other notions of difference that impact on governance? Up-to-date ethnicity mapping is long overdue, given age shifts, new migrations and other changes to the profile of ethnic demography. Challenges also need to be made to ideas such as 'self-segregation', co-ethnic and co-faith exclusion (or inclusion) through the development of demonstrable evidence. These, among many others, are necessary lines of enquiry if we are to understand the policy and practice issues thrown up by the new welfare arrangements for Black and ethnic minorities.

Towards a welfare society

What is clear from the discussion above is that considerable efforts are required at every level of society and across a broad spectrum of institutions if the general well-being of Britain's Black and minority ethnic peoples is to be secured. The achievement of a welfare society will inevitably rely on greater levels of overall material equality, the eradication of racism and racial discrimination and greater levels of solidarity achieved through respect for, and acceptance of, difference and diversity. This is clearly not going to be realized through the actions of the state alone. Its legislative and social policy instruments will always be too blunt to tackle the range of issues that lie within the structure, institutions and culture of society and the evident lack of political will represents a major countervailing force to transformatory change. Tackling inequalities of this nature implies not just state actions but collective action by a range of stakeholders including welfare professionals, users of services, activists and communities and neighbourhoods across the villages, towns and cities of the UK. It demands our actions as citizens, both individually and collectively. However, the organization of delivery systems that facilitate and promote such agency, the determining of processes to provide opportunities for involvement and encourage engagement and the establishment of the principles of engagement, are the functions of refreshed public services. In this respect, a decade on from the Parekh Report (Parekh Commission 2000) and its far-reaching recommendations, we would argue that greater opportunities do exist for the securing of a multicultural welfare system.

We have used the notion of a welfare society to suggest the forging of new sets of obligations across civil society and new relationships between the state, the individual and communities. For us this implies new and innovative ways of facilitating these interconnections within and between the welfare arenas, and the opening up of opportunities and sites for dialogue, struggle and contestation over welfare outcomes. We have been concerned in this text with delivery mechanisms, with the ways in which the sectors of the mixed economy of welfare are changing and the ways in which they are playing their part in response to identified needs of ethnic minorities. There is evidently a long way to go in establishing the framework for genuine engagement.

The achievement of strong, integrated and sustainable services to meet these needs will rely not on the development of ideal structures or standardized formulas for service delivery but on flexible arrangements forged by reference to agreed principles and processes. Formal structures will inevitably be doomed to fail and will be subject to change as governments change. The search for ideal structures is now in retreat; more significant to transformatory change is the contemporary shift to individuals and communities – to people and to a re-examination of the values and cultures of welfare. A welfare society must be people-led – led democratically and 'bottom up' by users and other welfare actors on the front line, from which structures will evolve merely as facilitating agency. We envisage the development of different structures evolving through engagements in different contexts and constellations against set, or at least communally agreed and equitable, outcomes, confident in the security of shared principles of welfare and minimum values. It behoves us therefore to briefly spell out what we see as some of the essential ingredients of a multicultural welfare system.

Transforming the public service culture

The process of forging new relationships between the various sectors in the mixed economy of welfare is under way. However, changes are required to *ways of working* and to bureaucratic processes in order to promote more openness and engagement of partners in the process of determining welfare outcomes. Greater shifts are needed by public servants in handing over power to users of services as relational citizens rather than the atomized individual of the neo-liberal politics, to moving away from assimilationist and universalist approaches and in responsiveness to difference. The token inclusion of a few 'users' in planning is not enough: the profile of control must reflect the diversity that exists among users. More sophisticated welfare practices are demanded by the contemporary reconfiguration of welfare delivery. This entails a commitment to developing new alliances in order to promote innovations and experimentation in service delivery.

Minimum values – embedded in quality measures

This acknowledges that in a plural society there are plural and often competing and conflicting value systems that must be negotiated. It challenges public services and public service professionals to expose as non-neutral the liberal monocultural values of their institution and confidently to reflect on the assumptive and normative ('white norms') world view which denies the value base of other cultures. These minimum values would rightly be based on a human rights culture.

It is necessary to make an explicit acknowledgement about this: silence over competition may mean that issues and needs are overlooked, and people from groups with a weaker bargaining position will be suspicious that their rights and needs are overlooked. A statement of minimum values would make clear that their rights and interests must be preserved, and would list the key 'strands' or parameters of inequality, including 'race', religion/faith/ spirituality, ethnic origin and sexuality, as is now commonly done in 'equality impact assessments' (EIA). Indeed, the holding of an EIA should now be part of the process of assuring minimum value quality standards, as those minimum values must include attention to equality of dignity. While some of those values are practised in the private realm and may not be shown publicly there is, especially in the field of welfare, an overlap between the public and the private – in order to assure minimum standards of welfare for all.

Flexible decentralized service delivery

Service delivery is gradually being taken closer to people but more effort needs to be made to support people from different ethnic groups to participate in localized service delivery. An ongoing commitment to ensuring more voice and representation in shaping public policy is needed and increased support will be required to engage previously excluded or 'hard to reach' groups which will only be achieved through sustained capacity building. The development of new processes has the potential to create fora and other mechanisms (perhaps using the new technologies) that allow for the expression of competing viewpoints and conflicts of interest to be worked through in a dialogue aimed at determining negotiated outcomes. The mobilization and sustainable development of the 'black' voluntary sector is crucial to this development.

Mutual understanding born out of experiential encounters

This is an acceptance of the significance of the politics of recognition to the power base of minority groups but is also an acknowledgement that diversity is dynamic and in constant flux. It works against the tendency to groupism or the rigid and stereotyped categorization of minority groups which defies their lived affiliations and identities. Accordingly it implies that models of meaning of racialization – i.e. those models on which we base our definitions of difference – are constantly changing and must not be fossilized and essentialized in care responses.

Confident and fine-tuned data

There is a ongoing need for accurate and fine-tuned data on ethnicity to guide policy intervention. As we have said above, there is no benefit in pretending that people are not different. Therefore, it is essential that when services are monitored and audited, or collect data for their own internal purposes, they should collect data on all aspects of diversity that may create inequality. This is especially true in relation to 'racialized' categories – where it is important that people are given the opportunity to select their own description ('self-assigned ethnicity') and that categories are used that reflect the reality and complexity of their lives. Crude labels such as 'Asian' conceal more than they inform, and it may be necessary to ask about religion, language and other dimensions, as well as adding categories (such as Arab, Vietnamese, etc.) to reflect changing populations, the growth of new migrations, and the needs of service provision to meet specific requirements and cultural values. This is as true in collection of routine monitoring data as it is in research. Such data can then inform both policy and practice.

A deracialised politics and refreshed discursive strategies

A commitment to the strategic development of a multicultural welfare must not be subject to or fuel popular sentiments, fears and anxieties about Black and minority ethnic peoples. Indeed, it requires a positive emphasis on the benefits of diversity and new inputs to the whole society. This requires a decoupling of immigration and domestic welfare policy and a retreat from a politics of assimilation that implies the levelling out of diversity. It implies more focused efforts on the building of socially mixed communities to foster encounters with difference and build solidarities. Greater emphasis should be given to the 'contributions' narrative over the 'drain on resources' narrative that has hitherto marked the story of 'race' and welfare.

Legal and ethical mandates on equalities and protection of rights

While legal measures alone cannot ensure the enforcement of rights, they are crucial to setting standards, laying down fundamental principles and providing minimum guarantees. As has been found, following the various rounds of 'privatization' and deregulation that public services have undergone since 1948, regulation is essential to ensure that the 'hidden hand' of the market does not overlook the needy and enforce essential quality standards that operate in the interests of a whole society rather than a select band of shareholders. Such measures provide the ground rules or framework within which to negotiate conflicts of rights between individuals or between society and groups of individuals and drive changes in behaviours. As such they are the bedrock on which dialogue, negotiation and an equalities and human rights culture can be built and lay down clear standards in relation to race equality.

These broad statements underpin what we would argue is a developmental process toward the co-production of a multicultural welfare system. In the current context communities themselves are becoming more governmental and gradually more equipped to participate in and shape systems of governance. It is as yet early days in terms of managing and negotiating the new welfare arrangements but particular concerns must be flagged about the lack of sustainability and inability of welfare professionals, policy makers and academics to capitalize on the strenuous efforts and gains made by black and minority ethnic organizations in civil society. While they experience a number of difficulties, both internal and external, these organizations are pivotal to the changes we outline. As we argued in our opening chapter, the challenge for public services is how to harness this resource toward transformative change effectively. Cultural diversity is not a problematic of the new welfare arrangements but a vital resource for its development.

References

Abrahamsson, A., Andersson, J. and Springett, J. (2009) Building bridges or negotiating tensions? Experiences from a project aimed at enabling migrant access to health and social care in Sweden, *Diversity in Health and Care*, 6 (2): 85–95.

Afiya Trust (2010) *Achieving Equality in Health and Social Care: A Framework for Action*. London: Afiya Trust. www.afiyatrust.org.uk.

Afshari, R. and Bhopal, R. S. (2010) Ethnicity has overtaken race in medical science: MEDLINE-based comparison of trends in the USA and the rest of the world 1965–2005, *International Journal of Epidemiology*, 1–3 (doi: 10.1093/ije/dyp382) [Advance access publication 20 Jan 2010].

Age Concern (2001) *Ethnic Elders: Access, Equality. The Impact of Government Policy for Black and Minority Ethnic Elders*. London: Age Concern.

Agyeman, J. and Spooner, R. (1997) Ethnicity and the rural environment, in P. Cloke and J. Little (eds), *Contested Countryside Cultures*. London: Routledge.

Ahmad, W.I.U. (1996) Family obligations and social change among Asian communities, in W.I.U. Ahmad and K. Atkin (eds) *Race and Community Care*. Buckingham: Open University Press.

Ahmad, W.I.U. (2000) *Ethnicity, Disability and Chronic Illness*. Buckingham: Open University Press.

Ahmad, W.I.U. and Atkin, K. (eds) (1996) *'Race' and Community Care*. Buckingham: Open University Press.

Ahmad, N., Pinnock, K., Morgan, A., Osidipe, T. *et al.* (2007) *Civic Participation: Potential Differences between Ethnic Groups*. London: Commission for Racial Equality.

Aldridge, J. and Becker, S. (1996) *Befriending Young Carers: A Pilot Study*. Loughborough: Young Carers Research Group for the Gulbenkian Foundation.

Alexander, Z. (1999) *Department of Health: Study of Black, Asian and Ethnic Minority Issues*. London: The Stationery Office.

Ali, N., Atkin, K., Craig, G., Dadze-Arthur, A. *et al.* (2006) *Ethnicity, Disability and Work*. London: RNIB.

Alibhai-Brown, Y. (2000) *After Multiculturalism*. London: Foreign Policy Centre.

Allan, H. and Larsen, J.A. (2003) *We Need Respect: Experiences of Internationally Recruited Nurses in the UK*. London: Royal College of Nursing. http://www.rcn.org.uk/__data/assets/pdf_file/0008/78587/002061.pdf [Accessed 26 February 2010].

Anderson, B. (2007) A very private business: exploring the demand for migrant domestic workers, *European Journal of Women's Studies*, 14: 247–64.

Anionwu, E.N. and Atkin, K. (2001) *The Politics of Sickle Cell and Thalassaemia*. Buckingham: Open University Press.

Anwar, M. (1979) *The Myth of Return: Pakistanis in Britain*. London: Heinemann.

Atkin, K. and Chattoo, S. (2007) The dilemmas of providing welfare in an ethnically diverse state: seeking reconciliation in the role of a 'reflexive practitioner', *Policy and Politics*, 35(3): 377–93.

Attwood, C., Singh, G., Prime, D., Creasey, R. *et al.* (2003) *2001 Home Office Citizenship Survey: People, Families and Communities, Home Office Research Study 270*. London: Home Office.

Audit Commission (2002) *Recruitment and Retention: A Public Service Workforce for the Twenty-first Century*. London: Audit Commission.

Bachrach, P. and Baratz, M.S. (1962) Two faces of power, *The American Political Science Review*, 56(4): 947–52.

Back, L., Keith, M., Khan, A., Shukra, K. and Solomos, J. (2002) The return of assimilationism: race, multiculturalism and New Labour, *Sociological Research Online*, 7(2) http://www.socresonline.org.uk/7/2/back.html [Accessed 18 April 2010].

Ballard, R. (1979) Ethnic minorities and the social services: what kind of service, in V.S. Khan (ed.) *Minority Families in Britain: Support and Stress*. London: Macmillan.

Bartnik, E. and Chalmers, R. (2007) It's about more than the money: local area coordination supporting people with disabilities, *Research Highlights in Social Work*, 49: 19–38.

Bashford, J. (2008a) A basic framework for cultural competency, in J. Fountain and J. Hicks (eds) *Delivering Race Equality in Mental Health Care: Report on the Findings and Outcomes of the Community Engagement Programme 2005–2008*. London: National Mental Health Development Unit.

Bashford, J. (2008b) An investigation into the effectiveness of organisational change management processes for implementing race equality post the Race Relations (Amendment) Act 2000. PhD thesis, University of Central Lancashire, Preston.

Baxter, C. (1997) The case for bilingual workers within the maternity services, *British Journal of Midwifery*, 5(9): 568–72.

Becker, S., Aldridge, J. and Dearden, C. (1998) *Young Carers and their Families*. Oxford: Blackwell Science.

Begum, N. (1992) *Something to be Proud Of: The Lives of Asian Disabled People and Carers in Waltham Forest*. London: Waltham Forest Race Relations Unit.

Begum, N. (2006) *Doing it for Themselves: Participation and Black and Minority Ethnic Service Users (Participation Report 14)*. London: Social Care Institute for Excellence and Race Equality Unit.

Beishon, S., Virdee, S. and Hagell, A. (1995) *Nursing in a Multi-ethnic NHS*. London: Policy Studies Institute.

Bhalla, A. and Blakemore, K. (1981) *Elders of the Minority Ethnic Groups*. Birmingham: AFFOR.

Bhattacharya, G. (2003) *Across All Boundaries: 25 Years of Asian Resource Centre in Birmingham*. Birmingham: Asian Resource Centre. http://www.asianresource. org.uk/anniv-book.pdf [Accessed 20 May 2009].

Bhavnani, R., Mirza, H.S. and Meetoo, V. (2005) *Tackling the Roots of Racism: Lessons for Success*. York: Joseph Rowntree Foundation.

Bhopal, K. (2006) Issues of rurality and good practice: gypsy traveller pupils in schools, in S. Neal and J. Agyeman (eds) *The New Countryside? Ethnicity, Nation and Exclusion in Contemporary Rural Britain*. Bristol: The Policy Press.

Bhopal, R. (2005) Hitler on race and health in *Mein Kampf*: a stimulus to anti-racism in the health professions, *Diversity in Health and Social Care*, 2(2): 119–26.

Bhui, K. and Sashidharan, S. (2003) Should there be separate psychiatric services for ethnic minority groups?, *British Journal of Psychiatry*, 182: 10–12.

Bhui, K., Warfa, N., Edonya, P., McKenzie, K. *et al*. (2007) Cultural competence in mental health care: a review of model evaluations, *BMC Health Services Research*, 7(15).

Black Carers Manifesto (2000) (National Black Carers Network and Afiya Trust). No longer available in print but cited in *Community Care* news item and posted at http://www.communitycare.co.uk/Articles/2001/03/01/30048/services-fail-black-carers.html [Accessed 13 August 2009].

Blunkett, D. (2001) From strength to strength: rebuilding the community through voluntary action, a speech to the Annual Conference of the National Council for Voluntary Organisations, 7 February, London.

Boeck, T., Fleming, J., Smith, R. and Thorp, L. (2009) *Volunteering and Faith Communities in England*. London: Volunteering England.

Bonnet, A. (2002) *Anti-Racism*. London: Routledge.

Boorman, S. (2009) *NHS Health and Well-being Final Report*. London: Department of Health. http://www.nhshealthandwellbeing.org/FinalReport.html [Accessed 26 February 2010].

Borrás-Alomar, S., Christiansen, T. and Rodríguez-Pose, A. (1994) Towards a 'Europe of the regions'? Visions and reality from a critical perspective', *Regional Politics and Policy*, 4(2): 1–27.

Bowler, I. (1993) 'They're not the same as us': midwives' stereotypes of South Asian descent maternity patients, *Sociology of Health and Illness*, 15(2): 157–78.

Bowler, I. (2004) Ethnic profile of doctors in the United Kingdom: a diverse group of doctors would appreciate the concerns of the population better, *British Medical Journal*, 32: 583–84.

Brackertz, N. (2007) Who is hard to reach and why? ISR Working Paper, Hawthorn, Victoria, Australia: Swinburne University of Technology, Institute for Social Research. http://www.sisr.net/publications/0701brackertz.pdf [Accessed 29 January 2010].

Bright, M. (2004) Plea to stem rural fears over asylum, *Observer*, 15 February.

Brown, C. and Lawton, J. (1991) Training for equality: a study of race relations and equal opportunities training, Discussion Paper 33. London: Policy Studies Institute.

Brown, R. (1995) Racism and immigration in Britain, *International Socialism Journal*, 68. http://pubs.socialistreviewindex.org.uk/isj68/brown.htm [Accessed 28 August 2009].

Bryan, B., Dadzie, S. and Scafe, S. (1985) *The Heart of the Race: Black Women's Lives in Britain.* London: Virago Press.

Burman, E., Smailers, S.L. and Chantler, K. (2004) 'Culture' as a barrier to service provision and delivery: domestic violence service for minoritized women, *Critical Social Policy*, 24(3): 332–57.

Busia, K. (1966) *Urban Churches in Britain.* London: Lutterworth Press for World Council of Churches.

Cabinet Office (2003) *Ethnic Minorities and the Labour Market: Final Report.* London: Cabinet Office. http://www.cabinetoffice.gov.uk/strategy/work_areas/ethnic_minorities.aspx [Accessed 26 February 2010].

Cabinet Office (2006) *Partnership in Public Services: An Action Plan for Third Sector Involvement.* London: Cabinet Office.

Campbell, C. and McLean, C. (2002) Ethnic identities, social capital and health inequalities: factors shaping African–Caribbean participation in local community networks in the UK, *Social Science and Medicine*, 55(4): 643–57.

Campinha-Bacote, J. (2003) Cultural desire: the key to unlocking cultural competence, *Journal of Nursing Education*, 42(6): 239–40.

Cangiano, A., Shutes, I., Spencer, S. and Leeson, G. (2009) *Migrant Care Workers in Ageing Societies: Research Findings in the United Kingdom.* Oxford: COMPAS.

Cantle, T. (2005) *Community Cohesion: A New Framework for Race and Diversity.* Basingstoke: Palgrave Macmillan.

Cantle, T. (2006) Community cohesion and the voluntary sector, National Association of Councils for Voluntary Service, *Circulation*, 3882(1).

Carers UK (2008) *NHS Next Stage Review: Policy Response from Carers UK*, January. http://www.carersuk.org.

Carnegie RARP (2009) Carnegie UK Trust Rural Action Research Programme. http://rural.carnegieuktrust.org.uk/rarp.

Carneiro, I.G., Ortega, A., Borg, V. and Høgh, A. (2009) Health and sickness absence in Denmark: a study of elderly-care immigrant workers, *Journal of Immigrant and Minority Health*, 12(1): 43–52.

Carr, J. (1996) *The Role of Management and Trade Unions in Promoting Equal Opportunities in Employment.* Strasbourg: Community Relations, Directorate of Social and Economic Affairs, Council of Europe Publishing.

Catto, G. (2008) A profession of equals, *Diversity in Health and Social Care*, 5(4): 235–6.

Caust, M., Berzins, K., Fleming, T., Kandola, M., Khan, A., Landry, C. *et al.* (2006) *Planning and Engaging with Intercultural Communities: Building the Knowledge and Skills Base.* London: Comedia and Academy for Sustainable Communities.

CCETSW (Central Council for Education and Training in Social Work) (1991) *One Small Step towards Racial Justice*. London: CCETSW.

CEMVO (Council for Ethnic Minority Voluntary Organizations) (2005) Understanding, accepting and valuing each other, report for NCVO, weblink no longer available. London: Council of Ethnic Minority Voluntary Organisations.

Chahal, K. (1999) *Minority Ethnic Homelessness in London: Findings from a Rapid Review*. London/Preston: Federation of Black Housing Organisations/University of Central Lancashire for NHS Executive.

Chahal, K. (2004) *Experiencing Ethnicity: Discrimination and Service Provision*. York: Joseph Rowntree Foundation.

Chakraborti, N. and Garland, J. (eds) (2004) *Rural Racism*. Uffculme, Devon: Willan Publishing.

Chan, C.K., Cole, B. and Bowpitt, G. (2007) Beyond silent organizations: a reflection of the UK Chinese people and their community organizations, *Critical Social Policy*, 27: 509–33.

Chaney, P. (2002) 'An absolute duty': the Assembly's Statutory Equality of Opportunity Imperative – Standing Committee on Equality of Opportunity, in J. Barry Jones, and J. Osmond, (eds) *Building a Civic Culture: Policy, Process and Institutional Change in the National Assembly*, Volume II, 2001–02. Cardiff: IWA.

Chaney, P. (2004) The Post-devolution equality agenda: the case of the Welsh Assembly's statutory duty to promote equality of opportunity, *Policy and Politics*, 32 (1): 37–52.

Chaney, P. (2009) *Equal Opportunities and Human Rights: The First Decade of Devolution*. Manchester: Equality and Human Rights Commission.

Channer, Y. and Doel, M. (2009) Beyond qualification: experiences of black social workers on a post-qualifying course, *Social Work Education*, 28(4): 396–412.

Chatterji, M. and Mumford, K. (2008) Flying high and laying low in the public and private sectors: a comparison of pay differentials for full-time male employees in Britain. University of Dundee Discussion Paper No. 209. Dundee: University of Dundee. http://www.dundee.ac.uk/econman/discussion/DDPE_209.pdf [Accessed 26 February 2010].

Chau, R.C.M. and Yu, S.W.K. (2001) Social exclusion of Chinese people in Britain, *Critical Social Policy*, 21(1): 103–25.

Cheung, S.Y. and Heath, A. (2007) Nice work if you can get it: ethnic penalties in Great Britain, *Proceedings of the British Academy*, 137: 507–50.

Chevannes, M. (2001) An evaluation of the recruitment of black and minority ethnic students to pre-registration nursing, *Nursing Times Research*, 6(2): 626–35.

Chouhan, K. (2004) One big equality mush. Britain's black communities don't trust a single super-quango to defend their rights. Will New Labour listen? *Guardian*, 30 November. http://www.guardian.co.uk/world/2004/nov/30/race.politics.

Chouhan, K. and Lusane, C. (2004) *Black Voluntary and Community Sector Funding: Its impact on Civic Engagement and Capacity Building*. York: Joseph Rowntree Foundation.

Clark, H., Gough, H. and McFarlane, A. (2004) *It Pays Dividends: Direct Payments and Older People*. Bristol: The Policy Press.

Clark, J. (2004) *Changing Welfare, Changing States: New Directions in Social Policy*. London: Sage Publications.

Clark, K. and Drinkwater, S. (2006) Changing patterns of minority ethnic self employment in Britain: evidence from census micro data, IZA Discussion Paper 2495. Bonn: IZA.

Clark, K. and Drinkwater, S. (2007) *Ethnic Minorities in the Labour Market: Dynamics and Diversity*. York: Joseph Rowntree Foundation. http://www.jrf.org.uk/sites/files/jrf/1986-ethnic-minorities-employment.pdf.

Clark, M., Owen, D., Szczepura, A. and Johnson, M. (1998) *Assessment of the Costs to the NHS Arising from the Need for Interpreter, Advocacy and Translation (IAT) Services*. Coventry: CHESS and CRER, University of Warwick, Report for the Technical Advisory Group and Advisory Committee on Resource Allocation, NHS Executive.

Clayton, T. (2005) 'Diasporic otherness': racism, sectarianism and 'national exteriority' in modern Scotland, *Social and Cultural Geography*, 6(1): 99–116.

Cloke, P. (2004) Rurality and racialised others: out of place in the countryside?, in S. Neal and J. Agyeman (eds) *The New Countryside? Ethnicity, Nation and Exclusion in Contemporary Rural Britain*. Bristol: The Policy Press.

Cloke, P., Goodwin, M. and Milbourne, P. (1998) Inside looking out: different experiences of cultural competences in rural lifestyles, in P. Boyle and K. Halfacre (eds) *Migration to Rural Areas*. Chichester: John Wiley.

Coker, N. (ed.) (2001) *Racism in Medicine: An Agenda for Change*. London: King's Fund.

Condor, S., Gibson, S. and Abell, J. (2006) English identity and ethnic diversity in the context of UK constitutional change, *Ethnicities*, 6(2): 123–58.

Connolly, P. (2006) 'It goes without saying (well, sometimes)': racism, Whiteness and identity in Northern Ireland in S. Neal and J. Agyeman (eds) *The New Countryside? Ethnicity, Nation and Exclusion in Contemporary Rural Britain*. Bristol: The Policy Press.

Connolly, P. and Keenan M. (2001) *The Hidden Truth about Racial Harassment in Northern Ireland*. http://www.paulconnolly.net/publications/pdf_files/thehiddentruth.pdf.

Connolly, P. and Keenan, M. (2002) *Tackling Racial Inequalities in Northern Ireland: Structures and Strategies*. Belfast: NISRA.

Craig, G. (2007a) Community capacity-building: Something old, something new . . .?, *Critical Social Policy*, 27(3): 335–59.

Craig, G. (2007b) 'Cunning, unprincipled and loathsome': the racist tail wags the welfare dog, *Journal of Social Policy*, 36(4): 605–23.

Craig, G. (2009) *Civil Society Associations and the Values of Social Justice: Report for the Carnegie UK Trust Inquiry into the Future of Civil Society in the UK and Ireland*. London: Carnegie Trust. http://www.carnegieuktrust.org.uk/files/main/Civil%

20society%20associations%20and%20the%20values%20of%20social%20jus tice%20-%20summary.pdf [Accessed 29 January 2010].

Craig, G. and Lachman, R. (2008) Black and minority ethnic voluntary and community sector organisations in rural areas and DEFRA: a thinkpiece from the North Yorkshire Black and Minority Ethnic Strategy Board (NYBSB) in response to the DEFRA Consultation Document. Gary.Craig@Garyc.demon.co.uk.

Craig, G. and Manthorpe, J. (2000) Unequal partners? Local government reorganization and the voluntary sector, *Social Policy and Administration*, 33(1): 55–72.

Craig, G. and Taylor, M. (2002) Dangerous Liaisons: Partnership Working and the Voluntary Sector, in C. Glendinning, M. Powell and K. Rummery (eds) *Partnerships, New Labour and the Governance of Welfare*. Bristol: The Policy Press.

Craig, G., Taylor, M., Wilkinson, M., Bloor, K. *et al.* (2002) *Contract or Trust? The Role of Compacts in Local Governance*. Bristol: The Policy Press.

CRE (Commission for Racial Equality)(1983) *Ethnic Minority Hospital Staff* (Report). London: Commission for Racial Equality.

CRE (1987) Memorandum submitted by the Commission for Racial Equality in response to the paper: Primary Health Care: an agenda for discussion. London: Commission for Racial Equality

CRE (2006) *Common Ground: Equality, Good Race Relations and Sites for Gypsies and Irish Travellers*. London: Commission for Racial Equality.

CRE (2007) *A Lot Done, A Lot to Do: Our Vision for an Integrated Britain*. London: Commission for Racial Equality.

Cruess, R.L., Cruess, S.R. and Johnston, S.E. (2000) Professionalism: an ideal to be sustained, *Lancet*, 356: 156–9.

CSCI (Commission for Social Care Inspection) (2009a) *Annual Report and Accounts 2008–9*. London: The Stationery Office. http://www.cqc.org.uk/_db/_documents/ 8251-CQC-CSCI-AR-Text.pdf.

CSCI (2009b) *Commission for Social Care Inspection State of Care Report (2007/8), article 694 National Action Plans and A8 migrants and Roma in Scotland*. Newcastle: Care Quality Commission. www.cqc.org.uCsp [Accessed 19 April 2010].

Culley, L. (2000) Working with diversity: beyond the factfile, in C. Davies, L. Finlay and A. Bullman, *Changing Practice in Health and Social Care*. London: Sage Publications/Open University Press.

Culley, L. and Dyson, S. (eds) (2001) *Ethnicity and Nursing Practice*. Basingstoke: Palgrave.

Culley, L., Dyson, S., Ham-Ying, S. and Young, W. (2001) Caribbean nurses and racism in the National Health Service, in L. Culley and S. Dyson (eds) *Ethnicity and Nursing Practice*. Basingstoke: Palgrave.

Dabydeen, D., Gilmore, J. and Jones, C. (2007) *The Oxford Companion to Black British History*. London: Oxford University Press.

Darr, A. (2001) The under-representation of Asian students on nursing, radiography and physiotherapy courses. Unpublished PhD Thesis, University of Bradford.

Darr, A. and Bharj, K. (1999) Addressing cultural diversities in health care – the challenge facing community nursing, in K. Atkin, N. Lunt and C. Thompson (eds) *Evaluating Community Nursing*. London: Bailliere Tindall.

Darr, A., Atkin, K., Johnson, M.R.D. and Archibong, U. (2007) *Improving the recruitment of people of South Asian origin into nursing: final report to the Department of Health*, unpublished report. Leeds: University of Leeds, Centre for Research in Primary Care.

Davis, S. and Cooke, V. (2002) *Why do Black Women Organise? A Comparative Analysis of Black Women's Voluntary Sector Organisations in Britain and their Relationship to the State*. London: Policy Studies Institute.

Day, G. (1998) A community of communities? Similarity and difference in Welsh rural community studies, *The Economic and Social Review*, 29(3): 233–57.

Day, G. (2006) Chasing the dragon? Devolution and the ambiguities of civil society in Wales, *Critical Social Policy*, 26(3): 642–55.

DCLG (Department of Communities and Local Government) (2006) *2005 Citizenship Survey, Active Communities Topic Report*. London: DCLG.

DCLG (Department for Communities and Local Government) (2007) *Preventing Violent Extremism: Winning Hearts and Minds*. London: DCLG.

DCLG (2009) *Tackling Race Inequalities Fund Prospectus*. London: DCLG.

DCLG (2010) *Tackling Race Inequality: A Statement on Race*. London: DCLG. http://www.communities.gov.uk/documents/communities/pdf/1432344.pdf [Accessed 18 April 2010].

De Lima, P. (2001) *Needs Not Numbers: An Exploration of Minority Ethnic Communities in Scotland*. London: CRE and Community Development Foundation.

De Lima, P. (2004) John O' Groats to Land's End: racial equality in Rural Britain?, in N. Chakroborti, and J. Garland, *Rural Racism*. Uffculme, Devon: Willan Publishing.

De Lima, P. and Wright, S. (2009) Welcoming migrants? Migrant labour in rural Scotland, *Social Policy and Society*, 8(3): 391–404.

Deakins, D., Ishaq, M., Smallbone, D., Whittam, G. and Wyper, J. (2007) Ethnic minority businesses in Scotland: the role of social capital, *International Small Business Journal*, 25(3): 307–26.

Dein, S. (2005) Opinions of medical practitioners completing a certificate in medical education with regard to 'culture' in the undergraduate medical training: a pilot project, *Diversity in Health and Social Care*, 2(1): 63–70.

Derbyshire, H. (1994) *Not in Norfolk: Tackling the Invisibility of Racism*. Norwich: Norwich and Norfolk Race Equality Council.

De Souza, P. (1991) A review of the experiences of black students in social work training, in CCETSW (eds) *One Small Step Towards Racial Justice*. London: CCETSW.

DH (Department of Health) (1999) *Caring about Carers: A National Strategy for Carers*. London: Department of Health.

DH (2000) *The NHS Plan: A Plan for Investment, a Plan for Reform*. London: Department of Health.

DH (2004) *The NHS Knowledge and Skills Framework (NHS KSF) and the Development Review Process.* Leeds: Department of Health.

Dhalech, M. (1999) *Challenging the Rural Idyll: Final Report of the Rural Racial Equality Project.* London: National Association of Citizens Advice Bureaux.

Dickens, L. (2007) The road is long: thirty years of equality legislation in Britain, *British Journal of Industrial Relations*, 45(3): 463–94.

Dinham, A., Furbey, R. and Lowndes, V. (eds) (2009) *Faith in the Public Realm: Controversies, Policies and Practices.* Bristol: The Policy Press.

Dogra, N. (2005) Cultural diversity teaching in the medical undergraduate curriculum, *Diversity in Health and Social Care*, 2(3): 233–45.

Dominelli, L. (1988) *Anti-racist Social Work.* London: Macmillan.

Drakeford, M. (2007) Private welfare, in M. Powell (ed.) *Understanding the Mixed Economy of Welfare.* Bristol: The Policy Press.

DTLR (Department for Transport, Local Government and the Regions) (2001) *Delivering Better Services for Citizens: A Review of Local Government Procurement in England.* London: Department for Transport, Local Government and the Regions.

Duffield, M.R. (1988) *Black Radicalism and the Politics of Deindustrialization: The Hidden History of Indian Foundry Workers in the West Midlands.* Aldershot: Avebury.

Dwyer, C. and Bressey, C. (2008) *New Geographies of Race and Racism.* Surrey: Ashgate.

Dyer, S., McDowell, L. and Batnitzky, A. (2008) Emotional labour/body work: the caring labours of migrants in the UK's National Health Service, *Geoforum*, 39(6): 2030–8.

EHRC (2009) *From Safety Net to Springboard: A New Approach to Care and Support for All Based on Equality and Human Rights.* London: Equality and Human Rights Commission. http://www.equalityhumanrights.com/uploaded_files/safetynet_ springboard.pdf [Accessed 26 February 2010].

Ellis, J. and Latif, S. (2006) *Capacity Building Black and Minority Ethnic Voluntary and Community Organisations: An Evaluation of CEMVO's London Pilot Programme.* York: Joseph Rowntree Foundation/Charities Evaluation Services.

Equalities Review (2007) *Fairness and Freedom: The Final Report of the Equalities Review.* London: The Stationery Office. http://archive.cabinetoffice.gov.uk/equalitiesreview/upload/assets/www.theequalitiesreview.org.uk/equality_review. pdf [Accessed 27 February 2010].

Esmail, A. (2001) Racism in admissions to medical school, in N. Coker (ed.) *Racism in Medicine.* London: Kings Fund.

Esmail, A. (2007) Asian doctors in the NHS: service and betrayal, *British Journal of General Practice*, 57(543): 827–34.

Esmail, A., Nelson, P. and Everington, S. (1996) Ethnic differences in applications to United Kingdom medical schools between 1990 and 1992, *New Community*, 22(3): 495–506.

ESRC/DTI/PSI Research Seminar Series (2005) Ethnicity and employment in the private sector, 26 January. http://www.psi.org.uk/eeps/seminar1.htm [Accessed 26 February 2010].

Evans, N. (2003) Immigrants and minorities in Wales 1840–1990: a comparative perspective, in C. Williams, N. Evans and P. O'Leary (eds) *A Tolerant Nation? Exploring Ethnic Diversity in Wales*. Cardiff: University of Wales Press.

Fanning, B. (2002) *Racism and Social Change in the Republic of Ireland*. Manchester: Manchester University Press.

Fanshawe, S. and Sriskandarajah, D. (2010) *'You Can't Put Me In a Box': Super-diversity and the End of Identity Politics in Britain*. London: IPPR.

Featherstone, L. (2010) *Race Equality and the Liberal Democrats: A Runnymede Platform Paper*. London: Runnymede Trust. www.runnymedetrust.org.

Finch, J. and Groves, D. (eds) (1983) *A Labour of Love: Women, Work and Caring*. London: Routledge and Kegan Paul.

Finney, N. and Simpson, L. (2009) *'Sleepwalking to Segregation'? Challenging Myths about Race and Migration*. Bristol: The Policy Press.

Firth, S. (2001) *Wider Horizons: Care of the Dying in a Multicultural Society*. London: National Council for Hospice and Specialist Palliative Care Services.

Fleming, E. and Gillibrand, W. (2009) An exploration of culture, diabetes, and nursing in the South Asian community: a metasynthesis of qualitative studies, *Journal of Transcultural Nursing*, 20(2): 146–55.

Flett, H. (1979) *Black Council Tenants in Birmingham: Working Papers on Ethnic Relations 12*. Bristol: SSRC Research Unit on Ethnic Relations, University of Bristol.

Foster, J. and Mirza, K. (1997) *By the People: Voluntary Activity by African– Caribbean and Asian Communities in Luton*. London: The National Centre for Volunteering.

Fraser, S. (ed.) (1995) *The Bell Curve Wars: Race, Intelligence, and the Future of America*. Scranton, PA: Harper Collins.

Friere, P. (1970) *The Pedagogy of the Oppressed*. New York: Continuum Publishing Company.

Fryer, P. (1984) *Staying Power*. London: Pluto Press.

Gaffin, J., Hill, D. and Penso, D. (1996) Opening doors: improving access to hospice and specialist palliative care services by members of the black and minority ethnic communities, *British Journal of Cancer (Supplement)*, 29: S 51–53.

Garland, J. and Chakraborti, N. (2002) *Tackling the Invisible Problem? An Examination of the Provision of Services to Victims of Racial Harassment in Rural Suffolk*. Leicester: Scarman Centre, University of Leicester.

Garland, J. and Chakraborti, N. (2006) 'Race', space and place: examining identity and cultures of exclusion in rural England, *Ethnicities*, 6(2): 159–77.

Garland, J. and Chakraborti, N. (2007) 'Protean times? Exploring the relationships between policing, community and 'race' in rural England, *Criminology and Criminal Justice*, 7(4): 347–65.

Garner, S. (2004) *Racism in the Irish Experience*. London: Pluto Press.

Genn, H. (1999) *Paths to Justice*. Oxford: Hart Publishing.

Gerrish, K., Husband, C. and Mackenzie, J. (1996) *Nursing for a Multi-ethnic Society*. Buckingham: Open University Press.

Gilroy, P. (1987) *There Ain't No Black in the Union Jack*. London: Hutchinson.

Ginn, J. and Arber, S. (2001) Pension prospects of minority ethnic groups: inequalities by gender and ethnicity, *British Journal of Sociology*, 52(3): 519–39.

Glendinning, C. (1983) *Unshared Care*. London: Routledge and Kegan Paul.

Goldacre, M.J., Davidson, J.M. and Lambert, T.W. (2004) Country of training and ethnic origin of UK doctors: database and survey studies, *BMJ*, 329: 597–60.

Goldstein, B. (2002) Black children with a white parent, *Social Work Education*, 21(5): 551–63.

Goodhart, D. (2004) Too diverse?, *Prospect*, 95: 1–6.

Gould, M. (2009) Better outcomes in diverse groups, *Health Service Journal*, 24 September: 20–1.

Graham, M. (2007) *Black Issues in Social Work and Social Care*. Bristol: The Policy Press.

Green, J. (1998) *Black Edwardians: Black People in Britain 1901–1914*. London: Frank Cass.

Green, M., Evandrou, M. and Falkingham, J. (2009) Older international migrants: who migrates to England and Wales in later life?, *Population Trends*, 137. http://www.statistics.gov.uk/articles/population_trends/MarcusGreenPT137web.pdf [Accessed 1 November 2009].

Grieve, D. (2010) *Conservatism and Community Cohesion: A Runnymede Platform Paper*. London: Runnymede Trust. www.runnymedetrust.org.

Hainsworth, P. (1998) *Divided Society: Ethnic Minorities and Racism in Northern Ireland*. London: Pluto Press.

Harris, M., Halfpenny, P. and Rochester, C. (2003) A social policy role for faith-based organisations? Lessons from the UK Jewish voluntary sector, *Journal of Social Policy*, 32(1): 93–112.

Hayes, D. (2000) Outsiders within: the role of welfare in the internal control of immigration, in B. Humphries and J. Batsleer (eds) *Welfare Exclusion and Political Agency*. London: Routledge.

Heath, A. (2001) *Ethnic Minorities in the Labour Market: Report to the Policy Implementation Unit, Cabinet Office*. Oxford: University of Oxford. http://www.cabinet office.gov.uk/media/cabinetoffice/strategy/assets/heathdata.pdf   [Accessed 17 August 2009].

Heath, A. and Cheung S.Y. (2006) Ethnic penalties in the labour market: employers and discrimination, Research Report No. 341. London: Department for Work and Pensions.

Heatherington, K. (2006) Visions of England: New Age Travellers and the idea of ethnicity, in S. Neal and J. Agyeman (eds) *The New Countryside: Ethnicity, Nation and Exclusion in Contemporary Rural Britain*. Bristol: The Policy Press.

Hechter, M. (1999) *Internal Colonialism: The Celtic Fringe in British National Development*. New Brunswick, NJ: Transaction Publishers.

Henderson, P. and Kaur, R. (eds) (1999) *Rural Racism in the UK*. London: Community Development Foundation.

Hills, J., Brewer, M., Jenkins, S., Lister, R. *et al.* (2010) *An Anatomy of Economic Inequality in the UK: Report of the National Equality Panel* (CASE Paper 60). London: Centre for Analysis of Social Exclusion, London School of Economics, for Government Equalities Office. http://sticerd.lse.ac.uk/dps/case/cr/CASEreport60.pdf [Accessed 26 February 2010].

Hirst, D. (2004) *Heart and Minds: The Health Effects of Caring*. London: Carers UK. http://www.york.ac.uk/inst/spru/pubs/pdf/HeartsandMinds.pdf [Accessed 3 March 2010].

HM Government (2007) The Equalities Review: Fairness and Freedom. Final Report of the Equalities Review. London: Cabinet Office. http://archive.cabinet-office.gov.uk/equalitiesreview/upload/assets/www.theequalitiesreview.org.uk/equality_review.pdf

HM Government (2008a) *Carers at the Heart of 21st-century Families and Communities: A Caring System On Your Side, A Life of your Own*. London: Department of Health.

HM Government (2008b) *Creating Strong, Safe and Prosperous Communities: Statutory Guidance*. http://www.communities.gov.uk/documents/localgovernment/pdf/885397.pdf.

HM Government (2009a) *The Equality Bill* (Bll 85 08–09), introduced to Parliament 24 April 2009, Volume 1. London: The Stationery Office. http://www.publications.parliament.uk/pa/cm200809/cmbills/085/voli/09085i.i-ii.html.

HM Government (2009b) *The Equality Bill* (Bll 85 08-09), introduced to Parliament 24 April 2009, Volume 2. London: The Stationery Office. http://www.publications.parliament.uk/pa/cm200809/cmbills/085/volii/09085ii.8-15.html [Accessed 29 January 2010].

HM Treasury (2007) *The Future Role of the Third Sector in Social and Economic Regeneration*. www.hm-treasury.gov.uk [Accessed 10 May 2010].

Hochschild, A.R. (2003) *The Commercialisation of Intimate Life*. Berkeley, CA: University of California Press.

Hodgson, L. (2004) Manufactured civil society, *Critical Social Policy*, 24(2): 130–64.

Hofstede, G. (2001) *Culture's Consequences: Comparing Values, Behaviors, Institutions, and Organizations across Nations*, 2nd ed. Thousand Oaks, CA: Sage Publications.

Hold, M. and Williams, C. (2007) *An Overview of the Race Equality Schemes and the Health, Social Care and Wellbeing Strategies Produced by Local Health Boards and Local Authorities, With a Focus on Representation, Consultation and Collaboration*. Wales Equality and Diversity in Health and Social Care Research and Support Service. www.wedhs.org.uk.

Holdaway, S. (1997) Constructing and sustaining 'race' within the police workforce, *British Journal of Sociology*, 48(1): 19–34.

Holder, D. and Lanao, C. (2002) *Other Voices: A Listening Session with a Rural Minority*

Ethnic Community in 2002. Belfast: Multi-cultural Resource Centre. http://www.mcrc-ni.org/PDFs/OtherVoices.pdf.

Home Office (2001) Black and Minority Ethnic Voluntary and Community Organisations: A Code of Good Practice. www.thecompact.org.uk.

Hudson, M. (2006) *The Hidden One in Five: Winning a Fair Deal for Britain's Vulnerable Workers*. London: TUC.

Hudson, M. and Parry, J. (2004) *Mapping the Terrain of the Private Sector in Relation to Race*. Report to the Commission for Racial Equality. London: Commission for Racial Equality.

Hussain, A. and Millar, W. (2006) *Multicultural Nationalism: Islamophobia, Anglophobia and Devolution*. Oxford: Oxford Scholarship Online Monographs. http://www.ingentaconnect.com/content/oso/1306561/2006/00000001/00000001/art00001 [Accessed 26 February 2010].

Hussain, Y., Atkin, K. and Ahmad, W. (2002) *South Asian Disabled Young People and their Families*. Bristol/York: The Policy Press/Joseph Rowntree Foundation.

Hussein, S. (2009) Social care workforce profile: age, gender and ethnicity, *Social Care Workforce Periodical 2*. http://www.kcl.ac.uk/content/1/c6/06/18/41/SCWPissue2FINAL.pdf [Accessed 26 February 2010].

ICC (Institute of Community Cohesion) and LGA (Local Government Association) (2007) Estimating the scale and impacts of migration at the local level, LGA Research Paper. http://www.lga.gov.uk/lga/aio/109536 [Accessed 18 April 2010].

Iganski, P. and Payne, G. (1996) Declining racial disadvantage in the British labour market, *Ethnic and Racial Studies*, 19(1): 113–34.

Iganski, P. and Payne, G. (1999) Socio-economic restructuring and employment: the case of minority ethnic groups, *British Journal of Sociology*, 50(2): 195–215.

Iganski, P., Mason, D., Humphreys, A. and Watkins, M. (2001) Equal opportunities and positive action in the British National Health Service: some lessons from the recruitment of minority ethnic groups into nursing and midwifery, *Ethnic and Racial Studies*, 24(2): 294–317.

Jacobs, S. (1985) Race, empire and the welfare state: council housing and racism, *Critical Social Policy*, 5(13): 6–28.

Jarman, N. (2002) *Overview Analysis of Racist Incidents Recorded in Northern Ireland by the RUC 1996–1999*. Northern Ireland: Office of the First Minister.

Jarman, N. and Monaghan, R. (2003) *Racist Harassment in Northern Ireland*. Belfast: Institute for Conflict Research.

Jay, E. (1992) *Keep Them in Birmingham: Challenging Racism in South West England*. London: Commission for Racial Equality.

Jefferys, S. (2007) Why do unions find fighting workplace racism difficult?, *Transfer*, 13(3): 377–91.

Jenkins, G. (1999) Labour and immigration: the badge of prejudice', *Socialist Review*, 234. http://pubs.socialistreviewindex.org.uk/sr234/jenkins.htm [Accessed 5 February 2010].

Jewson, N., Jeffers, S. and Kalra, U. (2003) *In Our Blood: Respite Services, Family Care and Asian Communities in Leicester*, 2nd edn. Leicester: Ethnicity Research Centre, University of Leicester.

Johns, N. (2004) Ethnic diversity policy: perceptions within the NHS, *Social Policy and Administration* 38(1): 73–88.

Johnson, M. and McGee, P. (2006) Developing culturally-competent services in palliative care: management perspectives, in R. Gatrad *et al.* (eds) *Valuing Diversity: Palliative Care for South Asians*. Swindon: Quay Books.

Johnson, M.R.D. (1986) Citizenship, social work and ethnic minorities, in S. Etherington, (ed.) *Social Work and Citizenship*. Birmingham: BASW.

Johnson, M.R.D. (1987) Housing as a process of racial discrimination, in S. Smith and J. Mercer (eds) *New Perspectives on Race and Housing in Britain*. Glasgow: Centre for Housing Research, Glasgow University.

Johnson, M.R.D. (1988) Mobility denied: Caribbean minorities in the UK labour market, in M. Cross and H. Entzinger (eds) *Lost Illusions*. London: Tavistock.

Johnson, M.R.D. (1991) The voluntary sector and race, in P. Lloyd, P.Marsden and D. Scott (eds) *Researching Voluntary and Community Action: Questions of Policy and Practice*. London: ARVAC.

Johnson, M.R.D. (1996) Ethnic Minorities, Health and Communication Research Paper in Ethnic Relations No. 24. Coventry: Centre for Research in Ethnic Relations, Warwick University (for NHS Executive and West Midlands Regional Health Authority).

Johnson, M.R.D. (1999) Offering an accessible service: Asian men's perceptions of primary health care staff, in *Practising Transcultural Healthcare: Integrating Race, Culture and Ethnicity into Healthcare Practice* (Proceedings of the Second National Conference of the Transcultural Nursing and Healthcare Association 1999). Birmingham: Health and Social Care Research Centre, University of Central England for TCNHCA and the Foundation of Nursing Studies.

Johnson, M.R.D. (2001) Ethnic monitoring and nursing, in L. Culley and S. Dyson (eds) *Ethnicity and Nursing Practice*. Basingstoke: Palgrave Macmillan.

Johnson, M.R.D. (2003a) *Asylum Seekers in Dispersal: Healthcare Issues*, Home Office Online Report 13/03, February. London: Home Office. www.homeoffice.gov.uk/rds/pdfs2/rdsolr1303.pdf.

Johnson, M.R.D. (2003b) Ethnic diversity in social context, in J. Kai (ed.) *Ethnicity, Health and Primary Care*. Oxford: Oxford University Press.

Johnson, M.R.D. (2008) Making difference count: ethnic monitoring in health (and social care), *Radical Statistics*, 96: 38–45.

Johnson, M.R.D. (2009) End of life care in ethnic minorities: providers need to overcome their fear of dealing with people from different backgrounds, *British Medical Journal*, 338: 489–90.

Johnson, M.R.D. and NBCCWN (ed.) (2008) *Beyond We Care Too: Putting Black Carers in the Picture*. London: Afiya Trust.

Johnson, M.R.D. and Verma, C. (1998) *It's Our Health Too: Asian Men's Health*

Perspectives, CRER Research Paper 26. Birmingham/Coventry: Southern Birmingham Community Health NHS Trust and NHS Executive Ethnic Health Unit/University of Warwick.

Johnson, M.R.D., Cross, M. and Cox, B. (1988) *Black Welfare and Local Government: Section 11 and Social Services Departments*, Policy Paper 12. Coventry: Centre for Research in Ethnic Relations, Warwick University.

Johnson, M.R.D., Cross, M. and Cox, B. (1989) Paying for change? Section 11 and local authority social services, *New Community*, 15(3): 371–90.

Johnson, M.R.D. with Chirico, S., Scott, M. and Pawar, A. (2000) *The Toolbox: Culturally Competent Organisations, Services and Care Pathways*. Bedford: Bedfordshire Health Promotion Agency

Johnson, M.R.D., Hamilton, P.M. and Essat, Z. (2008) *'Be Nice – Smile As You Do with Everyone'*, *Learning Multicultural Nursing in Leicester*, Seacole Research Paper No. 2. Leicester: Mary Seacole Research Centre.

Jones, K. and Smith, A.D. (1970) *The Economic Impact of Commonwealth Immigration*. Cambridge: Cambridge University Press.

JRSS (1983) Discussion on sources of statistics on ethnic minorities, *Journal of the Royal Statistical Society*, 146: 108.

Kable (2007) *Public Sector Outsourcing: The Big Picture to 2012*. London: Kable.

Karseras, P. and Hopkins, E. (1987) *British Asians' Health in the Community*. Chichester: John Wiley and Sons.

Katbamna, S., Ahmad, W., Bhakta, P. and Baker, R. (2004) Do they look after their own? Informal support for South Asian carers, *Health and Social Care in the Community*, 12(5): 398–406.

Katz, J.H. (1978) *White Awareness: A Handbook for Anti Racism Training*. Norman, OK: University of Oklahoma Press.

Katz, J.H. and Ivey, A. (1977) White awareness: the frontier of race awareness training, *Personnel and Guidance Journal*, 55(8): 485–9.

Kelly, F. and Papadopoulos, I. (2009) Enhancing the cultural competence of health-care professionals through an online course, *Diversity in Health and Care*, 6(2): 77–84.

Kenny, N. (1997) *It Doesn't Happen Here? A Report on Racial Harassment in Taunton Dean*. Somerset: Racial Equality Network.

Koskinen, L., Abdelhamid, P. and Likitalo, L. (2008) The simulation method for learning cultural awareness in nursing, *Diversity in Health and Social Care*, 5(1): 55–63.

Kyriakides, S. and Virdee, S. (2003) Migrant labour, racism and the British National Health Service, *Ethnicity and Health*, 8(4): 283–305.

Laing and Buisson (2007) *Care of Elderly People Market Survey 2007*. London: Laing and Buisson.

Laird, S.E. (2008) *Anti-oppressive Social Work: A Guide for Developing Cultural Competence*. London: Sage Publications.

Land, H. (2004) Privatisation, privatisation, privatisation: the British Welfare State since 1979, in N. Ellison, L. Bauld and M. Powell (eds) *Social Policy Review*, 16. Bristol: The Policy Press.

Law, I. (2009) Racism, ethnicity, migration and social security, in J. Millar (ed.) *Understanding Social Security*. Bristol: The Policy Press.

Layton Henry, Z. (1992) *The Politics of Immigration: Race and Race Relations in Post-war Britain*. Oxford: Blackwell.

Lee-Cunin, M. (1989) *Daughters of Seacole: A Study of Black Nurses in West Yorkshire*. Batley: West Yorkshire Low Pay Unit Ltd.

Leiberson, S. (1980) *A Piece of the Pie: Blacks and White Immigrants Since 1880*. Berkeley, CA: University of California Press.

Leigh, R. (2000) *Black Elders Project*. Leicester: Leicester Volunteer Centre.

Lemos, P. and Crane, G. (2000) *Tackling Racial Harassment in the NHS: Evaluating Black and Minority Ethnic Staff Attitudes and Experiences*. London: Department of Health.

Lentin, R. and McVeigh, R. (2002) *Racism and Anti-racism in Ireland*. Belfast: Beyond the Pale Publications.

Levitas, R. (2005) *The Inclusive Society: Social Exclusion and New Labour*. Basingstoke: Palgrave Macmillan.

Lewis, G. (2000a) *Race, Gender and Social Welfare: Encounters in a Postcolonial Society*. Cambridge: Polity Press.

Lewis, G. (2000b) Discursive histories: the pursuit of multiculturalism and social policy, in G. Lewis, S. Gerwirtz and J. Clark (eds) *Rethinking Social Policy*. London, Sage Publications.

Lewis, J. and Meredith, B. (1988) *Daughters Who Care*. London: Routledge and Kegan Paul.

LGA (Local Government Association) (2007) *Estimating the Scale and Impacts of Migration at the Local Level*. London: Local Government Association. http://news.bbc.co.uk/1/shared/bsp/hi/pdfs/01_11_07_immigration.pdf [Accessed 5 February 2010].

Li, P-L. and Logan, S. (1999) *The Mental Health Needs of Chinese People in England*. London: Chinese National Healthy Living Centre.

Like, R.C. (2008) Culturally competent medicine: an American perspective, *Diversity in Health and Social Care*, 5(2): 83–6.

Lipsky, M. (1980) *Street-level Bureaucracy: Dilemmas of the Individual in Public Services*. New York: Russell Sage Foundation.

Llwyd, A. (2005) *Cymru Ddu, Black Wales: A History*. Cardiff: Butetown History and Arts Centre.

Lukka, P. and Ellis, A. (2001) An exclusive construct? Exploring different cultural concepts of volunteering, *Journal of the Institute of Volunteering Research*, 3(3): 87–109.

Lustgarten, L. and Edwards, J. (1992) Racial equality and the limits of the law, in P. Braham, A. Rattansi and R. Skellington (eds) *Racism and Antiracism: Inequalities, Opportunities and Policies*. London: Sage Publications.

Luthra, M. and Oakley, R. (1991) *Combating Racism through Training: A Review of Approaches to Race Training in Organisations*, CRER Policy Paper No. 22. Coventry: University of Warwick.

Lyfar-Cisse, V. (2008) *Race Equality Service Review for NHS Trusts, PCTs and SHA in the NHS South East Coast Region*. Brighton: SECSHA Black and Minority Ethnic Network. http://www.miphealth.org.uk/_common/_core/server/svr-download.asp?fle=/ftp/articles-docs/BMENREServiceReviewSummaryReport.pdf [Accessed 29 January 2010].

Lynn, I.L. (1982) *The Chinese Community in Liverpool: Their Unmet Needs with respect to Education, Social Welfare and Housing*. Liverpool: University of Liverpool, Merseyside Area Profile Group.

McCleod, M., Owen, D. and Kahamis, C. (2001) *Black and Minority Ethnic Voluntary and Community Organisations: Their Role and Future Development in England and Wales*. London: Policy Studies Institute.

McClimont, B. and Grove, K. (2004) *Who Cares Now? An Updated Profile of the Independent Sector Home Care Workforce in England*. Sutton: United Kingdom Home Care Association Limited.

McCrone, D. (2006) Who do we think we are? In Commission for Racial Equality (ed.) *30: At the Turning of the Tide*. London: CRE.

MacEwen, M. (1991) *Housing, Race, and Law: The British Experience*. London: Routledge.

McGill, P. and Oliver, Q. (2002) *A Wake Up Call on Race: Implications of the Macpherson Report for Institutional Racism in Northern Ireland*. Belfast: The Equality Commission Northern Ireland. http://www.equalityni.org/archive/pdf/ECWakeUp.pdf.

McGlaughlin, E. and Neal, S. (2004) Misrepresenting the multicultural nation: the policy making process, news media management and the Parekh Report, *Policy Studies*, 25(3): 155–74.

McGregor, J. (2007) Joining the BBC (British Bottom Cleaners): Zimbabwean migrants and the UK care industry, *Journal of Ethnic and Migration Studies*, 33(5): 801–24.

Machin, J. (2005) *Volunteering and the Media: A Review of the Literature*. London: Institute for Volunteering Research for the Voluntary Action Media Unit.

McKay, S. and Winkelmann-Gleed, A. (2005) *Migrant Workers in the East of England: Project Report*. London: London Metropolitan University.

McLaughlin, E. (2005) Governance and social policy in Northern Ireland (1999–2004): the devolution years and postscript, in M. Powell, L. Bauld and K. Clarke (eds) *Social Policy Review 17: Anaysis and Debate in Social Policy* Bristol: The Policy Press.

McLaughlin, E. (2007) From negative to positive equality duties: the development and constitutionalisation of equality provisions in the UK, *Social Policy and Society*, 6(1): 111–21.

McLaughlin, E. and Baker, J. (2007) Equality, social justice and social welfare: a road map to the New Egalitarians, *Social Policy and Society*, 6(1): 53–68.

McLaughlin, K. (2005) From ridicule to institutionalisation: anti-oppression, the state and social work, *Critical Social Policy*, 25: 283–305.

Macpherson, W. (1999) *The Stephen Lawrence Inquiry: Report of an Inquiry by Sir William Macpherson of Cluny*. London: HMSO.

McVeigh, R. (1998) 'There's no racism because there's no black people here': racism and anti-racism in Northern Ireland, in P. Hainsworth (ed.) *Divided Society: Ethnic Minorities and Racism in Northern Ireland*. London: Pluto Press.

Magne, S. (2003) *Multi-ethnic Devon: A Rural Handbook. The Report of the Devon and Exeter Racial Equality Council's Rural Outreach Project*. Exeter: Devon and Exeter Racial Equality Council.

Malik, M. (2007) Modernising discrimination law: proposals for a single Equality Act for Great Britain, *International Journal of Discrimination and the Law*, 9(2): 73–94.

Marmot, M. (2010) *Fair Society, Healthy Lives: Strategic Review of Health Inequalities in England Post-2010*. London: University College of London Research Department of Epidemiology and Public Health. http://www.ucl.ac.uk/gheg/marmotreview [Accessed 26 February 2010].

Miles, R. and Dunlop, A. (1987) Racism in Britain: the Scottish dimension, in P. Jackson (ed.) *Race and Racism*. London: Urwin.

Miller, C. (2004) *Producing Welfare: A Modern Agenda*. Basingstoke: Palgrave Macmillan.

Mills, H. (2003) *Meeting the Needs of Black and Minority Ethnic Young Carers: A Literature Review and Research Study for the Willow Young Carers Service*. Essex: Barnardo's Policy, Research and Influencing Unit. http://www.barnardos.org.uk/meeting_needs_of_bme_young_carers_willow__040108.pdf [Accessed 5 February 2010].

Modood, T., Virdee, S. and Metcalf, H. (1996) *Asian Self-employment in Britain: The Interaction of Culture and Economics*. London: Policy Studies Institute. www.ukc.ac.uk/ESRC/papers/modood/modood1.html and www.ukc.ac.uk/ESRC/modrep.htm.

Modood, T., Berthoud, R., Lakey, J. and Nazroo, J. *et al.* (1997) *Ethnic Minorities in Britain: Diversity and Disadvantage (The Fourth National Study)*. PSI Report 843. London: Policy Studies Institute.

Mold, F., Fitzpatrick, J.M. and Roberts, J.D. (2005) Minority ethnic elders in care homes: a review of the literature, *Age and Ageing*, 34(2): 107–13.

Mooney, G. and Williams, C. (2006) Forging new 'ways of life': social policy and nation building in devolved Scotland and Wales, *Critical Social Policy*, 26(3): 608–29.

Mooney, G., Scott, G. and Williams, C. (2006) Introduction: rethinking social policy through devolution, *Critical Social Policy*, 26: 483–97.

Moore, M.H. (1995) *Creating Public Value Strategic Management in Government*. Boston, MA: Harvard University Press.

Morgan, R. (2003) Speech to the Global Britons Conference, Foreign Policy Institute, Cardiff, 11 February.

Morjaria-Keval, A. and Johnson, M.R.D. (2005) *Our Vision Too: Improving the Access of Ethnic Minority Visually Impaired People to Appropriate Services: Building a Supported Community Referral System*. Occasional Paper 10. London: Pocklington Trust /De Montfort University.

Murray, U. and Brown, D. (1998) *They Look After their Own, Don't They? Inspection of Community Care Services for Black and Minority Older People*. London: Department of Health Social Care Group and Social Services Inspectorate.

Nairn, T. (1977) *The Break-up of Britain: Crisis and Neo-nationalism*. London: NLB.

National Cancer Action Team (2009) *National BME Cancer Patient Experience Programme update*, 1: December.

National Cancer Equality Initiative (NCEI) (2009) *We Can: Reducing Inequalities in Commissioning Cancer Service. Principles and Practical Guidance for Good Equality Working*. London: National Cancer Equality Initiative (NCEI) for National Cancer Action Team.

National Children's Centre (1982) *The Silent Minority: The Report of a National Conference on Chinese Families in Great Britain*. London: Commonwealth Institute.

Navidi, U. (1997) *The Tables are Bare*. London: MSF.

Nazroo, J. (2010) Health and health care, in A. Bloch and J. Solomos (eds) *Race and Ethnicity in the Twenty-first Century*. Basingstoke: Palgrave Macmillan.

Nazroo, J.Y. (1997) *The Health of Britain's Ethnic Minorities*. London: Policy Studies Institute.

Nazroo, J.Y. (2003) 'The structuring of ethnic inequalities in health: economic position, racial discrimination and racism, *American Journal of Public Health*, 93(2): 277–84.

Nazroo, J.Y. (ed.) (2006) *Health and Social Research in Multicultural Societies*. Abingdon: Routledge.

NBCWN (National Black Carers Workers Network) (2000) *We Care Too*. London: Afiya Trust for National Black Carers Workers Network.

Neal, S. (2002) Rural landscapes, representations and racism: examining multicultural citizenship and policy making in the English countryside, *Ethnic and Racial Studies*, 25(3): 442–6.

Neal, S. and Agyeman, J. (2006) *The New Countryside: Ethnicity, Nation and Exclusion in Contemporary Rural Britain*. Bristol: The Policy Press.

Needham, C. and Carr, S. (2009) Co-production: an emerging evidence base for adult social care transformation. SCIE Research Briefing No. 31. London: Social Care Institute for Excellence. http://www.scie.org.uk/publications/briefings/files/briefing31.pdf [Accessed 5 February 2010].

Netto, G. (1999) 'I forget myself': the case for the provision of culturally sensitive respite care services for minority ethnic carers of older people, *Journal of Public Health Medicine*, 20(2): 221–8.

Netto, G. (2008) Multiculturalism in the devolved context: minority ethnic negotiation of identity through engagement in the arts in Scotland, *Sociology*, 42(1): 47–64.

Netto, G., Arshad, R., de Lima, P., Almeida Diniz, F. *et al.* (2001) *Audit of Research on Minority Ethnic Issues in Scotland from a 'Race' Perspective*. Edinburgh: Scottish Executive.

Newman, J. (2007) Rethinking 'the public' in troubled times: unsettling state, nation and the liberal public sphere, *Public Policy and Administration*, 22(1): 55–75.

NHS (2000) *The NHS Plan: A Plan for Investment, a Plan for Reform*, CM4818. London: Department of Health. http://www.dh.gov.uk/en/Publicationsandstatistics/Publications/PublicationsPolicyAndGuidance/DH_4002960.

NHSF (National Hindu Students Forum) (2009) *What is Sewa?* www.nhsf.org.uk [Accessed 19 November 2009].

NHS Health Scotland (2009) *Health in Our Multi-ethnic Scotland*. Glasgow: NHS Health Scotland. www.healthscotland.com/documents/3768.aspx [Accessed 26 February 2010].

Nizhar, P. (1995) *No Problem? Race Issues in Shropshire*. Shropshire: Telford and Shropshire Race Equality Forum.

NMC (2007) *Overseas Nurses Registration*. London: Nursing and Midwifery Council. http://www.nmc-uk.org/aArticle.aspx?ArticleID=1653 [Accessed 5 February 2010].

Obaze, D. (2000) *Noticeable by their Absence*. London: National Coalition for Black Volunteering.

O'Cinneide, C. (2001) The Race Relations (Amendment) Act 2000, *Public Law*: 220–32.

O'Cinneide, C. (2007) The commission for equality and human rights: a new institution for new and uncertain times, *Industrial Law Journal*, 36(2): 141–62.

OGC (Office of Government Commerce) (2008) *Buy and Make a Difference: How to Address Social Issues in Public Procurement*. London: OGC.

Ogenyi, E.O., Hirst, A. and Blankson, C. (2004) Food shopping behaviour among ethnic and non ethnic communities in Britain, *Journal of Food Products Marketing*, 10(4): 39–57.

O'Hagan, K. (2001) *Cultural Competence in the Caring Professions*. London: Jessica Kingsley.

ONS (Office for National Statistics) (2010) http://www.statistics.gov.uk/hub/index.html [Accessed 19 April 2010].

Orton, M. and Ratcliffe, P. (2005) New labour ambiguity, or neo-liberal consistency? The debate about racial inequality in employment and the use of contract compliance, *Journal of Social Policy*, 34(2): 255–72.

Osborne, H., Elliott, L. and Taylor, M. (2009) Councils 'not prepared for next wave of the recession', *Guardian*, 12 August. http://www.guardian.co.uk/jobsadvice/2009/aug/11/firms-hiring-migrant-workers-recession.

Osborne, R.D. (2003) Progressing the equality agenda in Northern Ireland, *Journal of Social Policy*, 32(3): 339–60.

Owen, D. (1993) The changing spatial distribution of ethnic minorities in Britain 1981–1991: analysis for National Ethnic Minority Data Archive. Unpublished report for University of Warwick, Coventry.

Owen, D. (1994) *Black People in Great Britain: Social and Economic Circumstances.* Census Statistical Paper No. 6. Coventry: National Ethnic Minority Data Archive.

Oxfam (2009) *Who Cares? How Best to Protect UK Care Workers Employed through Agencies and Gangmasters from Exploitation*, Briefing Paper No. 2. Oxford: Oxfam/Kalayaan.

Pacesetters (2008) *Making the Difference: The Pacesetters Beginner's Guide to Service Improvement for Equality and Diversity in the NHS*. London: Department of Health.

Pacione, M. (2005) The changing geography of ethnic minority settlement in Glasgow, 1951–2001, *Scottish Geographical Journal*, 121(2): 141–61.

Palese, A., Oliverio, F., Girardo, M.F., Fabbro, E. *et al.* (2004) Difficulties and workload of foreign caregivers: a descriptive analysis, *Diversity in Health and Social Care*, 2(1): 31–8.

Palese, A., Barba, M., Borghi, G., Mesaglio, M. *et al.* (2006) Romanian nurses' process of adaptation to Italian nursing practices during their first six months in Italy: a qualitative study, *Diversity in Health and Social Care*, 3(2): 123–30.

PAMECUS (2009) International Perspectives on Positive Action Measures: A Comparative Analysis in the European Union, Canada, the United States and South Africa. Luxembourg: Office for Official Publications of the European Communities.

Papps, E. and Ramsden, I (1996) Cultural safety in nursing: the New Zealand experience, *International Journal for Quality in Health Care*, 8(5): 491–7.

Parekh Commission (2000) *The Future of Multi-ethnic Britain* (Parekh Report). London: Profile Books.

Parker, G. (1992) Counting care: numbers and types of informal carers, in J. Twigg, (ed.) *Carers: Research and Practice*. London: HMSO.

Parker, G. and Lawton, D. (1994) *Different Types of Care, Different Types of Carer: Evidence from the General Household Survey*. London: HMSO.

Patel, N., Mirza, N.R., Lindblad, P. *et al.* (1998) *Dementia and Minority Ethnic Older People: Managing Care in the UK, Denmark and France*. Lyme Regis: Russell House Publishing.

Paul, K. (1998) *Whitewashing Britain: Race and Citizenship in the Post War Era*. Ithaca, NY and London: Cornell University Press.

Phillips, C. (2005) Facing inwards and outwards? Institutional racism, race equality and the role of Black and Asian professional Associations, *Criminal Justice*, 5(4): 357–77.

Phillips, M. and Phillips, T. (1998) *Windrush: The Irresistible Rise of Multi-racial Britain*. London: Harper Collins.

Phillips, T. (2000) Labour 'needs ethnic MP targets', BBC News, 22 May. http://news.bbc.co.uk/1/hi/uk_politics/758867.stm [Accessed 18 April 2010].

Phillips, T. (2004a) Interview, *Sunday Times*, 2 May.

Phillips, T. (2004b) Interview for *Today*, Radio 4, 8 October. http://news.bbc.co.uk/2/hi/uk_news/3725524.stm.

Phillips, T. (2005) After 7/7: sleep walking into segregation. Speech given to the Manchester Council for Community Relations, 22 September. http://www.humanities.manchester.ac.uk/socialchange/research/social-change/summer-workshops/documents/sleepwalking.pdf [Accessed 26 February 2010].

Poulton, J., Rylance, G. and Johnson, M.R.D. (1987) Medical teaching of the cultural aspects of ethnic minorities, *Medical Education*, 20: 492–7.

Powell, M. (2007) *Understanding the Mixed Economy of Welfare*. Bristol: The Policy Press.

PSMG (Public Sector Management Group) (1985) *Five Year Review of the Birmingham Inner City Partnership Inner City*. Research Paper No. 12. London: Department of the Environment.

Pugh, R. (2004) Difference and discrimination in rural areas, *Rural Social Work*, 9(1): 255–64.

Racial Justice Manifesto (2010) *The Price of Race Inequality: The Black Manifesto 2010*, published by a consortium of voluntary sector agencies at http://www.raceequalitypolicy.co.uk/ [Accessed 18 April 2010].

Raghuram, P. (2004) The difference that skills make: gender, family migration strategies and regulated labour markets, *Journal of Ethnic and Migration Studies*, 30(2): 303–23.

Ram, M. (1992) Coping with racism: Asian employers in the inner city, *Work, Employment and Society*, 6: 601–16.

Ram, M. and Jones, T. (2008) Ethnic-minority businesses in the UK: a review of research and policy developments, *Environment and Planning C: Government and Policy*, 26(2): 352–74.

Ram, M. and Smallbone, D. (2003) Policies to support ethnic minority enterprise: the English experience, *Entrepreneurship and Regional Development*, 15(2): 151–66.

Randhawa, G., Owens, A., Fitches, R. and Khan, Z. (2003) Communication in the development of culturally competent palliative care services in the UK: a case study, *International Journal of Palliative Nursing*, 9(1): 24–31.

RARP (Rural Action Research Project) (2009) *Building Inclusive Communities*. Dunfermline: Carnegie UK Trust. http://rural.carnegieuktrust.org.uk/publications/the_rural_action_research_programme_briefing_series-_building_inclusive_communities [Accessed 19 April 2010].

Ratcliffe, P. (2004) *Race, Ethnicity and Difference: Imagining the Inclusive Society*. Maidenhead: Open University Press.

Rawles, S. (2008) Portraits of respect, *Guardian*, 26 March. http://www.guardian.co.uk/society/2008/mar/26/longtermcare.socialcare [Accessed 19 April 2010].

Raynor, J. (2005) Grim truth about race hate, *Observer*, 27 March.

Rees, T. and Parken, A. (2003) *Mainstreaming Equality: The Things You Really Need to Know but have been Afraid to Ask*. Manchester: Equal Opportunities Commission.

Rex, J. (1969) Race as a social category, *Journal of Biosocial Science Supplement*, 1: 145–52.

Rex, J. (2001) The basic elements of a systematic theory of ethnic relations, *Sociological Research Online*, 6(1). http://www.socresonline.org.uk/6/1/rex.html [Accessed 28 Aug 2009].

Richards, J.K., Griffiths, S. and Nicholas, M. (1985) *Survey of Racism Awareness*. Nottingham: Trent Polytechnic Papers in Education.

Robinson, V. and Garner, R. (2004) Unravelling a stereotype: the lived experience of black and minority ethnic people in rural Wales, in N. Chakraborti, and J. Garland (eds) *Rural Racism*. Uffculme, Devon: Willan Publishing.

Robinson, V. and Garner, H. (2006) Place matters: exploring the distinctiveness of racism in rural Wales, in S. Neal and J. Agyeman (eds) *The New Countryside: Ethnicity, Nation and Exclusion in Contemporary Britain*. Bristol: The Policy Press.

Runnymede Trust (1980) *Britain's Black Population*. London: Heinemann Educational Books for Runnymede Trust and Radical Statistics Group.

Runnymede Trust (1986) *The Chinese Community in Britain: The Home Affairs Committee Report in Context*. London: Runnymede Trust.

Runnymede Trust (2007) *Personal Accounts: Implications for Black, Asian and Minority Ethnic Communities*. London: Runnymede Trust. www.runnymedetrust.org.uk [Accessed 19 April 2010].

Saeed, A., Blain, N. and Forbes, D. (1999) New ethnic and national questions in Scotland: post-British identities among Glasgow Pakistani teenagers, *Ethnic and Racial Studies*, 22(5): 821–44.

Sakamoto, I. and Pitner, R.O. (2005) Use of critical consciousness in anti-oppressive social work practice: disentangling power dynamics at personal and structural levels, *British Journal of Social Work*, 35(4): 435–52.

Saltus, R. (2005) Scoping study to explore the feasibility of a health and social care research development network covering black and minority ethnic groups in Wales. Cardiff: Wales Office of Research and Development, Welsh Assembly Government.

Santry, C. (2008) Minority staff get worse deal on jobs, pay and grievances, *Health Service Journal*, 7 August.

Sashidharan, S.P. (2003) *Inside Outside: Improving Mental Health Services for Black and Minority Ethnic Communities in England*. Leeds: Department of Health.

Scarman, Lord (1981) *The Brixton Disorders 10–12 April 1981: Report of an Inquiry*, Cmnd 8427. London: HMSO.

SCIE (Social Care Institute for Excellence) (2009a) *At a Glance 6: Personalisation Briefing. Implications for Commissioners*. London: Social Care Institute for Excellence.

SCIE (2009b) *At a Glance 10: Personalisation Briefing. Implications for Carers.* London: Social Care Institute for Excellence. http://www.scie.org.uk/publications/ataglance/ataglance10.asp [Accessed 5 February 2010].

Scottish Executive (2002) *Racist Crime and Victimisation in Scotland.* Edinburgh: The Stationery Office.

Scottish Executive (2005) *Scottish Executive Review of Race Equality Work in Scotland: A Summary of the Review and the Way Forward.* Edinburgh: The Stationery Office. http://www.scotland.gov.uk/Publications/2005/11/1881943/19435.

Scourfield, J. and Davies, A. (2005) Children's accounts of Wales as racialised and inclusive, *Ethnicities*, 5(1): 83–107.

Scourfield, J., Beynon, H., Evans, J. and Shah, W. (2002) *Not a Black and White Issue: The Experiences of Black and Minority Ethnic Children Living in the South Wales Valley.* Cardiff: Barnardo's Cymru.

SECSHA BMEN (South East Coast Strategic Health Authority Black and Minority EthnicNetwork)(2008)*RaceEqualityServiceReview:ActionPlan.*www.sabp.nhs.uk/aboutus/diversity-inclusion/BMENActionPlan%20(2).pdf. [Accessed 21 May 2010].

Sen, A.K. (1997) *On Economic Inequality.* Oxford: Oxford University Press.

Sen, A.K. (2005) Human rights and capabilities, *Journal of Human Development*, 6(2): 151–66.

Shah, R. and Hatton, C. (1999) *Caring Alone: Young Carers in South Asian Communities.* London: Barnardo's.

Shieh, J. (2006) Reaching out to Vietnamese communities, *A Life in the Day*, 10(3): 16–19.

Shields, M.A. and Price, S.W. (2003) Racial harassment, job satisfaction and intentions to quit: evidence from the British nursing profession, *Economica*, 69(274): 295–326.

Sibley, D. (1998) Problematizing exclusion: reflections on space, difference and knowledge, *International Planning Studies*, 3 (1): 93–100.

Sims, J.M. (2007) *Mixed Heritage: Identity, Policy and Practice.* London: Runnymede Trust.

Sivanandan, A. (1985) RAT and the degradation of black struggle, *Race and Class*, 26(4): 1–33.

Sivanandan, A. (2006) Britain's shame: from multiculturalism to nativism, interview, *Institute of Race Relations News*, 22 May. http://www.irr.org.uk/2006/may/ha000024.html [Accessed 26 February 2010].

Smith, J.D., Ellis, A., Howlett, S. and O'Brien, J. (2004) *Volunteering for All? Exploring the Link between Volunteering and Social Exclusion.* London: Institute for Volunteering Research.

Sparrow, A. and Owen, P. (2010) Minister: ethnic minorities 'no longer automatically disadvantaged', *Guardian*, 14 January. www.Guardian.co.uk.

Spratt, E.R. and James, M. (2008) *Faith, Cohesion and Community Development:*

Faith Communities Capacity Building Fund, Final Evaluation Report. London: Community Development Foundation.

Steele, A. and Sodhi, D. (2004) Black and minority ethnic contractors and consultants and UK housing associations' contracting power, *Construction Management and Economics*, 22(2): 151–7.

Steventon, A. and Sanchez, C. (2008) *The Under Pensioned: Disabled People and People from Ethnic Minorities*, Research Report No. 5. London: Pensions Policy Institute, Equality and Human Rights Commission.

Stuart, O. (2006) Will community-based support services make direct payments a viable option for black and minority ethnic service users and carers? SCIE Race Equality Discussion Paper 01. London: Social Care Institute for Excellence. http://www.scie.org.uk/publications/raceequalitydiscussionpapers/redp01.asp [Accessed 5 February 2010].

Stubbs, P. (1985) The Employment of black social workers: from 'ethnic sensitivity' to anti-racism?, *Critical Social Policy*, 12: 6–27.

Svensson, L.G. (2006) New professionalism, trust and competence: some conceptual and empirical data, *Current Sociology*, 54(4): 579–93.

Syed, A., Craid, G. and Taylor, M. (2002) *Black and Minority Ethnic Organisations' Experience of Local Compacts*. York: Joseph Rowntree Foundation.

Szczepura A., Johnson M.R.D., Clark, M. and Owen, D. (1998) *The Unavoidable Costs of Ethnicity*. Report to the Advisory Group on Resource Allocation, National Health Service Executive 1998. Coventry: Centre for Evidence in Ethnicity, Health and Diversity, University of Warwick.

Tamkin, P. (2000) Institutional racism: daring to open Pandora's box, *Equal Opportunities Review*, June.

Tamkin, P., Ashton, J., Cummings, J., Hokker, H. *et al.* (2002) *A Review of Training in Racism Awareness and Valuing Cultural Diversity, RDS on-line report 09/02*. London:HomeOffice.http://www.homeoffice.gov.uk/rds/pdfs2/rdsolr0902.pdf [Accessed 5 February 2010].

Tamkin, P., Pollard, E., Tackey, N.D., Strebler, M. *et al.* (2003) *A Review of Community Race Relations (CRR) Training in the Metropolitan Police Service*. London: Institute for Employment studies for Metropolitan Police Authority.

Taylor, P.(1993) Minority ethnic groups and gender in access to higher education, *New Community*, 19(3): 425–40.

Theodore, N.C. (1995) Strengthening Business Opportunities Project, Chicago Urban League, Chicago, Illinois, *International Journal of Public Administration*, 18(7): 1115–40.

Thomas, M. and Morton-Williams, J. (1972) *Overseas Nurses in Britain: A PEP Survey for the UK*. Council Broadsheet No. 539. London: Political and Economic Planning (now Policy Studies Institute).

Tomlins, R., Johnson, M.R.D., Line, B., Brown, T., Owen, D. and Ratcliffe, P. (2000) *Building Futures: Meeting the Needs of our Vietnamese Communities*. London: An Viet Housing Association.

Tomlins, R., Johnson, M.R.D. and Owen, D. (2002) The resource of ethnicity in the housing careers and preferences of the Vietnamese communities in London, *Housing Studies*, 17(3): 505–19.

Tomlinson, S. (2008) *Race and Education: Policy and Politics in Britain*. Maidenhead: Open University Press.

TOPPS UK Partnership (2002) *National Occupational Standards for Social Work*. http://www.skillsforcare.org.uk/developing_skills/National_Occupational_-Standards/ social_work.aspx. [Accessed 24 August 2009].

TUC (Trades Union Congress) (2003) *Overworked, Underpaid and Over Here: Migrant Workers in Britain*. London: TUC. www.tuc.org.uk.

TUC (2009) *Tackling Racial Inequalities Consultation: A TUC Response*. London: TUC. http://www.tuc.org.uk/equality/tuc-16463-f0.pdf [Accessed 26 February 2010].

Twigg, J. and Atkin, K. (1994) *Carers Perceived*. Maidenhead: Open University Press.

Tylor, E.B. (1891) *Primitive Culture*, 3rd revised ed. London: J. Murray.

UCAS (Universities and Colleges Application Service) (2005) Chapter 8 data supplied by Universities and Colleges Application Service.

UNESCO (United Nations Educational, Scientific and Cultural Organization) (1968) UNESCO statement on race and racial prejudice, *Race and Class*, 9(3): 365–8.

Ungerson, C. (1987) *Policy is Personal: Sex, Gender and Informal Care*. New York: Tavistock.

UNISON (2008) *Submission to the National Debate on Care and Support*. London: Unison.

Van Stolk, C., Starkey, T., Shehabi, A. and Hassan, E. (2009) *NHS Workforce Health and Wellbeing Review: Staff Perception Research*. London: The Work Foundation, Rand Europe and Aston Business School for Department of Health. http://www.nhshealthandwellbeing.org/pdfs/NHS_HWB_Survey_Report_Final.pdf [Accessed 26 February 2010].

Vellins, S. (1982) South Asian students in British universities: a statistical note, *New Community*, 10: 206–12.

Vernon, P. (2009) A manifesto for change in health and social care for BME Communities, *Diversity in Health and Care*, 6(3): 145–6.

Vertovec, S. (1999) Minority associations, networks and public policies: reassessing relationships, *Journal of Ethnic and Migration Studies*, 25(1): 21–42.

Vertovec, S. (2007) Super-diversity and its implications, *Ethnic and Racial Studies*, 30: 1024–54.

Vidler, E. and Clark, J. (2005) Creating citizen consumers: New Labour and the remaking of public services, *Public Policy and Administration*, 20(2): 19–37. http://ppa.sagepub.com/cgi/content/abstract/20/2/19 [Accessed 5 February 2010].

Virdee, S. (2000) A Marxist critique of black radical theories of trade-union racism, *Sociology*, 34(3): 545–65.

Visram, R. (1986) *Ayahs, Lascars, and Princes: Indians in Britain, 1700–1947*. London: Pluto Press.

WAG (Welsh Assembly Government) (2004) *Making the Connections: Delivering Better Services in Wales*. Cardiff: Welsh Assembly Government.

Walby, S., Armstrong, J. and Humphreys, L. (2008) *Review of Equality Statistics*, Research Report No. 1. London: Equality and Human Rights Commission. http://www.equalityhumanrights.com/uploaded_files/research/1_review_of_ equality_statistics_241008.pdf [Accessed 5 February 2010].

Walker, R., Cromarty, H., Kelly, L. and St Pierre-Hansen, N. (2008) Achieving cultural safety in Aboriginal health services: implementation of a cross-cultural safety model in a hospital setting, *Diversity in Health and Social Care*, 6(1): 11–22.

Webster, W. (1998) *Imagining Home: Gender, 'Race' and National Identity 1945–1964*. London: UCL Press Ltd.

Werbner, P. (1990) *The Migration Process: Capital, Gifts and Offerings among British Pakistanis*. London: Berg.

Whitehead, E., Purdy, D. and Mascharenas-Keyes, S. (2006) *Ethnic Minority Businesses in England: Report on the Annual Small Business Survey 2003 Ethnic Boost*. London: Small Business Service.

Williams, C. (1995) Race and racism: some reflections on the Welsh context, *Contemporary Wales*, 8: 113–31.

Williams, C. (2004a) Access to justice and social inclusion: the policy challenges in Wales, *Journal of Social Welfare and Family Law*, 26(1): 53–68.

Williams, C. (2004b) Passions and pathologies in the politics of minority ethnic participation in governance, *Wales, Journal of Law and Policy*, 3(2): 157–73.

Williams, C. (2006) The dilemmas of civil society: black and ethnic minority associations in Wales, in G. Day, D. Dunkerley and A. Thompson (eds) *Civil Society in Wales*. Cardiff: University of Wales Press.

Williams, C. (2007a) Revisiting the rural/race debates: a view from the Welsh countryside, *Ethnic and Racial Studies*, 30(5): 741–66.

Williams, C, (ed.) (2007b) *Social Policy for Social Welfare Practice in a Devolved Wales*. Birmingham: BASW/Venture Press.

Williams, C. (2010) *Cultural Competency, Race Equality and Social Work Education*. Pontypridd: Wales Equality and Diversity in Health and Social Care. www.wedhs.org.uk [Accessed 26 February 2010].

Williams, C. and Chaney, P. (2001a) Devolution and identities: the experience of ethnic minorities in Wales, *Soundings*, 18: 169–83.

Williams, C. and Chaney, P. (2001b) Inclusive government for excluded groups: ethnic minorities, in P. Chaney, T. Hall and A. Pithouse (eds) *New Governance – New Democracy?* Cardiff: University of Wales Press.

Williams, C. and De Lima, P. (2006) Devolution, multicultural citizenship and race equality: from laissez faire to nationally responsible policies, *Critical Social Policy*, 26(3): 483–97.

Williams, C. and Hong Baker, T. (2009) *Developing Effective Engagement for Consultation with Black and Ethnic Minorities in Rural Areas*. London: Carnegie UK

Trust Building Inclusive Rural Communities Rural Action Research Programme. www.carnegie.org.uk [Accessed 26 February 2010].

Williams, C. with, Hold, M., Turunen, S. and Jeffries, J. (2005) *The BEST Report: Ethnic Minorities in North Wales: A Mapping Exercise.* Commissioned by Black and Ethnic Minorities Support Team – Scarman Trust, MEWN Cymru, AWEMA, BVSNW and Welsh Assembly Government. http://www.mewn-cymru.org.uk/PDF/BESTReportExecutiveSummary.pdf [Accessed 19 April 2010].

Williams, C., Merrell J., Rance J., Olumide, G., Saltus, R. and Hawthorne, K. (2007) A critical reflection on the research priorities for improving the health and social care of black and minority ethnic groups in Wales, *Diversity in Health and Social Care*, 4 (3):193–9.

Williams, F. (1989) *Social Policy: A Critical Introduction.* Cambridge: Polity Press.

Wilson, W.J. (1978) *The Declining Significance of Race: Blacks and Changing American Institutions.* Chicago, IL: University of Chicago Press.

Wilson, W.J. (2009) *More Than Just Race: Being Black and Poor in the Inner City.* New York: W.W. Norton and Co.

Winckler, V. (ed.) (2009) *Equality Issues in Wales: A Research Review*, Research Report 11. London: Equality and Human Rights Commission. http://www.equalityhumanrights.com/uploaded_files/research/11_equality_issues_in_wales_-_ a_research_review.pdf [Accessed 5 February 2010].

Worley, C. (2005) It's not about race. It's about the community: New Labour and 'community cohesion', *Critical Social Policy*, 25(4): 483–96.

Wrench, J. (2004) Trade union responses to immigrants and ethnic inequality in Denmark and the UK: the context of consensus and conflict, *European Journal of Industrial Relations*, 10(1): 7–30.

Wrench, J. (2007) *Diversity Management and Discrimination: Immigrants and Ethnic Minorities in the EU.* Aldershot: Ashgate Publishing.

Wrench, J. and Taylor, P. (1994) *A Research Manual on the Evaluation of Anti-Discrimination Training Activities.* Geneva: International Labour Office.

Yeandle, L., Bennet, C., Butcher, L., Fry, G. *et al.* (2007) *Diversity in Caring: Towards Equality for Carers.* Leeds: University of Leeds.

Yeandle, S. and Stiell, B. (2007) Issues in the development of the Direct Payments scheme for older people in England, in Ungerson, C. and Yeandle, S. (eds) *Cash for Care in Developed Welfare States.* Basingstoke: Palgrave Macmillan.

Index

Related books from Open University Press

Purchase from www.openup.co.uk or order through your local bookseller

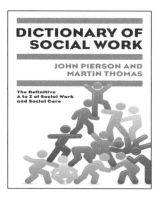

DICTIONARY OF SOCIAL WORK
The Definitive A to Z of Social
Work and Social Care

John Pierson and Martin Thomas

9780335238811 (Paperback)
September 2010

eBook also available

With over 1500 entries, this popular dictionary provides concise and up to date explanations of the theories, approaches and terminology that define front-line social work and social care. These entries explain, in jargon-free language, how key concepts can be used to improve practice. Clear explanations outline significant developments such as Every Child Matters and the personalization of adult services.

Key features:

- Entries are helpfully cross referenced and are evidence based
- Written by specialists in the field
- Specific focus on the most recent legislation and policy guidance from government

www.openup.co.uk

**AN INTRODUCTION TO
APPLYING SOCIAL WORK
THEORIES AND METHODS**

Barbra Teater

9780335237784 (Paperback)
July 2010

eBook also available

This practical book provides a basic introduction to the most
commonly used theories and methods in social work practice. The
book explores the concept of a theory and a method, the difference
between the two and the ways in which they are connected. Teater
also discusses the social worker-client relationship and offers a handy
overview of anti-oppressive practice.

Key features:

- Each chapter explores a single theory or method in depth
- Uses a variety of interactive tools to encourage exploration of
  thoughts and beliefs
- Step-by-step illustrations show how to apply the theory/method to
  a social work case

www.openup.co.uk

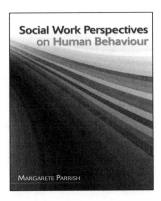

SOCIAL WORK PERSPECTIVES ON HUMAN BEHAVIOUR

Margarete Parrish

9780335223671 (Paperback)
2009

eBook also available

The capacity to observe, interpret and understand human behaviour is vital for effective social work practice. By choosing to enter a profession that requires high levels of astute observation and listening skills in the interpretation of people's behaviour, social work students have undertaken a demanding task.

Using a bio-psychosocial framework, this fascinating book provides a wide basis of perspectives on human behaviour on which to build understanding of and responses to people's behaviours, along with an enhanced appreciation of some of the circumstances that shape behaviour.

Key features:

- Exercises for students to complete
- Chapter summary points
- Discussion questions

www.openup.co.uk